Praise for David Allen

"*Getting Things Done* describes an incredibly practical process that can help busy people regain control of their lives. It can help you be more successful. Even more important, it can help you have a happier life!"

—Marshall Goldsmith, coeditor, *The Leader of the Future* and *Coaching for Leadership*

"When I'm flat-out stressed about the volume and complexity of my work, I open this book and find immediate ways to gain a sense of control. That's really a critical need for decision making. David made me what I am today: headstrong and proud of it."

—Pat Carlyle, senior vice president, human resources, Headstrong

"David Allen's *Getting Things Done* offers as much to knowledge workers as Machiavelli's *The Prince* to politicians."

—Eric Rose, M.D., chairman, Columbia University Department of Surgery

"A true skeptic of most management fixes, I have to say David's program is a winner!"

—Joline Godfrey, CEO, Independent Means, Inc., and author of *Our Wildest Dreams*

"WARNING: Reading *Getting Things Done* can be hazardous to your old habits of procrastination. David Allen's approach is refreshingly simple and intuitive. He provides the systems, tools, and tips to achieve profound results."

—Carola Endicott, director, Quality Resources, New England Medical Center

"David Allen said, 'Small things done consistently over time have major impact.' I continue to be amazed at his insights and practical everyday lessons. If you want to stay unproductive, don't read this book. If you want your life to be easier, read it twice."

—Sara Larch, FACMPE, chief operating officer, University Physicians, Inc.

GETTING THINGS DONE

GETTING THINGS DONE

HOW TO ACHIEVE
STRESS-FREE PRODUCTIVITY

DAVID ALLEN

First published in the USA by Viking
of the Penguin Group

First published in the UK in 2001 by
Piatkus Books Ltd
5 Windmill Street
London W1T 2JA
e-mail: info@piatkus.co.uk

Reprinted 2002, 2003 (twice), 2004 (three times), 2005 (four times), 2006 (twice)

The moral right of the author has been asserted

*A catalogue record for this book is
available from the British Library*

ISBN 0 7499 2264 8

Text Design by Sara E. Stemen

This book has been printed on paper manufactured
with respect for the environment using wood from
managed sustainable resources

Printed in Great Britain by
MPG Books Ltd, Bodmin, Cornwall

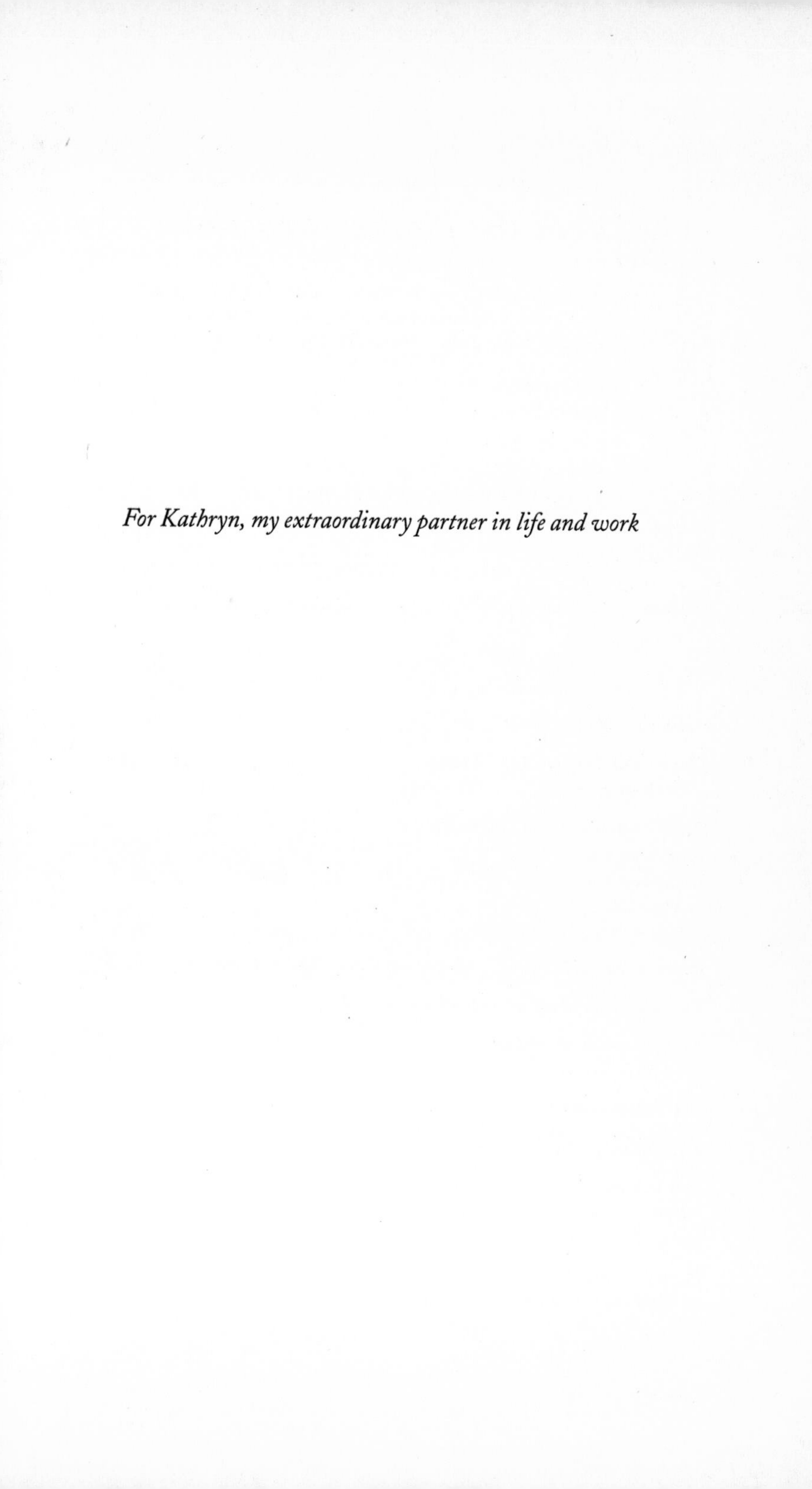

For Kathryn, my extraordinary partner in life and work

Acknowledgments

Many mentors, partners, colleagues, staff, and friends have contributed over the years to my understanding and development of the principles in *Getting Things Done.* George Mayer, Michael Bookbinder, Ted Drake, Dean Acheson, and Russell Bishop played key roles along my path of personal and professional growth. Ron Medved, Sally McGhee, Leslie Boyer, Tom Boyer, Pam Tarrantine, and Kelly Forrister contributed in their own ways to my work as it matured.

In addition, tens of thousands of clients and workshop participants have helped validate and fine-tune these models. Particular thanks go to the senior human resource strategists who early on recognized the significance of this material in changing their corporate cultures, and who gave me the opportunity to do that—in particular: Michael Winston, Ben Cannon, Susan Valaskovic, Patricia Carlyle, Manny Berger, Carola Endicott, Klara Sztucinski, and Elliott Kellman. The administrative and moral support that Shar Kanan and Andra Carasso gave me over many years was priceless.

This book itself could not have happened the way it has without the unique energies and perspectives of Tom Hagan, John and Laura McBride, Steve Lewers, Doe Coover, Greg Stikeleather, Steve Shull, and Marian Bateman. And much credit is due my editor, Janet Goldstein, who has been a marvelous (and patient) instructor in the art and craft of book writing.

Finally, deepest thanks go to my spiritual coach, J-R, for being such an awesome guide and consistent reminder of my real priorities; and to my incredible wife, Kathryn, for her trust, love, hard work, and the beauty she has brought into my life.

Contents

Welcome to *Getting Things Done*

WELCOME TO A gold mine of insights into strategies for how to have more energy, be more relaxed, and get a lot more accomplished with much less effort. If you're like me, you like getting things done and doing them well, and yet you also want to savor life in ways that seem increasingly elusive if not downright impossible if you're working too hard. This doesn't have to be an either-or proposition. It *is* possible to be effectively *doing* while you are delightfully *being*, in your ordinary workaday world.

I think efficiency is a good thing. Maybe what you're doing is important, interesting, or useful; or maybe it isn't but it has to be done anyway. In the first case you want to get as much return as you can on your investment of time and energy. In the second, you want to get on to other things as fast as you can, without any nagging loose ends.

> *The art of resting the mind and the power of dismissing from it all care and worry is probably one of the secrets of our great men.*
> —*Captain J. A. Hatfield*

And *whatever* you're doing, you'd probably like to be more relaxed, confident that whatever you're doing at the moment is just what you need to be doing—that having a beer with your staff after hours, gazing at your sleeping child in his or her crib at midnight, answering the e-mail in front of you, or spending a few informal minutes with the potential new client after the meeting is exactly what you *ought* to be doing, as you're doing it.

Teaching you how to be maximally efficient and relaxed, whenever you need or want to be, was my main purpose in writing this book.

I have searched for a long time, as you may have, for answers to the questions of *what* to do, *when* to do it, and *how* to do it. And after twenty-plus years of developing and applying new methods for personal and organizational productivity, alongside years of rigorous exploration in the self-development arena, I can attest that there is no single, once-and-for-all solution. No software, seminar, cool personal planner, or personal mission statement will simplify your workday or make your choices for you as you move through your day, week, and life. What's more, just when you learn how to enhance your productivity and decision-making at one level, you'll graduate to the next accepted batch of responsibilities and creative goals, whose new challenges will defy the ability of any simple formula or buzzword-du-jour to get you what you want, the way you want to get it.

But if there's no single means of perfecting personal organization and productivity, there *are* things we can do to facilitate them. As I have personally matured, from year to year, I've found deeper and more meaningful, more significant things to focus on and be aware of and do. And I've uncovered simple processes that we can all learn to use that will vastly improve our ability to deal proactively and constructively with the mundane realities of the world.

What follows is a compilation of more than two decades' worth of discoveries about personal productivity—a guide to maximizing output and minimizing input, and to doing so in a world in which work is increasingly voluminous and ambiguous. I have spent many thousands of hours coaching people "in the trenches" at their desks, helping them process and organize all of their work at hand. The methods I have uncovered have proved to be highly effective in all types of organizations, at every job level, across cultures, and even at home and school. After twenty years of coaching and training some of the world's most sophisticated and productive professionals, I know the world is hungry for these methods.

Executives at the top are looking to instill "ruthless execution" in themselves and their people as a basic standard. They know, and I know, that behind closed doors, after hours, there remain unanswered calls, tasks to be delegated, unprocessed issues from meetings and conversations, personal responsibilities unmanaged, and dozens of e-mails still not dealt with. Many of these businesspeople are successful because the crises they solve and the opportunities they take advantage of are bigger than the problems they allow and create in their own offices and briefcases. But given the pace of business and life today, the equation is in question.

On the one hand, we need proven tools that can help people focus their energies strategically and tactically without letting anything fall through the cracks. On the other, we need to create work environments and skills that will keep the most invested people from burning out due to stress. We need positive work-style standards that will attract and retain the best and brightest.

We know this information is sorely needed in organizations. It's also needed in schools, where our kids are still not being taught how to process information, how to focus on outcomes, or what actions to take to make them happen. And for all of us individually, it's needed so we can take advantage of all the opportunities we're given to add value to our world in a sustainable, self-nurturing way.

The power, simplicity, and effectiveness of what I'm talking about in *Getting Things Done* are best experienced *as* experiences, in real time, with real situations in your real world. Necessarily, the book must put the essence of this dynamic art of workflow management and personal productivity into a linear format. I've tried to organize it in such a way as to give you both the inspiring big-picture view and a taste of immediate results as you go along.

The book is divided into three parts. Part 1 describes the whole game, providing a brief overview of the system and an explanation of why it's unique and timely, and then presenting the basic methodologies themselves in their most condensed and basic form. Part 2 shows you how to implement the system. It's your personal coaching, step by step, on the nitty-gritty application of the models. Part 3 goes even deeper, describing the subtler and more profound results you can expect when you incorporate the methodologies and models into your work and your life.

I want you to hop in. I want you to test this stuff out, even challenge it. I want you to find out for yourself that what I promise is not only possible but instantly accessible to you personally. And I want you to know that everything I propose is *easy to do.* It involves no new skills at all. You already know how to focus, how to write things down, how to decide on outcomes and actions, and how to review options and make choices. You'll validate that many of the things you've been doing instinctively and intuitively all along are *right.* I'll give you ways to leverage those basic skills into new plateaus of effectiveness. I want to inspire you to put all this into a new behavior set that will blow your mind.

Throughout the book I refer to my coaching and seminars on this material. I've worked as a "management consultant" for the last two decades, alone and in small partnerships. My work has consisted primarily of doing private productivity coaching and conducting seminars based on the methods presented here. I (and my colleagues) have coached more than a thousand individuals, trained hundreds of thousands of professionals, and delivered many hundreds of public seminars. This is the background from which I have drawn my experience and examples.

The promise here was well described by a client of mine who wrote, "When I habitually applied the tenets of this program it *saved* my life . . . when I faithfully applied them, it *changed* my life. This is a vaccination against day-to-day fire-fighting (the so-called urgent and crisis demands of any given workday) and an antidote for the imbalance many people bring upon themselves."

part 1

The Art of Getting Things Done

1

A New Practice for a New Reality

IT'S POSSIBLE FOR a person to have an overwhelming number of things to do and still function productively with a clear head and a positive sense of relaxed control. That's a great way to live and work, at elevated levels of effectiveness and efficiency. It's also becoming a critical operational style required of successful and high-performing professionals. You already know how to do everything necessary to achieve this high-performance state. If you're like most people, however, you need to apply these skills in a more timely, complete, and systematic way so you can get on top of it all instead of feeling buried. And though the method and the techniques I describe in this book are immensely practical and based on common sense, most people will have some major work habits that must be modified before they can implement this system. The small changes required—changes in the way you clarify and organize all the things that command your attention—could represent a significant shift in how you approach some key aspects of your day-to-day work. Many of my clients have referred to this as a significant paradigm shift.

> *Anxiety is caused by a lack of control, organization, preparation, and action.*
>
> —*David Kekich*

The methods I present here are all based on two key objectives: (1) capturing *all* the things that need to get done—now, later, someday, big, little, or in between—into a logical and trusted system outside of your head and off your mind; and (2) disciplining yourself to make front-end decisions about all of the "inputs" you let into your life so that you will always have a plan for "next actions" that you can implement or renegotiate at any moment.

This book offers a proven method for this kind of high-performance workflow management. It provides good tools, tips, techniques, and tricks for implementation. As you'll discover, the principles and methods are instantly usable and applicable to everything you have to do in your personal as well as your professional life.* You can incorporate, as many others have before you, what I describe as an ongoing dynamic style of operating in your work and in your world. Or, like still others, you can simply use this as a guide to getting back into better control when you feel you need to.

The Problem: New Demands, Insufficient Resources

Almost everyone I encounter these days feels he or she has too much to handle and not enough time to get it all done. In the course of a single recent week, I consulted with a partner in a major global investment firm who was concerned that the new corporate-management responsibilities he was being offered would stress his family commitments beyond the limits; and with a midlevel human-resources manager trying to stay on top of her 150-plus e-mail requests per day fueled by the goal of doubling the company's regional office staff from eleven hundred to two thousand people in one year, all as she tried to protect a social life for herself on the weekends.

A paradox has emerged in this new millennium: people have

---

*I consider "work," in its most universal sense, as meaning anything that you want or need to be different than it currently is. Many people make a distinction between "work" and "personal life," but I don't: to me, weeding the garden or updating my will is just as much "work" as writing this book or coaching a client. All the methods and techniques in this book are applicable across that life/work spectrum—to be effective, they need to be.

enhanced quality of life, but at the same time they are adding to their stress levels by taking on more than they have resources to handle. It's as though their eyes were bigger than their stomachs. And most people are to some degree frustrated and perplexed about how to improve the situation.

Work No Longer Has Clear Boundaries

A major factor in the mounting stress level is that the actual nature of our jobs has changed much more dramatically and rapidly than have our training for and our ability to deal with work. In just the last half of the twentieth century, what constituted "work" in the industrialized world was transformed from assembly-line, make-it and move-it kinds of activity to what Peter Drucker has so aptly termed "knowledge work."

I try to take one day at a time, but sometimes several days attack me at once.
—Ashley Brilliant

In the old days, work was self-evident. Fields were to be plowed, machines tooled, boxes packed, cows milked, widgets cranked. You knew what work had to be done—you could see it. It was clear when the work was finished, or not finished.

Now, for many of us, there are no edges to most of our projects. Most people I know have at least half a dozen things they're trying to achieve right now, and even if they had the rest of their lives to try, they wouldn't be able to finish these to perfection. You're probably faced with the same dilemma. How good could that conference potentially be? How effective could the training program be, or the structure of your executives' compensation package? How inspiring is the essay you're writing? How motivating the staff meeting? How functional the reorganization? And a last question: How much available data could be relevant to doing those projects "better"? The answer is, an infinite amount, easily accessible, or at least potentially so, through the Web.

Almost every project could be done *better,* and an infinite quantity of information is now available that could make that happen.

On another front, the lack of edges can create *more* work for everyone. Many of today's organizational outcomes require cross-divisional communication, cooperation, and engagement. Our individual office silos are crumbling, and with them is going the luxury of not having to read cc'd e-mails from the marketing department, or from human resources, or from some ad hoc, deal-with-a-certain-issue committee.

Our Jobs Keep Changing

The disintegrating edges of our projects and our work in general would be challenging enough for anyone. But now we must add to that equation the constantly shifting definition of our jobs. I often ask in my seminars, "Which of you are doing only what you were hired to do?" Seldom do I get a raised hand. As amorphous as edgeless work may be, if you had the chance to stick with some specifically described job long enough, you'd probably figure out what you needed to do—how much, at what level—to stay sane. But few have that luxury anymore, for two reasons:

1 | The organizations we're involved with seem to be in constant morph mode, with ever-changing goals, products, partners, customers, markets, technologies, and owners. These all, by necessity, shake up structures, forms, roles, and responsibilities.

2 | The average professional is more of a free agent these days than ever before, changing careers as often as his or her parents once changed jobs. Even fortysomethings and fiftysomethings hold to standards of continual growth. Their aims are just more integrated into the mainstream now, covered by the catchall "professional, management, and executive development"—which simply means they won't keep doing what they're doing for any extended period of time.

We can never really be prepared for that which is wholly new. We have to adjust ourselves, and every radical adjustment is a crisis in self-esteem: we undergo a test, we have to prove ourselves. It needs subordinate self-confidence to face drastic change without inner trembling.
—*Eric Hoffer*

Little seems clear for very long anymore, as far as what our work is and what or how much input may be relevant to doing it well. We're allowing in huge amounts of information and communication from the outer world and generating an equally large volume of ideas and agreements with ourselves and others from our inner world. And we haven't been well equipped to deal with this huge number of internal and external commitments.

> *The hurrier I go, the behinder I get.*
> —*Anonymous*

The Old Models and Habits Are Insufficient

Neither our standard education, nor traditional time-management models, nor the plethora of organizing tools available, such as personal notebook planners, Microsoft Outlook, or Palm personal digital assistants (PDAs), has given us a viable means of meeting the new demands placed on us. If you've tried to use any of these processes or tools, you've probably found them unable to accommodate the speed, complexity, and changing priority factors inherent in what you are doing. The ability to be successful, relaxed, and in control during these fertile but turbulent times demands new ways of thinking and working. There is a great need for new methods, technologies, and work habits to help us get on top of our world.

> *The winds and waves are always on the side of the ablest navigators.*
> —*Edward Gibbon*

The traditional approaches to time management and personal organization were useful in their time. They provided helpful reference points for a workforce that was just emerging from an industrial assembly-line modality into a new kind of work that included choices about what to do and discretion about when to do it. When "time" itself turned into a work factor, personal calendars became a key work tool. (Even as late as the 1980s many professionals considered having a pocket Day-Timer the essence of being organized, and many people today think of their calendar as the central tool for being in control.) Along with discretionary time also came the need to make good choices about what to do. "ABC" priority codes and daily "to-do" lists were key techniques that people developed to help them sort through their choices in some meaningful way. If you had the freedom to decide what to do, you also had the responsibility to make good choices, given your "priorities."

What you've probably discovered, at least at some level, is that a calendar, though important, can really effectively manage only a small portion of what you need to organize. And daily to-do lists and simplified priority coding have proven inadequate to deal with the volume and variable nature of the average professional's workload. More and more people's jobs are made up of dozens or even hundreds of e-mails a day, with no latitude left to ignore a single request, complaint, or order. There are few people who can (or even should) expect to code everything an "A," a "B," or a "C" priority, or who can maintain some predetermined list of to-dos that the first telephone call or interruption from their boss won't totally *un*do.

The "Big Picture" vs. the Nitty-Gritty

At the other end of the spectrum, a huge number of business books, models, seminars, and gurus have championed the "bigger view" as the solution to dealing with our complex world. Clarifying major goals and values, so the thinking goes, gives order, meaning, and direction to our work. In practice, however, the well-intentioned exercise of values thinking too often does not achieve its desired results. I have seen too many of these efforts fail, for one or more of the following three reasons:

1 | There is too much distraction at the day-to-day, hour-to-hour level of commitments to allow for appropriate focus on the higher levels.
2 | Ineffective personal organizational systems create huge subconscious resistance to undertaking even bigger projects and goals that will likely not be managed well, and that will in turn cause even *more* distraction and stress.
3 | When loftier levels and values actually *are* clarified, it raises

the bar of our standards, making us notice that much more that needs changing. We are already having a serious negative reaction to the overwhelming number of things we have to do. And what created much of the work that's on those lists in the first place? Our values!

Focusing on values does *not* simplify your life. It gives meaning and direction—and a lot more complexity.

Focusing on primary outcomes and values *is* a critical exercise, certainly. But it does not mean there is less to do, or fewer challenges in getting the work done. Quite the contrary: it just ups the ante in the game, which still must be played day to day. For a human-resources executive, for example, deciding to deal with quality-of-work-life issues in order to attract and keep key talent does *not* make things simpler.

There has been a missing piece in our new culture of knowledge work: a system with a coherent set of behaviors and tools that functions effectively at the level at which work really happens. It must incorporate the results of big-picture thinking as well as the smallest of open details. It must manage multiple tiers of priorities. It must maintain control over hundreds of new inputs daily. It must save a lot more time and effort than are needed to maintain it. It must make it easier to get things done.

The Promise: The "Ready State" of the Martial Artist

Reflect for a moment on what it actually might be like if your personal management situation were totally under control, at all levels and at all times. What if you could dedicate fully 100 percent of your attention to whatever was at hand, at your own choosing, with no distraction?

It *is* possible. There *is* a way to get a grip on it all, stay relaxed, and get meaningful things done with minimal effort,

Life is denied by lack of attention, whether it be to cleaning windows or trying to write a masterpiece.
—Nadia Boulanger

across the whole spectrum of your life and work. You *can* experience what the martial artists call a "mind like water" and top athletes refer to as the "zone," within the complex world in which you're engaged. In fact, you have probably already been in this state from time to time.

It's a condition of working, doing, and being in which the mind is clear and constructive things are happening. It's a state that is accessible by everyone, and one that is increasingly needed to deal effectively with the complexity of life in the twenty-first century. More and more it will be a required condition for high-performance professionals who wish to maintain balance and a consistent positive output in their work. World-class rower Craig Lambert has described how it feels in *Mind Over Water* (Houghton Mifflin, 1998):

Your ability to generate power is directly proportional to your ability to relax.

> *Rowers have a word for this frictionless state: swing. . . . Recall the pure joy of riding on a backyard swing: an easy cycle of motion, the momentum coming from the swing itself. The swing carries us; we do not force it. We pump our legs to drive our arc higher, but gravity does most of the work. We are not so much swinging as being swung. The boat swings you. The shell wants to move fast: Speed sings in its lines and nature. Our job is simply to work with the shell, to stop holding it back with our thrashing struggles to go faster. Trying too hard sabotages boat speed. Trying becomes striving and striving undoes itself. Social climbers strive to be aristocrats but their efforts prove them no such thing. Aristocrats do not strive; they have already arrived. Swing is a state of arrival.*

The "Mind Like Water" Simile

In karate there is an image that's used to define the position of perfect readiness: "mind like water." Imagine throwing a pebble into a still pond. How does the water respond? The answer is, totally appropriately to the force and mass of the input; then it returns to calm. It doesn't overreact or underreact.

If your mind is empty, it is always ready for anything; it is open to everything.
—Shunryu Suzuki

The power in a karate punch comes from speed, not muscle; it comes from a focused "pop" at the end of the whip. That's why petite people can learn to break boards and bricks with their hands: it doesn't take calluses or brute strength, just the ability to generate a focused thrust with speed. But a tense muscle is a slow one. So the high levels of training in the martial arts teach and demand balance and relaxation as much as anything else. Clearing the mind and being flexible are key.

Anything that causes you to overreact or underreact can control you, and often does. Responding inappropriately to your e-mail, your staff, your projects, your unread magazines, your thoughts about what you need to do, your children, or your boss will lead to less effective results than you'd like. Most people give either more or less attention to things than they deserve, simply because they don't operate with a "mind like water."

Anything that causes you to overreact or underreact can control you, and often does.

There is one thing we can do, and the happiest people are those who can do it to the limit of their ability. We can be completely present. We can be all here. We can . . . give all our attention to the opportunity before us.
—Mark Van Doren

Can You Get into Your "Productive State" When Required?

Think about the last time you felt highly productive. You probably had a sense of being in control; you were not stressed out; you were highly focused on what you were doing; time tended to disappear (lunchtime already?); and you felt you were making noticeable progress toward a meaningful outcome. Would you like to have more such experiences?

And if you get seriously far *out* of that state—and start to feel out of control, stressed out, unfocused, bored, and stuck—do you have the ability to get yourself back *into* it? That's where the methodology of *Getting Things Done* will have the greatest impact on your life, by showing you how to get back to "mind like water," with all your resources and faculties functioning at a maximum level.

The Principle: Dealing Effectively with Internal Commitments

A basic truism I have discovered over twenty years of coaching and training is that most of the stress people experience comes from inappropriately managed commitments they make or accept. Even those who are not consciously "stressed out" will invariably experience greater relaxation, better focus, and increased productive energy when they learn more effectively to control the "open loops" of their lives.

You've probably made many more agreements with yourself than you realize, and every single one of them—big or little—is being tracked by a less-than-conscious part of you. These are the "incompletes," or "open loops," which I define as anything pulling at your attention that doesn't belong where it is, the way it is. Open loops can include everything from really big to-do items like "End world hunger" to the more modest "Hire new assistant" to the tiniest task such as "Replace electric pencil sharpener."

It's likely that you also have more internal commitments currently in play than you're aware of. Consider how many things you feel even the smallest amount of responsibility to change, finish, handle, or do something about. You have a commitment, for instance, to deal in some way with every new communication landing in your e-mail, on your voice-mail, and in your in-basket. And surely there are numerous projects that you sense need to be defined in your areas of responsibility, as well as goals and directions to be clarified, a career to be managed, and life in general to be kept in balance. You have accepted some level of internal responsibility for every-

Anything that does not belong where it is, the way it is, is an "open loop" pulling on your attention.

thing in your life and work that represents an open loop of any sort.

In order to deal effectively with all of that, you must first identify and collect all those things that are "ringing your bell" in some way, and then plan how to handle them. That may seem like a simple thing to do, but in practice most people don't know how to do it in a consistent way.

The Basic Requirements for Managing Commitments

Managing commitments well requires the implementation of some basic activities and behaviors:

- First of all, if it's on your mind, your mind isn't clear. Anything you consider unfinished in any way must be captured in a trusted system outside your mind, or what I call a collection bucket, that you know you'll come back to regularly and sort through.

- Second, you must clarify exactly what your commitment is and decide what you have to do, if anything, to make progress toward fulfilling it.

- Third, once you've decided on all the actions you need to take, you must keep reminders of them organized in a system you review regularly.

An Important Exercise to Test This Model

I suggest that you *write down the project or situation that is most on your mind at this moment.* What most "bugs" you, distracts you, or interests you, or in some other way consumes a large part of your conscious attention? It may be a project or problem that is really "in your face," something you are being pressed to handle, or a situation you feel you must deal with sooner rather than later.

Maybe you have a vacation trip coming up that you need to make some major last-minute decisions about. Or perhaps you just inherited six million dollars and you don't know what to do with the cash. Whatever.

Got it? Good. Now describe, in a single written sentence, your intended successful outcome for this problem or situation. In other words, what would need to happen for you to check this "project" off as "done"? It could be as simple as "Take the Hawaii vacation," "Handle situation with customer X," "Resolve college situation with Susan," "Clarify new divisional management structure," or "Implement new investment strategy." All clear? Great.

Now write down the *very next physical action required to move the situation forward*. If you had nothing else to do in your life but get closure on this, where would you go right now, and what visible action would you take? Would you pick up a phone and make a call? Go to your computer and write an e-mail? Sit down with pen and paper and brainstorm about it? Talk face-to-face with your spouse, your secretary, your attorney, or your boss? Buy nails at the hardware store? What?

Got the answer to that? Good.

Was there any value for you in these two minutes of thinking? If you're like the vast majority of people who complete that drill during my seminars, you'll be experiencing at least a tiny bit of enhanced control, relaxation, and focus. You'll also be feeling more motivated to actually *do* something about that situation you've merely been thinking about till now. Imagine that motivation magnified a thousandfold, as a way to live and work.

Think like a man of action, act like a man of thought.
—Henry Bergson

If anything at all positive happened for you in this little exercise, think about this: What changed? What happened to create that improved condition within your own experience? The situation itself is no further along, at least in the physical world. It's certainly not finished yet. What probably happened is that you acquired a clearer definition of the outcome desired and the next action required.

But what created that? The answer is, *thinking*. Not a lot, just enough to solidify your commitment and the resources required to fulfill it.

The Real Work of Knowledge Work

Welcome to the real-life experience of "knowledge work," and a profound operational principle: *You have to think about your stuff more than you realize but not as much as you're afraid you might.* As Peter Drucker has written, "In knowledge work . . . the task is not given; it has to be determined. 'What are the expected results from this work?' is . . . the key question in making knowledge workers productive. And it is a question that demands risky decisions. There is usually no right answer; there are choices instead. And results have to be clearly specified, if productivity is to be achieved."

The ancestor of every action is a thought.
—Ralph Waldo Emerson

Most people have a resistance to initiating the burst of energy that it will take to clarify the real meaning, for them, of something they have let into their world, and to decide what they need to do about it. We're never really taught that we have to think about our work before we can do it; much of our daily activity is already defined for us by the undone and unmoved things staring at us when we come to work, or by the family to be fed, the laundry to be done, or the children to be dressed at home. Thinking in a concentrated manner to define desired outcomes is something few people feel they have to do. But in truth, outcome thinking is one of the most effective means available for making wishes reality.

Why Things Are on Your Mind

Most often, the reason something is "on your mind" is that you want it to be different than it currently is, and yet:

- you haven't clarified exactly what the intended outcome is;
- you haven't decided what the very next physical action step is; and/or
- you haven't put reminders of the outcome and the action required in a system you trust.

That's why it's on your mind. Until those thoughts have been clarified and those decisions made, and the resulting data has been stored in a system that you *absolutely* know you will think about as often as you need to, your brain can't give up the job. You can fool everyone else, but you can't fool your own mind. It knows whether or not you've come to the conclusions you need to, and whether you've put the resulting outcomes and action reminders in a place that can be trusted to resurface appropriately within your conscious mind. If you haven't done those things, it won't quit working overtime. Even if you've already decided on the next step you'll take to resolve a problem, your mind can't let go until and unless you write yourself a reminder in a place it *knows* you will, without fail, look. It will keep pressuring you about that untaken next step, usually when you can't do anything about it, which will just add to your stress.

This constant, unproductive preoccupation with all the things we have to do is the single largest consumer of time and energy.
—*Kerry Gleeson*

Your Mind Doesn't Have a Mind of Its Own

At least a portion of your mind is really kind of stupid, in an interesting way. If it had any innate intelligence, it would remind you of the things you needed to do *only when you could do something about them.*

Do you have a flashlight somewhere with dead batteries in it? When does your mind tend to remind you that you need new batteries? When you notice the dead ones! That's not very smart. If your mind had any innate intelligence, it would remind you about those dead batteries only when you passed live ones in a store. And ones of the right size, to boot.

Between the time you woke up today and now, did you think of anything you needed to do that you still haven't done? Have you had that thought more than once? Why? It's a waste of time and energy to keep thinking about something that you make no progress on. And it only adds to your anxieties about what you should be doing and aren't.

It seems that most people let their minds run a lot of the show, especially where the too-much-to-do syndrome is concerned. You've probably given over a lot of your "stuff," a lot of your open loops, to an entity on your inner committee that is incapable of dealing with those things effectively the way they are—your mind.

Rule your mind or it will rule you.
—Horace

The Transformation of "Stuff"

Here's how I define "stuff": anything you have allowed into your psychological or physical world that doesn't belong where it is, but for which you haven't yet determined the desired outcome and the next action step. The reason most organizing systems haven't worked for most people is that they haven't yet transformed all the "stuff" they're trying to organize. As long as it's still "stuff," it's not controllable.

We need to transform all the "stuff" we're trying to organize into actionable stuff we need to do.

Most of the to-do lists I have seen over the years (when people had them at all) were merely listings of "stuff," not inventories of the resultant real work that needed to be done. They were partial reminders of a lot of things that were unresolved and as yet untranslated into outcomes and actions—that is, the real outlines and details of what the list-makers had to "do."

"Stuff" is not inherently a bad thing. Things that command our attention, by their very nature, usually show up as "stuff." But once "stuff" comes into our lives and work, we have an inherent commitment to ourselves to define and clarify its meaning. That's our responsibility as knowledge workers; if "stuff" were already transformed and clear, our value, other than physical labor, would probably not be required.

At the conclusion of one of my seminars, a senior manager of a major biotech firm looked back at the to-do lists she had come in with and said, "Boy, that was an amorphous blob of undoability!" That's the best description I've ever heard of what passes for organizing lists in most personal systems. The vast majority of people have been trying to get organized by rearranging incomplete lists of unclear things; they haven't yet realized how much and what they need to organize in order to get the real payoff. They need to gather everything that requires thinking about and then *do* that thinking if their organizational efforts are to be successful.

The Process: Managing Action

You can train yourself, almost like an athlete, to be faster, more responsive, more proactive, and more focused in knowledge work. You can think more effectively and manage the results with more ease and control. You can minimize the loose ends across the whole spectrum of your work life and personal life and get a lot more done with less effort. And you can make front-end decision-making about all the "stuff" you collect and create standard operating procedure for living and working in this new millennium.

Before you can achieve any of that, though, you'll need to get in the habit of keeping nothing on your mind. And the way to do *that,* as we've seen, is not by managing time, managing information, or managing priorities. After all:

- you don't manage five minutes and wind up with six;
- you don't manage information overload—otherwise you'd walk into a library and die, or the first time you connected to the Web, or even opened a phone book, you'd blow up; and
- you don't manage priorities—you *have* them.

Instead, the key to managing all of your "stuff" is managing your *actions.*

Managing Action Is the Prime Challenge

What you *do* with your time, what you *do* with information, and what you *do* with your body and your focus relative to your priorities—those are the real options to which you must allocate your limited resources. The real issue is how to make appropriate choices about what to *do* at any point in time. The real issue is how we manage *actions*.

That may sound obvious. However, it might amaze you to discover how many next actions for how many projects and commitments remain undetermined by most people. It's extremely difficult to manage actions you haven't identified or decided on. Most people have dozens of things that they need to do to make progress on many fronts, but they don't yet know what they are. And the common complaint that "I don't have time to ____" (fill in the blank) is understandable because many projects seem overwhelming—and *are* overwhelming because you can't *do* a project at all! You can only do an action related to it. Many actions require only a minute or two, in the appropriate context, to move a project forward.

The beginning is half of every action.
—Greek proverb

In training and coaching thousands of professionals, I have found that lack of time is not the major issue for them (though they themselves may think it is); the real problem is a lack of clarity and definition about what a project really is, and what the associated next-action steps required are. Clarifying things on the front end, when they first appear on the radar, rather than on the back end, after trouble has developed, allows people to reap the benefits of managing action.

Things rarely get stuck because of lack of time. They get stuck because the doing of them has not been defined.

The Value of a Bottom-Up Approach

I have discovered over the years the practical value of working on personal productivity improvement from the bottom up, starting with the most mundane, ground-floor level of current activity and commitments. Intellectually, the most appropriate way *ought* to be to work from the top down, first uncovering personal and corporate missions, then defining critical objectives, and finally focusing on the details of implementation. The trouble is, however, that most people are so embroiled in commitments on a day-to-day level that their ability to focus successfully on the larger horizon is seriously impaired. Consequently, a bottom-up approach is usually more effective.

Getting current on and in control of what's in your in-basket and on your mind right now, and incorporating practices that can help you *stay* that way, will provide the best means of broadening your horizons. A creative, buoyant energy will be unleashed that will better support your focus on new heights, and your confidence will increase to handle what that creativity produces. An immediate sense of freedom, release, and inspiration naturally comes to people who roll up their sleeves and implement this process.

You'll be better equipped to undertake higher-focused thinking when your tools for handling the resulting actions for implementation are part of your ongoing operational style. There are more meaningful things to think about than your in-basket, but if your management of that level is not as efficient as it could be, it's like trying to swim in baggy clothing.

Vision is not enough; it must be combined with venture. It is not enough to stare up the steps; we must step up the stairs.
—Vaclav Havel

Many executives I have worked with during the day to clear the decks of their mundane "stuff" have spent the following evening having a stream of ideas and visions about their company and their future. This happens as an automatic consequence of unsticking their workflow.

Horizontal and Vertical Action Management

You need to control commitments, projects, and actions in two ways—horizontally and vertically. "Horizontal" control maintains coherence across all the activities in which you are involved. Imagine your psyche constantly scanning your environment like police radar; it may land on any of a thousand different items that invite or demand your attention during any twenty-four-hour period: the drugstore, the housekeeper, your aunt Martha, the strategic plan, lunch, a wilting plant in the office, an upset customer, shoes that need shining. You have to buy stamps, deposit that check, make the hotel reservation, cancel a staff meeting, see a movie tonight. You might be surprised at the volume of things you actually think about and have to deal with just in one day. You need a good system that can keep track of as many of them as possible, supply required information about them on demand, and allow you to shift your focus from one thing to the next quickly and easily.

"Vertical" control, in contrast, manages thinking up and down the track of individual topics and projects. For example, your inner "police radar" lands on your next vacation as you and your spouse talk about it over dinner—where and when you'll go, what you'll do, how to prepare for the trip, and so on. Or you and your boss need to make some decisions about the new departmental reorganization you're about to launch. Or you just need to get your thinking up to date on the customer you're about to call. This is "project planning" in the broad sense. It's focusing in on a single endeavor, situation, or person and fleshing out whatever ideas, details, priorities, and sequences of events may be required for you to handle it, at least for the moment.

The goal for managing horizontally and vertically is the same: to get things off your mind and get things done. Appropriate action management lets you feel comfortable and in control as you move through your broad spectrum of work and life, while appropriate project focusing gets you clear about and on track with the specifics needed.

The Major Change: Getting It All Out of Your Head

There is no real way to achieve the kind of relaxed control I'm promising if you keep things only in your head. As you'll discover, the individual behaviors described in this book are things you're already doing. The big difference between what I do and what others do is that I capture and organize 100 percent of my "stuff" *in and with objective tools at*

> There is usually an inverse proportion between how much something is on your mind and how much it's getting done.

hand, not in my mind. And that applies to *everything*—little or big, personal or professional, urgent or not. Everything.

I'm sure that at some time or other you've gotten to a place in a project, or in your life, where you just *had* to sit down and *make a list*. If so, you have a reference point for what I'm talking about. Most people, however, do that kind of list-making drill only when the confusion get too unbearable and they just *have* to do something about it. They usually make a list only about the specific area that's bugging them. But if you made that kind of review a characteristic of your ongoing life- and work style, and you maintained it across all areas of your life (not just the most "urgent"), you'd be practicing the kind of "black belt" management style I'm describing.

There is no reason ever to have the same thought twice, unless you like having that thought.

I try to make intuitive choices based on my options, instead of trying to think about what those options *are*. I need to have *thought* about all of that already and captured the results in a trusted way. I don't want to waste time thinking about things more than once. That's an inefficient use of creative energy and a source of frustration and stress.

And you can't fudge this thinking. Your mind will keep working on anything that's still in that undecided state. But there's a limit to how much unresolved "stuff" it can contain before it blows a fuse.

The short-term-memory part of your mind—the part that tends to hold all of the incomplete, undecided, and unorganized "stuff"—functions much like RAM on a personal computer. Your conscious mind, like the computer screen, is a focusing tool, not a storage place. You can think about only two or three things at once. But the incomplete items are still being stored in the short-term-memory space. And as with RAM, there's limited capacity; there's only so much "stuff" you can store in there and still have that part of your brain function at a high level. Most people walk around with their RAM bursting at the seams. They're constantly distracted, their focus disturbed by their own internal mental overload.

For example, in the last few minutes, has your mind wandered off into some area that doesn't have anything to do with what you're reading here? Probably. And most likely where your mind went was to some open loop, some incomplete situation that you have some investment in. All that situation did was rear up out of the RAM part of your brain and yell at you, internally. And what did you do about it? Unless you wrote it down and put it in a trusted "bucket" that you know you'll review appropriately sometime soon, more than likely you *worried* about it. Not the most effective behavior: no progress was made, and tension was increased.

> *It is hard to fight an enemy who has outposts in your head.*
>
> *—Sally Kempton*

The big problem is that your mind keeps reminding you of things when you can't *do* anything about them. It has no sense of past or future. That means that as soon as you tell yourself that you need to do something, and store it in your RAM, there's a part of you that thinks you should be doing that something *all the time*. Everything you've told yourself you ought to do, it thinks you should be doing *right now*. Frankly, as soon as you have two things to do stored in your RAM, you've generated personal failure, because you can't do them both at the same time. This produces an all-pervasive stress factor whose source can't be pinpointed.

Most people have been in some version of this mental stress state so consistently, for so long, that they don't even know they're *in* it. Like gravity, it's ever-present—so much so that those who experience it usually aren't even aware of the pressure. The only time most of them will realize how much tension they've been under is when they get rid of it and notice how different they feel.

Can you get rid of that kind of stress? You bet. The rest of this book will explain how.

2

Getting Control of Your Life: The Five Stages of Mastering Workflow

THE CORE PROCESS I teach for mastering the art of relaxed and controlled knowledge work is a five-stage method for managing workflow. No matter what the setting, there are five discrete stages that we go through as we deal with our work. We (1) *collect* things that command our attention; (2) *process* what they mean and what to do about them; and (3) *organize* the results, which we (4) *review* as options for what we choose to (5) *do*. This constitutes the management of the "horizontal" aspect of our lives—incorporating everything that has our attention at any time.

The knowledge that we consider knowledge proves itself in action. What we now mean by knowledge is information in action, information focused on results.
—Peter F. Drucker

The method is straightforward enough in principle, and it is generally how we all go about our work in any case, but in my experience most people can stand significantly to improve their handling of each one of the five stages. The quality of our workflow management is only as good as the weakest link in this five-phase chain, so all the links must be integrated together and supported with consistent standards. Most people have major leaks in their *collection* process. Many have collected things but haven't *processed* or decided what action to take about them. Others make good decisions about "stuff" in the moment but lose the value of that thinking because they don't efficiently *organize* the results. Still others have good systems but don't *review* them consistently enough to keep them functional. Finally, if any one of these links is weak, what someone is likely to choose to *do* at any point in time may not be the best option.

The dynamics of these five stages need to be understood, and good techniques and tools implemented to facilitate their functioning at an optimal level. I have found it very helpful, if not essential, to separate these stages as I move through my day. There are times when I want only to collect input and not decide what to do with it yet. At other times I may just want to process my notes from a meeting. Or I may have just returned from a big trip and need to distribute and organize what I collected and processed on the road. Then there are times when I want to review the whole inventory of my work, or some portion of it. And obviously a lot of my time is spent merely doing something that I need to get done.

I have discovered that one of the major reasons many people haven't had a lot of success with "getting organized" is simply that they have tried to do all five phases at one time. Most, when they sit down to "make a list," are trying to collect the "most important things" in some order that reflects priorities and sequences, without setting out many (or any) real actions to take. But if you don't decide what needs to be done about your secretary's birthday, because it's "not that important" right now, that open loop will take up energy and prevent you from having a totally effective, clear focus on what is important.

This chapter explains the five phases in detail. Chapters 4 through 8 provide a step-by-step program for implementing an airtight system for each phase, with lots of examples and best practices.

Collect

It's important to know what needs to be collected and how to collect it most effectively so you can process it appropriately. In order for your mind to let go of the lower-level task of trying to hang on to everything, you have to know that you have truly captured *everything* that might represent something you have to do, and that at some point in the near future you will process and review all of it.

Gathering 100 Percent of the "Incompletes"

In order to eliminate "holes in the bucket," you need to collect and gather together placeholders for or representations of all the things you consider incomplete in your world—that is, anything personal or professional, big or little, of urgent or minor importance, that you think ought to be different than it currently is and that you have any level of internal commitment to changing.

Many of the things you have to do are being collected *for* you as you read this. Mail is coming into your mailbox, memos are being routed to your in-basket, e-mail is being funneled into your computer, and messages are accumulating on your voice-mail. But at the same time, you've been "collecting" things in your environment and in your psyche that don't belong where they are, the way they are, for all eternity. Even though it may not as obviously "in your face" as your e-mail, this "stuff" still requires some kind of resolution—a loop to be closed, something to be done. Strategy ideas loitering on a legal pad in a stack on your credenza, "dead" gadgets in your desk drawers that need to be fixed or thrown away, and out-of-date magazines on your coffee table all fall into this category of "stuff."

As soon as you attach a "should," "need to," or "ought to" to an item, it becomes an incomplete. Decisions you still need to make about whether or not you are going to do something, for example, are already incompletes. This includes all of your "I'm going to"s, where you've decided to do something but haven't started moving on it yet. And it certainly includes all pending and in-progress items, as well as those things on which you've done everything you're ever going to do except acknowledge that you're finished with them.

In order to manage this inventory of open loops appropriately, you need to capture it into "containers" that hold items in abeyance until you have a few moments to decide what they are and what, if anything, you're going to do about them. Then you must empty these containers regularly to ensure that they remain viable collection tools.

Basically, everything is already being collected, in the larger sense. If it's not being directly managed in a trusted external system of yours, then it's resident *somewhere* in your psyche. The fact that you haven't put an item in your in-basket doesn't mean you haven't *got* it. But we're talking here about making sure that everything you need is collected somewhere *other* than in your head.

The Collection Tools

There are several types of tools, both low- and high-tech, that can be used to collect your incompletes. The following can all serve as versions of an in-basket, capturing self-generated input as well as information coming from outside:

- Physical in-basket
- Paper-based note-taking devices
- Electronic note-taking devices
- Voice-recording devices
- E-mail

The Physical In-Basket

The standard plastic, wood, leather, or wire tray is the most common tool for collecting paper-based materials and anything else physical that needs some sort of processing: mail, magazines, memos, notes, phone slips, receipts—even flashlights with dead batteries.

Writing Paper and Pads

Loose-leaf notebooks, spiral binders, and steno and legal pads all work fine for collecting random ideas, input, things to do, and so on. Whatever kind fits your taste and needs is fine.

Electronic Note-Taking

Computers can be used to type in notes for processing later. And as character-recognition technology advances, a parade of digital tools designed to capture data continues to be introduced. Handheld devices (personal digital assistants, or PDAs) and electronic legal pads can both be used to collect all kinds of input.

Auditory Capture

Available auditory devices include answering machines, voicemail, and dictating equipment, such as digital or microcassette recorders. All of these can be useful for preserving an interim record of things you need to remember or deal with.

E-mail

If you're wired to the rest of the world through e-mail, your software contains some sort of holding area for incoming messages and files, where they can be stored until they are viewed, read, and processed. Pagers and telephones can capture this kind of input as well.

Higher-Tech Devices

Now you can dictate into computers as well as hand-write into them. As more and more communication is morphed into digital and wireless formats, it will become easier to capture ideas (with a corresponding increase in the amount of data reaching us that we need to manage!).

"Computer!"

"Yes, David?"

"I need bread."

"Yes, David."

My needed grocery item has been *collected*. And as the *organizing* part of the action-management process is further digitized, "bread" will automatically be added to my electronic grocery list, and maybe even ordered and delivered.

Whether high-tech or low-tech, all of the tools described above serve as similar in-baskets, capturing potentially useful information, commitments, and agreements for action. You're probably already using some version of most of them.

The Collection Success Factors

Unfortunately, merely having an in-basket doesn't make it functional. Most people *do* have collection devices of some sort, but usually they're more or less out of control. Let's examine the three requirements to make the collection phase work:

1 | Every open loop must be in your collection system and out of your head.
2 | You must have as few collection buckets as you can get by with.
3 | You must empty them regularly.

Get It All Out of Your Head

If you're still trying to keep track of too many things in your RAM, you likely won't be motivated to use and empty your in-baskets with integrity. Most people are relatively careless about these tools because they know they don't represent discrete, whole systems anyway: there's an incomplete set of things in their in-basket and an incomplete set in their mind, and they're not getting any payoff from either one, so their thinking goes. It's like trying to play pinball on a machine that has big holes in the table, so the balls keep falling out: there's little motivation to keep playing the game.

These collection tools should become part of your life-style. Keep them close by so no matter where you are you can collect a potentially valuable thought—think of them as being as indispensable as your toothbrush or your driver's license or your glasses.

Minimize the Number of Collection Buckets

You should have as many in-baskets as you need and as few as you can get by with. You need this function to be available to you in every context, since things you'll want to capture may show up almost anywhere. If you have too many collection zones, however, you won't be able to process them easily or consistently.

An excess of collection buckets is seldom a problem on the high-tech end; the real improvement opportunity for most people is on the low-tech side, primarily in the areas of note-taking and physical in-basket collection. Written notes need to be corralled and processed instead of left lying embedded in stacks, notebooks, and drawers. Paper materials need to be funneled into physical in-baskets instead of being scattered over myriad piles in all the available corners of your world.

Men of lofty genius when they are doing the least work are the most active.
—Leonardo da Vinci

Implementing standard tools for capturing ideas and input will become more and more critical as your life and work become more sophisticated. As you proceed in your career, for instance, you'll probably notice that your best ideas about work will not come to you *at* work. The ability to leverage that thinking with good collection devices that are always at hand is key to increased productivity.

Empty the Buckets Regularly

The final success factor for *collecting* should be obvious: if you don't empty and process the "stuff" you've collected, your buckets aren't serving any function other than the storage of amorphous material. Emptying the bucket does not mean that you have to *finish* what's in your voice-mail, e-mail, or in-basket; it just means you have to take it out of the container, decide what it is and what should be done with it, and, if it's still unfinished, organize it into your system. You don't put it back into "in"! Not emptying your in-basket is like having garbage cans that nobody ever dumps—you just have to keep buying new ones to hold all your trash.

In order for you to get "in" to empty, your total action-management system must be in place. Too much "stuff" is left piled in in-baskets because of a lack of effective systems "downstream" from there. It often seems easier to leave things in "in" when you know you have to do something about them but can't do it right then. The in-basket, especially for paper and e-mail, is the best that many people can do in terms of organization—at least they know that *somewhere* in there is a reminder of something they still have to do. Unfortunately, that safety net is lost when the piles get out of control or the inventory of e-mails gets too extensive to be viewed on one screen.

When you master the next phase and know how to process your incompletes easily and rapidly, "in" can return to its original function. Let's move on to how to get those in-baskets and e-mail systems *empty* without necessarily having to *do* the work now.

Process

Teaching them the item-by-item thinking required to get their collection buckets empty is perhaps the most critical improvement I have made for virtually all the people I've worked with. When the head of a major department in a global corporation had finished processing all her open items with me, she sat back in awe and told me that though she had been able to relax about what meetings to go to thanks to her trust in her calendar, she had never felt that same relief about all the many other aspects of her job, which we had just clarified together. The actions and information she needed to be reminded of were now identified and entrusted to a concrete system.

What do you need to ask yourself (and answer) about each e-mail, voice-mail, memo, or self-generated idea that comes your way? This is the component of action management that forms the basis for your personal organization. Many people try to "get organized" but make the mistake of doing it with incomplete batches of "stuff." You can't organize what's incoming—you can only collect it and process it. Instead, you organize the actions you'll need to take based on the decisions you've made about what needs to be done. The whole deal—both the *processing* and

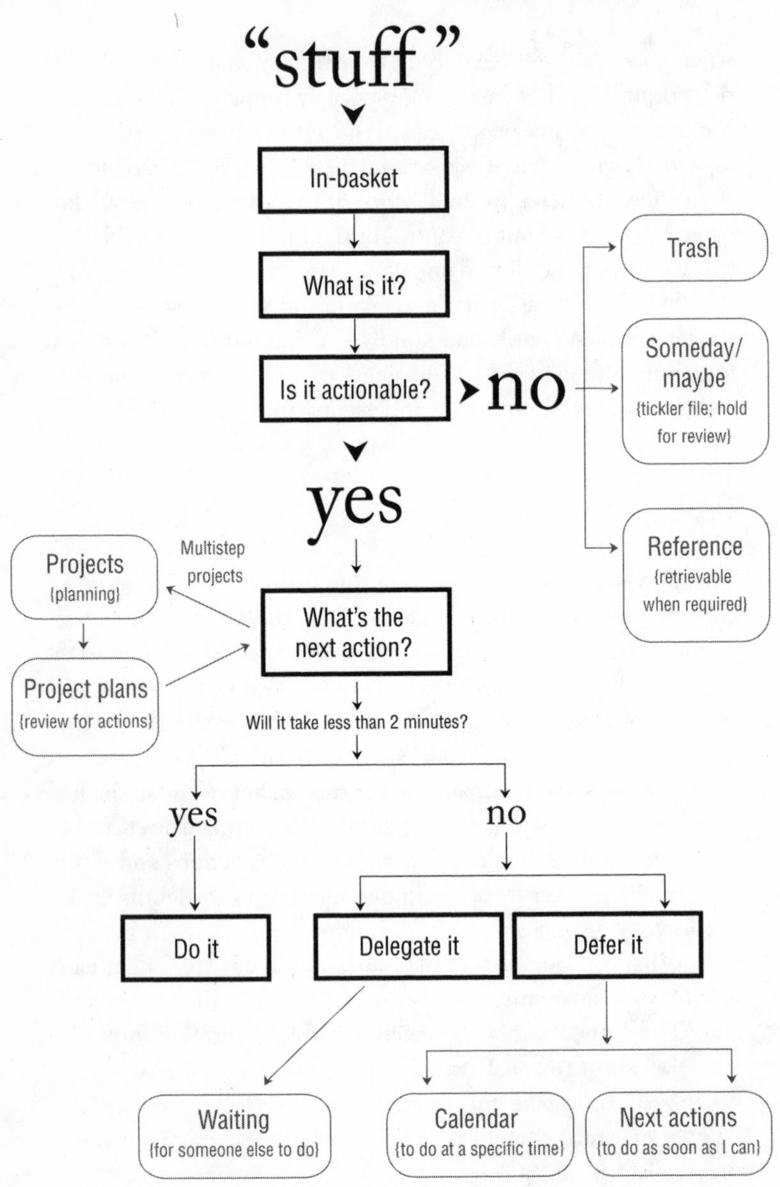

WORKFLOW DIAGRAM—PROCESSING

organizing phases—is captured in the center "trunk" of the decision-tree model shown here.

In later chapters, I'll coach you in significant detail through each element of the process. For now, though, I suggest you select a to-do list or a pile of papers from your in-basket and assess a few items as we take an overview.

What Is It?

This is not a dumb question. We've talked about "stuff." And we've talked about collection buckets. But we haven't discussed what stuff *is* and what to do about it. For example, many of the items that tend to leak out of our personal organizing systems are amorphous forms that we receive from the government or from our company—do we actually need to *do* something about them? And what about that e-mail from human resources, letting us know that blah-blah about the blah-blah is now the policy of blah-blah? I've unearthed piles of messages in stacks and desk drawers that were tossed there because the client didn't take just a few seconds to figure out what in fact the communication or document was really about. Which is why the next decision is critical.

Is It Actionable?

There are two possible answers for this: YES and NO.

No Action Required If the answer is NO, there are three possibilities:

1 | It's trash, no longer needed.
2 | No action is needed now, but something might need to be done later (incubate).
3 | The item is potentially useful information that might be needed for something later (reference).

These three categories can themselves be managed; we'll get into that in a later chapter. For now, suffice it to say that you need a trash basket and <Del> key for trash, a "tickler" file or calendar for material that's incubating, and a good filing system for reference information.

Actionable This is the YES group of items, stuff about which something needs to be done. Typical examples range from an e-mail requesting your participation in a corporate service project on such-and-such a date to the notes in your in-basket from your face-to-face meeting with the group vice president about a significant new project that involves hiring an outside consultant.

Two things need to be determined about each actionable item:

1 | What "project" or outcome have you committed to? and
2 | What's the next action required?

If It's About a Project . . . You need to capture that outcome on a "Projects" list. That will be the stake in the ground that reminds you that you have an open loop. A Weekly Review of the list (see page 46) will bring this item back to you as something that's still outstanding. It will stay fresh and alive in your management system until it is completed or eliminated.

It does not take much strength to do things, but it requires a great deal of strength to decide what to do.
—Elbert Hubbard

What's the Next Action? This is the critical question for anything you've collected; if you answer it appropriately, you'll have the key substantive thing to organize. The "next action" is the next physical, visible activity that needs to be engaged in, in order to move the current reality toward completion.

Some examples of next actions might be:

- Call Fred re tel. # for the garage he recommended.
- Draft thoughts for the budget-meeting agenda.
- Talk to Angela about the filing system we need to set up.
- Research database-management software on the Web.

These are all real physical activities that need to happen. Reminders of these will become the primary grist for the mill of your personal productivity-management system.

Do It, Delegate It, or Defer It Once you've decided on the next action, you have three options:

1 | *Do it.* If an action will take less than two minutes, it should be *done* at the moment it is defined.
2 | *Delegate it.* If the action will take longer than two minutes, ask yourself, Am I the right person to do this? If the answer is no, *delegate* it to the appropriate entity.
3 | *Defer it.* If the action will take longer than two minutes, and you are the right person to do it, you will have to *defer* acting on it until later and track it on one or more "Next Actions" lists.

Organize

The outer ring of the workflow diagram shows the eight discrete categories of reminders and materials that will result from your processing all your "stuff." Together they make up a total system for organizing just about everything that's on your plate, or could be added to it, on a daily and weekly basis.

For nonactionable items, the possible categories are *trash, incubation tools,* and *reference storage.* If no action is needed on something, you toss it, "tickle" it for later reassessment, or file it so you can find the material if you need to refer to it at another time. To manage actionable things, you will need a *list of projects, storage or files for project plans and materials,* a *calendar,* a *list of reminders of next actions,* and a *list of reminders of things you're waiting for.*

All of the organizational categories need to be physically contained in some form. When I refer to "lists," I just mean some sort of reviewable set of reminders, which could be lists on

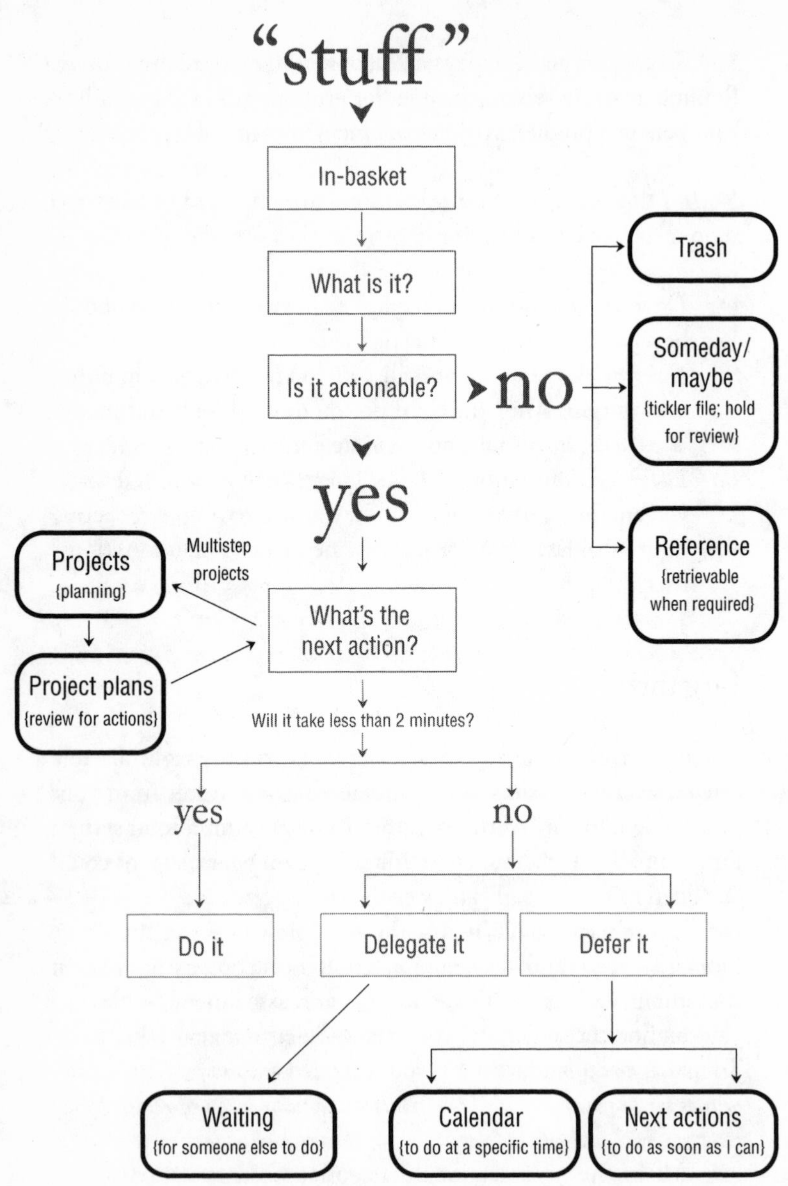

WORKFLOW DIAGRAM—ORGANIZING

notebook paper or in some computer program or even file folders holding separate pieces of paper for each item. For instance, the list of current projects could be kept on a page in a Day Runner; it could be a "To Do" category on a PDA; or it could be in a file labeled "Projects List." Incubating reminders (such as "after March 1 contact my accountant to set up a meeting") may be stored in a paper-based "tickler" file or in a paper- or computer-based calendar program.

Projects

I define a *project* as any desired result that requires more than one action step. This means that some rather small things that you might not normally call projects are going to be on your "Projects" list. The reasoning behind my definition is that if one step won't complete something, some kind of stake needs to be placed in the ground to remind you that there's something still left to do. If you don't have a placeholder to remind you about it, it will slip back into RAM. Another way to think of this is as a list of open loops.

A Partial "Projects" List

Get new staff person on board
August vacation
Staff off-site retreat
Publish book
Finalize computer upgrades
Update will
Finalize budgets
Finalize new product line
Get comfortable with new contact-management software
Get reprints of *Fortune* article
Get a publicist
Finish new orchard planting
R&D joint-venture video project
Produce new training compact disk
Establish next year's seminar schedule
Orchestrate a one-hour keynote presentation
Get proficient with videoconferencing access
Finalize employment agreements
Install new backyard lights
Establish formal relationships with South American rep
Finalize staff policies and procedures
Get a new living-room chair

Projects do not need to be listed in any particular order, whether by size or by priority. They just need to be on a master list so you can review them regularly enough to ensure that appropriate next actions have been defined for each of them.

You don't actually *do* a project; you can only do action steps *related* to it. When enough of the right action steps have been taken, some situation will have been created that matches your initial picture of the outcome closely enough that you can call it "done." The list of projects is the compilation of finish lines we put before us, to keep our next actions moving on all tracks appropriately.

Project Support Material

For many of your projects, you will accumulate relevant information that you will want to organize by theme or topic or project name. Your "Projects" list will be merely an index. All of the details, plans, and supporting information that you may need as you work on your various projects should be contained in separate file folders, computer files, notebooks, or binders.

Support Materials and Reference Files Once you have organized your project support material by theme or topic, you will probably find that it is almost identical to your reference material and could be kept in the same reference file system (a "Wedding" file could be kept in the general-reference files, for instance). The only difference is that in the case of active projects, support material may need to be reviewed on a more consistent basis to ensure that all the necessary action steps are identified.

I usually recommend that people store their support materials out of sight. If you have a good working reference file system close enough at hand, you may find that that's the simplest way to organize them. There will be times, though, when it'll be more convenient to have the materials out and instantly in view and available, especially if you're working on a hot project that you need to check references for several times during the day. File folders in wire standing holders or in stackable trays within easy reach can be practical for this kind of "pending" paperwork.

The Next-Action Categories

As the Workflow Diagram makes clear, the next-action decision is central. That action needs to be the next physical, visible behavior, without exception, on every open loop.

Any less-than-two-minute actions that you perform, and all other actions that have already been completed, do not, of course, need to be tracked; they're done. What *does* need to be tracked is every action that has to happen at a specific time or on a specific day (enter these in your calendar); those that need to be done as soon as they can (add these to your "Next Actions" lists); and all those that you are waiting for others to do (put these on a "Waiting For" list).

Calendar

Reminders of actions you need to take fall into two categories: those about things that have to happen on a specific day or time, and those about things that just need to get done as soon as possible. Your calendar handles the first type of reminder.

Three things go on your calendar:

- time-specific actions;
- day-specific actions; and
- day-specific information.

Time-Specific Actions This is a fancy name for appointments. Often the next action to be taken on a project is attending a meeting that has been set up to discuss it. Simply tracking that on the calendar is sufficient.

Day-Specific Actions These are things that you need to do *sometime* on a certain day, but not necessarily at a *specific* time. Perhaps you told Mioko you would call her on Friday to check that the report you're sending her is OK. She won't have the report until Thursday, and she's leaving the country on Saturday, so Friday is the time window for taking the action—but anytime Friday will be fine. That should be tracked on the calendar for Friday but not tied to any particular time slot—it should just go on the day. It's useful to have a calendar on which you can note both time-specific and day-specific actions.

Day-Specific Information The calendar is also the place to keep track of things you want to *know* about on specific days—not necessarily *actions* you'll have to take but rather *information* that may be useful on a certain date. This might include directions for appointments, activities that other people (family or staff) will be involved in then, or events of interest. It's also helpful to put short-term "tickler" information here, too, such as a reminder to call someone after the day they return from a vacation.

No More "Daily To-Do" Lists Those three things are what go on the calendar, and nothing else! I know this is heresy to traditional time-management training, which has almost universally taught that the "daily to-do list" is key. But such lists don't work, for two reasons.

Blessed are the flexible, for they shall not be bent out of shape.
—Michael McGriffy, M.D.

First, constant new input and shifting tactical priorities reconfigure daily work so consistently that it's virtually impossible to nail down to-do items ahead of time. Having a working game plan as a reference point is always useful, but it must be able to be renegotiated at any moment. Trying to keep a list in writing on the calendar, which must then be rewritten on another day if items don't get done, is demoralizing and a waste of time. The "Next Actions" lists I advocate will hold all of those action reminders, even the most time-sensitive ones. And they won't have to be rewritten daily.

Second, if there's something on a daily to-do list that doesn't absolutely *have* to get done that day, it will dilute the emphasis on the things that truly *do*. If I *have* to call Mioko on Friday because that's the only day I can reach her, but then I add five other, less important or less time-sensitive calls to my to-do list, when the day gets crazy I may never call Mioko. My brain will have to take back the reminder that that's the one phone call I won't get another chance at. That's not utilizing the system appropriately. The way I look at it, the calendar should be sacred territory. If you write something there, it must get done that day or not at all. The only rewriting should be for changed appointments.

The "Next Actions" List(s)

So where do all your action reminders go? On "Next Actions" lists, which, along with the calendar, are at the heart of daily action-management organization.

Any longer-than-two-minute, nondelegatable action you have identified needs to be tracked somewhere. "Call Jim Smith re budget meeting," "Phone Rachel and Laura's moms about sleepaway camp," and "Draft ideas re the annual sales conference" are all the kinds of action reminders that need to be kept in appropriate lists, or buckets, to be assessed as options for what we will do at any point in time.

If you have only twenty or thirty of these, it may be fine to keep them all on one list labeled "Next Actions," which you'll review whenever you have any free time. For most of us, however, the number is more likely to be fifty to 150. In that case it makes sense to subdivide your "Next Actions" list into categories, such as "Calls" to make when you're at a phone or "Project Head Questions" to be asked at your weekly briefing.

Everything should be made as simple as possible, but not simpler.
—Albert Einstein

Nonactionable Items

You need well-organized, discrete systems to handle the items that require no action as well as the ones that do. No-action systems fall into three categories: *trash, incubation,* and *reference.*

Trash

Trash should be self-evident. Throw away anything that has no potential future action or reference value. If you leave this stuff mixed in with other categories, it will seriously undermine the system.

Incubation

There are two other groups of things besides trash that require no immediate action, but this stuff you will want to *keep*. Here again, it's critical that you separate nonactionable from actionable items; otherwise you will tend to go numb to your piles, stacks, and lists and not know where to start or what needs to be done.

Say you pick up something from a memo, or read an e-mail, that gives you an idea for a project you *might* want to do someday, but not now. You'll want to be reminded of it again later so you can reassess the option of doing something about it in the future. For example, a brochure arrives in the mail for the upcoming season of your local symphony. On a quick browse, you see that the program that really interests you is still four months away—too distant for you to move on it yet (you're not sure what your travel schedule will be that far out), but if you *are* in town, you'd like to go. What should you do about that?

There are two kinds of "incubate" systems that could work for this kind of thing: "Someday/Maybe" lists and a "tickler" file.

"Someday/Maybe" It can be useful and inspiring to maintain an ongoing list of things you might want to do at some point but not now. This is the "parking lot" for projects that would be impossible to move on at present but that you don't want to forget about entirely. You'd like to be reminded of the possibility at regular intervals.

Typical Partial "Someday/Maybe" List

Get a bass-fishing boat
Learn Spanish
Take a watercolor class
Get a sideboard for the kitchen
Build a lap pool
Get Kathryn a scooter
Take a balloon ride
Build a wine cellar
Take a trip through Montana
Learn Photoshop software capabilities
Set up a not-for-profit foundation
Create promotional videos of staff
Find Stafford Lyons
Get a digital video camera
Northern Italy trip
Apprentice with my carpenter
Spotlight our artwork
Build a koi pond
Digitize old photos and videos
Have a neighborhood party
Set up remote-server access at home

You'll probably have some subcategories in your master "Someday/Maybe" list, such as

- CDs I might want
- Videos to rent
- Books to read
- Wine to taste
- Weekend trips to take
- Things to do with the kids
- Seminars to take

You must review this list periodically if you're going to get the most value from it. I suggest you include a scan of the contents in your Weekly Review (see page 46).

"Tickler" File The most elegant version of holding for review is the "tickler" file, sometimes also referred to as a "suspended" or "follow-on" file. This is a system that allows you to almost literally mail something to yourself, for receipt on some designated day in the future.

Your calendar can serve the same function. You might remind yourself on your calendar for March 15, for example, that your taxes are due in a month; or for September 12, that *Swan Lake* will be presented by the Bolshoi at the Civic Auditorium in six weeks.

For further details, refer to chapter 7.

Reference Material

Many things that come your way require no action but have intrinsic value as information. You will want to keep and be able to retrieve these as needed. They can be stored in paper-based or digital form.

Paper-based material—anything from the menu for a local take-out deli to the plans, drawings, and vendor information for a landscape project—is best stored in efficient physical-retrieval systems. These can range from pages in a loose-leaf planner or notebook, for a list of favorite restaurants or the phone numbers of the members of a school committee, to whole file cabinets dedicated to the due-diligence paperwork for a corporate merger.

Electronic storage can include everything from networked database information to ad hoc reference and archive folders located in your communication software.

The most important thing to remember here is that reference should be exactly that—information that can be *easily* referred to when required. Reference systems generally take two forms: (1) topic- and area-specific storage, and (2) general-reference files. The first types usually define themselves in terms of how they are stored—for example, a file drawer dedicated to contracts, by date; a drawer containing only confidential employee-compensation information; or a series of cabinets for closed legal cases that might need to be consulted during future trials.

General-Reference Filing The second type of reference system is one that everyone needs close at hand for storing ad hoc information that doesn't belong in some predesignated category. You need somewhere to keep the instruction manual for your cell phone, the notes from the meeting about the Smith project, and those few yen that you didn't get to change at the end of your last trip to Tokyo (and that you'll use when you go back there).

The lack of a good general-reference file can be one of the biggest bottlenecks in implementing an efficient personal action-management system. If filing isn't easy and fast (and even fun!), you'll tend to stack things instead of filing them. If your reference material doesn't have a nice clean edge to it, the line between actionable and nonactionable items will blur, visually and psychologically, and your mind will go numb to the whole business. Establishing a good working system for this category of material is critical to ensuring stress-free productivity; we will explore it in detail in chapter 7.

Review

It's one thing to write down that you need milk; it's another to be at the store and *remember* it. Likewise, writing down that you need to call a friend for the name of an estate attorney is different from remembering it when you're at a phone and have some discretionary time.

You need to be able to review the whole picture of your life and work at appropriate intervals and appropriate levels. For most people the magic of workflow management is realized in the consistent use of the review phase. This is where you take a look at all your outstanding projects and open loops, at what I call the 10,000-foot level (see page 51), on a weekly basis. It's your chance to scan all the defined actions and options before you, thus radically increasing the efficacy of the choices you make about what you're doing at any point in time.

What to Review When

If you set up a personal organization system structured as I recommend, with a "Projects" list, a calendar, "Next Actions" lists, and a "Waiting For" list, not much will be required to maintain that system.

The item you'll probably review most frequently is your calendar, which will remind you about the "hard landscape" for the day—that is, what things will die if you don't do them. This doesn't mean that the things written on there are the most "important" in some grand sense—only that they have to get done. At at any point in time, knowing what *has* to get done, and when, creates a terrain for maneuvering. It's a good habit, as soon as you conclude an action on your calendar (a meeting, a phone call, the final draft of a report), to check and see what else remains to be done.

After checking your calendar, you'll most often turn to your "Next Actions" lists. These hold the inventory of predefined actions that you can take if you have any discretionary time during the day. If you've organized them by context ("At Home," "At Computer," "In Meeting with George"), they'll come into play only when those contexts are available.

Review your lists as often as you need to, to get them off your mind.

"Projects," "Waiting For," and "Someday/Maybe" lists need to be reviewed only as often as you think they have to be in order to stop you from wondering about them.

Critical Success Factor: The Weekly Review

Everything that might potentially require action must be reviewed on a frequent enough basis to keep your mind from taking back the job of remembering and reminding. In order to trust the rapid and intuitive judgment calls that you make about actions from moment to moment, you must consistently retrench at some more elevated level. In my experience (with thousands of people), that translates into a behavior critical for success: the Weekly Review.

All of your open loops (i.e., projects), active project plans, and "Next Actions," "Agendas," "Waiting For," and even "Someday/Maybe" lists should be reviewed once a week. This also gives you an opportunity to ensure that your brain is clear and that all the loose strands of the past few days have been collected, processed, and organized.

If you're like most people, you've found that things can get relatively out of control during the course of a few days of operational intensity. That's to be expected. You wouldn't want to distract yourself from too much of the work at hand in an effort to stay totally "squeaky clean" all the time. But in order to afford the luxury of "getting on a roll" with confidence, you'll probably need to clean house once a week.

The affairs of life embrace a multitude of interests, and he who reasons in any one of them, without consulting the rest, is a visionary unsuited to control the business of the world.
—James Fenimore Cooper

The Weekly Review is the time to

- Gather and process all your "stuff."
- Review your system.
- Update your lists.
- Get clean, clear, current, and complete.

Most people don't have a really complete system, and they get no real payoff from reviewing things for just that reason: their overview isn't total. They still have a vague sense that something may be missing. That's why the rewards to be gained from implementing *this* whole process are at least geometric: the more complete the system is, the more you'll trust it. And the more you trust it, the more complete you'll be motivated to *keep* it. The Weekly Review is a master key to maintaining that standard.

Most people feel best about their work when they've cleaned up, closed up, clarified, and renegotiated all their agreements with themselves and others. Do this weekly instead of yearly.

Most people feel best about their work the week before their vacation, but it's not because of the vacation itself. What do you do the last week before you leave on a big trip? You clean up, close up, clarify, and renegotiate all your agreements with yourself and others. I just suggest that you do this weekly instead of yearly.

Do

The basic purpose of this workflow-management process is to facilitate good choices about what you're *doing* at any point in time. At 10:33 A.M. Monday, deciding whether to call Sandy, finish the proposal, or process your e-mails will always be an intuitive call, but with the proper preplanning you can feel much more confident about your choices. You can move from *hope* to *trust* in your actions, immediately increasing your speed and effectiveness.

Every decision to act is an intuitive one. The challenge is to migrate from *hoping* it's the right choice to *trusting* it's the right choice.

Three Models for Making Action Choices

Let's assume for a moment that you're not resisting any of your "stuff" out of insecurity or procrastination. There will always be a large list of actions that you are *not* doing at any given moment. So how will you decide what to *do* and what *not* to do, and feel good about both?

The answer is, by trusting your intuition. If you have *collected*, *processed*, *organized*, and *reviewed* all your current commitments, you can galvanize your intuitive judgment with some intelligent and practical thinking about your work and values.

You have more to do than you can possible do. You just need to feel good about your choices.

I have developed three models that will be helpful for you to incorporate in your decision-making about what to do. They won't tell you answers—whether you call Frederick, e-mail your son at school, or just go have an informal "how are you?" conversation with your secretary—but they will assist you in framing your options more intelligently. And that's something that the simple time- and priority-management panaceas *can't* do.

1. The Four-Criteria Model for Choosing Actions in the Moment
At 3:22 on Wednesday, how do you choose what to do? There are four criteria you can apply, in this order:

1 | Context
2 | Time available
3 | Energy available
4 | Priority

Context A few actions can be done anywhere (like drafting ideas about a project with pen and paper), but most require a specific location (at home, at your office) or having some productivity tool at hand, such as a phone or a computer. These are the first factors that limit your choices about what you *can* do in the moment.

Time Available When do you have to do something *else*? Having a meeting in five minutes would prevent doing many actions that require more time.

Energy Available How much energy do you have? Some actions you have to do require a reservoir of fresh, creative mental energy. Others need more physical horsepower. Some need very little of either.

Priority Given your context, time, and energy available, what action will give you the highest payoff? You have an hour, you're in your office with a phone and a computer, and your energy is 7.3 on a scale of 10. Should you call the client back, work on the proposal, process your voice-mails and e-mails, or check in with your spouse to see how his or her day is going?

This is where you need to access your intution and begin to rely on your judgment call in the moment. To explore that concept further, let's examine two more models for deciding what's "most important" for you to be doing.

2. The Threefold Model for Evaluating Daily Work

When you're getting things done, or "working" in the universal sense, there are three different kinds of activities you can be engaged in:

- Doing predefined work
- Doing work as it shows up
- Defining your work

Doing Predefined Work When you're doing predefined work, you're working off your "Next Actions" lists—completing tasks that you have previously determined need to be done, managing your workflow. You're making the calls you need to make, drafting ideas you want to brainstorm, or preparing a list of things to talk to your attorney about.

Doing Work as It Shows Up Often things come up ad hoc—unsuspected, unforeseen—that you either have to or choose to respond to as they occur. For example, your partner walks into your office and wants to have a conversation about the new product launch, so you talk to her instead of doing all the other things you could be doing. Every day brings surprises—unplanned-for things that just show up, and you'll need to expend at least *some* time and energy on many of them. When you follow these leads, you're deciding by default that these things are more important than anything else you have to do.

Defining Your Work Defining your work entails clearing up your in-basket, your e-mail, your voice-mail, and your meeting notes and breaking down new projects into actionable steps. As you process your inputs, you'll no doubt be taking care of some less-than-two-minute actions and tossing and filing numerous things (another version of doing work as it shows up). A good portion of this activity will consist of identifying things that need to get done sometime, but not right away. You'll be adding to all of your lists as you go along.

Once you have defined all your work, you can trust that your lists of things to do are complete. And your context, time, and energy available still allow you the option of more than one thing to do. The final thing to consider is the nature of your work, and its goals and standards.

3. The Six-Level Model for Reviewing Your Own Work

Priorities should drive your choices, but most models for determining them are not reliable tools for much of our real work activity. In order to know what your priorities are, you have to know what your work is. And there are at least six different perspectives from which to define that. To use an aerospace analogy, the conversation has a lot to do with the altitude.

- 50,000+ feet: Life
- 40,000 feet: Three- to five-year vision
- 30,000 feet: One- to two-year goals
- 20,000 feet: Areas of responsibility
- 10,000 feet: Current projects
- Runway: Current actions

Let's start from the bottom up:

Runway: Current Actions This is the accumulated list of all the actions you need to take—all the phone calls you have to make, the e-mails you have to respond to, the errands you've got to run, and the agendas you want to communicate to your boss and your spouse. You'd probably have three hundred to five hundred hours' worth of these things to do if you stopped the world right now and got no more input from yourself or anyone else.

10,000 Feet: Current Projects Creating many of the actions that you currently have in front of you are the thirty to one hundred projects on your plate. These are the relatively short-term outcomes you want to achieve, such as setting up a home computer, organizing a sales conference, moving to a new headquarters, and getting a dentist.

20,000 Feet: Areas of Responsibility You create or accept most of your projects because of your responsibilities, which for most people can be defined in ten to fifteen categories. These are the key areas within which you want to achieve results and maintain standards. Your job may entail at least implicit commitments for things like strategic planning, administrative support, staff development, market research, customer service, or asset management. And your personal life has an equal number of such focus arenas: health, family, finances, home environment, spirituality, recreation, etc. Listing and reviewing these responsibilities gives a more comprehensive framework for evaluating your inventory of projects.

30,000 Feet: One- to Two-Year Goals What you want to be experiencing in the various areas of your life and work one to two years from now will add another dimension to defining your work. Often meeting the goals and objectives of your job will require a shift in emphasis of your job focus, with new areas of responsibility emerging. At this horizon personally, too, there probably are things you'd like to accomplish or have in place, which could add importance to certain aspects of your life and diminish others.

40,000 Feet: Three- to Five-Year Vision Projecting three to five years into the future generates thinking about bigger categories: organization strategies, environmental trends, career and life-transition circumstances. Internal factors include longer-term career, family, and financial goals and considerations. Outer-world issues could involve changes affecting your job and organization, such as technology, globalization, market trends, and competition. Decisions at this altitude could easily change what your work might look like on many levels.

50,000+ Feet: Life This is the "big picture" view. Why does your company exist? Why do *you* exist? The primary purpose for anything provides the core definition of what its "work" really is. It is the ultimate job description. All the goals, visions, objectives, projects, and actions derive from this, and lead toward it.

These altitude analogies are somewhat arbitrary, and in real life the important conversations you will have about your focus and your priorities may not fit exactly to one horizon or another. They can provide a useful framework, however, to remind you of the multilayered nature of your "job" and resulting commitments and tasks.

Obviously, many factors must be considered before you feel comfortable that you have made the best decision about what to do and when. "Setting priorities" in the traditional sense of focusing on your long-term goals and values, though obviously a necessary core focus, does not provide a practical framework for a vast majority of the decisions and tasks you must engage in day to day. Mastering the flow of your work at all the levels you experience that work provides a much more holistic way to get things done, and feel good about it.

Part 2 of this book will provide specific coaching about how to use these three models for making action choices, and how the best practices for collecting, processing, planning, organizing, and reviewing all contribute to your greatest success with them.

3

Getting Projects Creatively Under Way: The Five Phases of Project Planning

You've got to think about the big things while you're doing small things, so that all the small things go in the right direction.
—Alvin Toffler

THE KEY INGREDIENTS of relaxed control are (1) clearly defined outcomes (projects) and the next actions required to move them toward closure, and (2) reminders placed in a trusted system that is reviewed regularly. This is what I call horizontal focus. Although it may seem simple, the actual application of the process can create profound results.

Enhancing "Vertical" Focus

Horizontal focus is all you'll need in most situations, most of the time. Sometimes, however, you may need greater rigor and focus to get a project under control, to identify a solution, or to ensure that all the right steps have been determined. This is where vertical focus comes in. Knowing how to think productively in this more "vertical" way and how to integrate the results into your personal system is the second powerful behavior set needed for knowledge work.

The goal is to get projects and situations off your mind, but not to lose any potentially useful ideas.

This kind of thinking doesn't have to be elaborate. Most of the thinking you'll need to do is informal, what I call back-of-the-envelope planning—the kind of thing you do literally on the back of an envelope in a coffee shop with a colleague as you're hashing out the agenda and structure of a sales presentation. In my experience this tends to be the most productive kind of planning you can do in terms of your output relative to the energy you put into it. True, every once in a while you may need to develop a more formal structure or plan to clarify components, sequences, or priorities. And more detailed outlines will also be necessary to coordinate more complex situations—if teams need to collaborate about various project pieces, for example, or if business plans need to be drafted to convince an investor you know what you're doing. But as a general rule, you can be pretty creative with nothing more than an envelope and a pencil.

The greatest need I've seen in project thinking in the professional world is not for more formal models; usually the people who need those models already have them or can get them as part of an academic or professional curriculum. Instead, I've found the biggest gap to be the lack of a project-focusing model for "the rest of us." We need ways to validate and support our thinking, no matter how informal. Formal planning sessions and high-horsepower planning tools (such as project software) can certainly be useful, but too often the participants in a meeting will need to have *another* meeting—a back-of-the-envelope session—to actually get a piece of work fleshed out and under control. More formal and structured meetings also tend to skip over at least one critical issue, such as *why* the project is being done in the first place. Or they don't allow adequate time for brainstorming, the development of a bunch of ideas nobody's ever thought about that would make the project more interesting, more profitable, or just more fun. And finally, very few such meetings bring to bear sufficient rigor in determining action steps and accountabilities for the various aspects of a project plan.

The good news is, there *is* a productive way to think about projects, situations, and topics that creates maximum value with minimal expenditure of time and effort. It happens to be the way we *naturally* think and plan, though not necessarily the way we *normally* plan when we consciously try to get a project under control. In my experience, when people do more planning, more informally and naturally, they relieve a great deal of stress *and* obtain better results.

The Natural Planning Model

You're already familiar with the most brilliant and creative planner in the world: your brain. You yourself are actually a planning machine. You're planning when you get dressed, eat lunch, go to the store, or simply talk. Although the process may seem somewhat random, a quite complex series of steps in fact has to occur before your brain can make anything happen physically. Your mind goes through five steps to accomplish virtually any task:

The most experienced planner in the world is your brain.

1 | Defining purpose and principles
2 | Outcome visioning
3 | Brainstorming
4 | Organizing
5 | Identifying next actions

A Simple Example: Planning Dinner Out

The last time you went out to dinner, what initially caused you to think about doing it? It could have been any number of things—the desire to satisfy hunger, socialize with friends, celebrate a special occasion, sign a business deal, or develop a romance. As soon as any of these turned into a real inclination that you wanted to move on, you started planning. Your intention was your ***purpose***, and it automatically triggered your internal planning process. Your ***principles*** created the boundaries of your plan. You probably didn't consciously think *about* your principles regarding going out to dinner, but you thought *within* them: standards of food and service, affordability, convenience, and comfort all may have played a part. In any case, your purpose and principles were the defining impetus and boundaries of your planning.

Once you decided to fulfill your purpose, what were your first substantive thoughts? Probably not "point II.A.3.b. in plan." Your first ideas were more likely things like "Italian food at Giovanni's," or "Sitting at a sidewalk table at the Bistro Café." You probably also imagined some positive picture of what you might experience or how the evening would turn out—maybe the people involved, the atmosphere, and/or the outcome. That was your ***outcome visioning***. Whereas your purpose was the *why* of your going out to dinner, your vision was an image of the *what*—of the physical world's looking, sounding, and feeling the ways that best fulfilled your purpose.

Once you'd identified with your vision, what did your mind naturally begin doing? What did it start to think about? "What time should we go?" "Is it open tonight?" "Will it be crowded?" "What's the weather like?" "Should we change clothes?" "Is there gas in the car?" "How hungry are we?" That was ***brainstorming***. Those questions were part of the naturally creative process that happens once you commit to some outcome that hasn't happened yet. Your brain noticed a gap between what you were looking toward and where you actually were at the time, and it began to resolve that "cognitive dissonance" by trying to fill in the blanks. This is the beginning of the "how" phase of natural planning. But it did the thinking in a somewhat random and ad hoc fashion. Lots of different aspects of going to dinner just occurred to you. You almost certainly didn't need to actually write all of them down on a piece of paper, but you did a version of that process in your mind.*

Once you had generated a sufficient number of ideas and details, you couldn't help but start to ***organize*** them. You may

---

*If, however, you were handling the celebration for your best friend's recent triumph, the complexity and detail that might accrue in your head should warrant *at least* the back of an envelope!

have thought or said, "First we need to find out if the restaurant is open", or "Let's call the Andersons and see if they'd like to go out with us." Once you've generated various thoughts relevant to the outcome, your mind will automatically begin to sort them by components (subprojects), priorities, and/or sequences of events. *Components* would be: "We need to handle logistics, people, and location." *Priorities* would be: "It's critical to find out if the client really would like to go to dinner." *Sequences* would be: "First we need to check whether the restaurant is open, then call the Andersons, then get dressed."

Finally (assuming that you're really committed to the project—in this case, going out to dinner), you focus on the ***next action*** that you need to take to make the first component actually happen. "Call Suzanne's to see if it's open, and make the reservation."

These five phases of project planning occur naturally for everything you accomplish during the day. It's how you create things—dinner, a relaxing evening, a new product, or a new company. You have an urge to make something happen; you image the outcome; you generate ideas that might be relevant; you sort those into a structure; and you define a physical activity that would begin to make it a reality. And you do all of that naturally, without giving it much thought.

Natural Planning Is Not Necessarily Normal

But is the process described above the way your committee is planning the church retreat? Is it how your IT team is approaching the new system installation? Is it how you're organizing the wedding or thinking through the potential merger?

Have you clarified the primary purpose of the project and communicated it to everyone who ought to know it? And have you agreed on the standards and behaviors you'll need to adhere to to make it successful?

Have you envisioned wild success lately?

Have you envisioned success and considered all the innovative things that might result if you achieved it?

Have you gotten all possible ideas out on the table—everything you need to take into consideration that might affect the outcome?

Have you identified the mission-critical components, key milestones, and deliverables?

Have you defined all the aspects of the project that could be moved on right now, what the next action is for each part, and who's responsible for what?

If you're like most people I interact with in a coaching or consulting capacity, the collective answer to these questions is, probably not. There are likely to be at least some components of the natural planning model that you haven't implemented.

In some of my seminars I get participants to actually plan a current strategic project that uses this model. In only a few minutes they walk themselves through all five phases, and usually end up being amazed at how much progress they've made compared with what they have tried to do in the past. One gentleman came up afterward and told me, "I don't know whether I should thank you or be angry. I just finished a business plan I've been telling myself would take months, and now I have no excuses for not doing it!"

You can try it for yourself right now if you like. Choose one project that is new or stuck or that could simply use some improvement. Think of your purpose. Think of what a successful outcome would look like: where would you be physically, financially, in terms of reputation, or whatever? Brainstorm potential steps. Organize your ideas. Decide on the next actions. Are you any clearer about where you want to go and how to get there?

The Unnatural Planning Model

To emphasize the importance of utilizing the natural planning model for the more complex things we're involved with, let's contrast it with the more "normal" model used in most environments—what I call unnatural planning.

When the "Good Idea" Is a Bad Idea

Have you ever heard a well-intentioned manager start a meeting with the question, "OK, so who's got a good idea about this?"

What is the assumption here? Before any evaluation of what's a "good idea" can be trusted, the purpose must be clear, the vision must be well defined, and all the relevant data must have been collected (brainstormed) and analyzed (organized). "What's a good idea?" is a good question, but only when you're about 80 percent of the way through your thinking! *Starting* there would probably blow anyone's creative mental fuses.

If you're waiting to have a good idea before you have any ideas, you won't have many ideas.

Trying to approach any situation from a perspective that is not the natural way your mind operates will be difficult. People do it all the time, but it almost always engenders a lack of clarity and increased stress. In interactions with others, it opens the door for egos, politics, and hidden agendas to take over the discussion (generally speaking, the most verbally aggressive will run the show). And if it's just you, attempting to come up with a "good idea" before defining your purpose, creating a vision, and collecting lots of initial bad ideas is likely to give you a case of creative constipation.

Let's Blame Mrs. Williams

If you're like most people in our culture, the only formal training you've ever had in planning and organizing proactively was in the fourth or fifth grade. And even if that wasn't the *only* education you've had in this area, it was probably the most emotionally intense (meaning it sank in the deepest).

Mrs. Williams, my fourth-grade teacher, had to teach us about organizing our thinking (it was in her lesson plans). We were going to learn to write *reports*. But in order to write a well-organized, successful report, what did we have to write first? That's right—an *outline*!

Outlines were easy, as long as you wrote the report first.

Did you ever have to do that, create an outline to begin with? Did you ever stare at a Roman numeral I at the top of your page for a torturous period of time and decide that planning and organizing ahead of time were for people very different from you? Probably.

In the end, I did learn to write outlines. I just wrote the report first, then made up an outline from the report, after the fact.

That's what most people learned about planning from our educational system. And I still see outlines done after the fact, just to please the authorities. In the business world, they're often headed "Goals" and "Objectives." But they still have very little to do with what people are doing or what they're inspired about. These documents are sitting in drawers and in e-mails somewhere, bearing little relationship to operational reality.

The Reactive Planning Model

The unnatural planning model is what most people consciously think of as "planning," and because it's so often artificial and irrelevant to real work, people just don't plan. At least not on the front end: they resist planning meetings, presentations, and strategic operations until the last minute.

But what happens if you don't plan ahead of time? In many cases, crisis! ("Didn't you get the tickets? I thought you were going to do that?!") Then, when the urgency of the last minute is upon you, the reactive planning model ensues.

When you find yourself in a hole, stop digging.
—Will Rogers

What's the first level of focus when the stuff hits the fan? ***Action!*** Work harder! Overtime! More people! Get busier! And a lot of stressed-out people are thrown at the situation.

Then, when having a lot of busy people banging into each other doesn't resolve the situation, someone gets more sophisticated and says, "We need to get ***organized!***" (Catching on now?) Then people draw boxes around the problem and label them. Or *redraw* the boxes and *relabel* them.

Don't just do something. Stand there.
—Rochelle Myer

At some point they realize that just redrawing boxes isn't really doing much to solve the problem. Now someone (much more sophisticated) suggests that more creativity is needed. "Let's ***brainstorm!***" With everyone in the room, the boss asks, "So, who's got a *good* idea here?" (Thank you, Mrs. Williams.)

When not much happens, the boss may surmise that his staff has used up most of its internal creativity. Time to hire a consultant! Of course, if the consultant is worth his salt, at some point he is probably going to ask the big question: "So, what are you really trying to *do* here, anyway?" (***vision, purpose***).

The reactive style is the *reverse* of the natural model. It will always come back to a top-down focus. It's not a matter of *whether* the natural planning will be done—just *when,* and at what cost.

Natural Planning Techniques: The Five Phases

It goes without saying, but still it must be said again: thinking in more effective ways about projects and situations can make things happen sooner, better, and more successfully. So if our minds plan naturally anyway, what can we learn from that? How can we use that model to facilitate getting more and better results in our thinking?

Let's examine each of the five phases of natural planning and see how we can leverage these contexts.

Purpose

It never hurts to ask the "why?" question. Almost anything you're currently doing can be enhanced and even galvanized by more scrutiny at this top level of focus. Why are you going to your next meeting? What's the purpose of your task? Why are you having friends over for a barbeque in the backyard? Why are you hiring a marketing director? Why do you have a budget?

Fanaticism consists of redoubling your efforts when you have forgotten your aim.
—George Santayana

I admit it: this is nothing but advanced common sense. To know and to be clear about the purpose of any activity are prime directives for clarity, creative development, and cooperation. But it's common sense that's not commonly practiced, simply because it's so easy for us to create things, get caught up in the form of what we've created, and let our connection with our real and primary intentions slip.

I know, based upon thousands of hours spent in many offices with many sophisticated people, that the "why?" question cannot be ignored. When people complain to me about having too many meetings, I have to ask, "What is the purpose of the meetings?" When they ask, "Who should I invite to the planning session?" I have to ask, "What's the purpose of the planning session?" Until we have the answer to *my* questions, there's no possible way to come up with an appropriate response to *theirs*.

The Value of Thinking About "Why"

Here are just some of the benefits of asking "why?":

- It defines success.
- It creates decision-making criteria.
- It aligns resources.
- It motivates.
- It clarifies focus.
- It expands options.

People love to win. If you're not totally clear about the purpose of what you're doing, you have no chance of winning.

Let's take a closer look at each of these in turn.

It Defines Success People are starved for "wins" these days. We love to play games, and we like to win, or at least be in a position where we *could* win. And if you're not totally clear about the purpose of what you're doing, you have no chance of winning. Purpose defines success. It's the primal reference point for any investment of time and energy, from deciding to run for elective office to designing a form.

Celebrate any progress. Don't wait to get perfect.
—Ann McGee Cooper

Ultimately you can't feel good about a staff meeting unless you know what the purpose of the meeting was. And if you want to sleep well, you'd better have a good answer when your board asks why you fired your V.P. of marketing or hired that hotshot M.B.A. as your new finance director. You won't really know whether or not your business plan is any good until you hold it up against the success criterion that you define by answering the question "Why do we need a business plan?"

It Creates Decision-Making Criteria How do you decide whether to spend the money for a five-color brochure or just go with a two-color? How do you know whether it's worth hiring a major Web design firm to handle your new Web site?

Often the only way to make a hard decision is to come back to the purpose.

It all comes down to purpose. Given what you're trying to accomplish, are these resource investments required, and if so, which ones? There's no way to know until the purpose is clarified.

It Aligns Resources How should we spend our staffing allocation in the corporate budget? How do we best use the cash flow right now to maximize our viability as a retailer over the next year? Should we spend more money on the luncheon or the speakers for the monthly association meeting?

In each case, the answer depends on what we're really trying to accomplish—the *why*.

It Motivates Let's face it: if there's no good *reason* to be doing something, it's not worth doing. I'm often stunned by how many people have forgotten *why* they're doing what they're doing—and by how quickly a simple question like "Why are you doing that?" can get them back on track.

It Clarifies Focus When you land on the real purpose for anything you're doing, it makes things clearer. Just taking two minutes and writing out your primary reason for doing something invariably creates an increased sharpness of vision, much like bringing a telescope into focus. Frequently, projects and situations that have begun to feel scattered and blurred grow clearer when someone brings it back home by asking, "What are we really trying to accomplish here?"

It Expands Options Paradoxically, even as purpose brings things into pinpoint focus, it opens up creative thinking about wider possibilities. When you really know the underlying "why"—for the conference, for the staff party, for the elimination of the management position, or for the merger—it expands your thinking about how to make the desired result happen. When people write out their purpose for a project in my seminars, they often claim it's like a fresh breeze blowing through their mind, clarifying their vision of what they're doing.

> If you're not sure why you're doing something, you can never do enough of it.

Is your purpose clear and specific enough? If you're truly experiencing the benefits of a purpose focus—motivation, clarity, decision-making criteria, alignment, and creativity—then your purpose probably *is* specific enough. But many "purpose statements" are too vague to produce such results. "To have a good department," for example, might be too broad a goal. After all, what constitutes a "good department"? Is it a group of people who are highly motivated, collaborating in healthy ways, and taking initiative? Or is it a department that comes in under budget? In other words, if you don't really know when you've met your purpose or when you're off track, you don't have a viable directive. The question "How will I know when this is off-purpose?" must have a clear answer.

Principles

Of equal value as prime criteria for driving and directing a project are the standards and values you hold. Although people seldom think about these consciously, they are always there. And if they are violated, the result will inevitably be unproductive distraction and stress.

Simple, clear purpose and principles give rise to complex and intelligent behavior. Complex rules and regulations give rise to simple and stupid behavior.
—Dee Hock

A great way to think about what your principles are is to complete this sentence: "I would give others totally free rein to do this as long as they . . ."—what? What policies, stated or unstated, will apply to your group's activities? "As long as they stayed within budget"? "satisfied the client"? "ensured a healthy team"? "promoted a positive image"?

It can be a major source of stress when others engage in or allow behavior that's outside your standards. If you never have to deal with this issue, you're truly graced. If you do, some constructive conversation about and clarification of principles could align the energy and prevent unnecessary conflict. You may want to begin by asking yourself, "What behavior might undermine what I'm doing, and how can I prevent it?" That will give you a good starting point for defining your standards.

Another great reason for focusing on principles is the clarity and reference point they provide for positive conduct. How do you want or need to work with others on this project to ensure its success? You yourself are at your best when you're acting how?

Whereas purpose provides the juice and the direction, principles define the parameters of action and the criteria for excellence of behavior.

Vision/Outcome

In order most productively to access the conscious and unconscious resources available to you, you must have a clear picture in your mind of what success would look, sound, and feel like. Purpose and principles furnish the impetus and the monitoring, but vision provides the actual blueprint of the final result. This is the "what?" instead of the "why?" What will this project or situation really be like when it successfully appears in the world?

For example, graduates of your seminar are demonstrating consistently applied knowledge of the subject matter. Market share has increased 2 percent within the northeastern region over the last fiscal year. Your daughter is clear about your guidelines and support for her first semester in college.

The Power of Focus

Since the 1960s thousands of books have expounded on the value of appropriate positive imagery and focus. Forward-looking focus has even been a key element in Olympic-level sports training, with athletes imagining the physical effort, the positive energy, and the successful result to ensure the highest level of unconscious support for their performance.

We know that the focus we hold in our minds affects what we perceive and how we perform. This is as true on the golf course as it is in a staff meeting or during a serious conversation with a spouse. My interest lies in providing a model for focus that is dynamic in a practical way, especially in project thinking.

Imagination is more important than knowledge.
—Albert Einstein

When you focus on something—the vacation you're going to take, the meeting you're about to go into, the product you want to launch—that focus instantly creates ideas and thought patterns you wouldn't have had otherwise. Even your physiology will respond to an image in your head as if it were reality.

The Reticular Activating System The May 1957 issue of *Scientific American* contained an article describing the discovery of the reticular formation at the base of the brain. The reticular formation is basically the gateway to your conscious awareness; it's the switch that turns on your perception of ideas and data, the thing that keeps you asleep even when music's playing but wakes you if a special little baby cries in another room.

> *Your automatic creative mechanism is teleological. That is, it operates in terms of goals and end results. Once you give it a definite goal to achieve, you can depend upon its automatic guidance system to take you to that goal much better than "you" ever could by conscious thought. "You" supply the goal by thinking in terms of end results. Your automatic mechanism then supplies the means whereby.*
> *—Maxwell Maltz*

Just like a computer, your brain has a search function—but it's even more phenomenal than a computer's. It seems to be programmed by what we focus on and, more primarily, what we identify with. It's the seat of what many people have referred to as the paradigms we maintain. We notice only what matches our internal belief systems and identified contexts. If you're an optometrist, for example, you'll tend to notice people wearing eyeglasses across a crowded room; if you're a building contractor, you may notice the room's physical details. If you focus on the color red right now and then just glance around your environment, if there is any red at all, you'll see even the tiniest bits of it.

The implications of how this filtering works—how we are unconsciously made conscious of information—could fill a weeklong seminar. Suffice it to say that something automatic and extraordinary happens in your mind when you create and focus on a clear picture of what you want.

Clarifying Outcomes

There is a simple but profound principle that emerges from understanding the way your perceptive filters work: *you won't see how to do it until you see yourself doing it.*

It's easy to envision something happening if it has happened before or you have had experience with similar successes. It can be quite a challenge, however, to identify with images of success if they represent new and foreign territory—that is, if you have few reference points about what an event might actually look like and little experience of your own ability to make it happen.

You often need to make it up in your mind before you can make it happen in your life.

Many of us hold ourselves back from imaging a desired outcome unless someone can show us *how to get there.* Unfortunately, that's backward in terms of how our minds work to generate and recognize solutions and methods.

One of the most powerful skills in the world of knowledge work, and one of the most important to hone and develop, is creating clear outcomes. This is not as self-evident as it may sound. We need to constantly define (and redefine) what we're trying to accomplish on many different levels, and consistently reallocate resources toward getting these tasks completed as effectively and efficiently as possible.

I always wanted to be somebody. I should have been more specific.
—Lily Tomlin

What will this project look like when it's done? How do you want the client to feel, and what do you want him to know and do, after the presentation? Where will you be in your career three years from now? How would the ideal V.P. of finance do his job? What would your Web site really look like and have as capabilities if it could be the way you wanted it?

Outcome/vision can range from a simple statement of the project, such as "Finalize computer-system implementation," to a completely scripted movie depicting the future scene in all its glorious detail. Here are three basic steps for developing a vision:

1 | View the project from beyond the completion date.
2 | Envision "WILD SUCCESS"! (Suspend "Yeah, but . . .")
3 | Capture features, aspects, qualities you imagine in place.

When I get people to focus on a successful scenario of their project, they usually experience heightened enthusiasm and think of something unique and positive about it that hadn't occurred to them before. "Wouldn't it be great if . . ." is not a bad way to start thinking about a situation, at least for long enough to have the option of getting an answer.

The best way to get a good idea is to get lots of ideas.
—Linus Pauling

Brainstorming

Once you know what you want to have happen, *and why,* the "how" mechanism is brought into play. When you identify with some picture in your mind that is different from your current reality, you automatically start filling in the gaps, or brainstorming. Ideas begin to pop into your head in somewhat random order—little ones, big ones, not-so-good ones, good ones. This process usually goes on internally for most people about most things, and that's often sufficient. For example, you think about what you want to say to your boss as you're walking down the hall to speak to her. But there are many other instances when writing things down, or capturing them in some external way, can give a tremendous boost to productive output and thinking.

Your mind wants to fill in the blanks between here and there, but in somewhat random order.

Capturing Your Ideas

Over the last few decades, a number of graphics-oriented brainstorming techniques have been introduced to help develop creative thinking about projects and topics. They've been called things like mind-mapping, clustering, patterning, webbing, and fish-boning. Although the authors of these various processes may portray them as being different from one another, for most of us end-users the basic premise remains the same: give yourself permission to capture and express *any* idea, and then later on figure out how it fits in and what to do with it. If nothing else (and there is plenty of "else"), this practice adds to your efficiency—when you have the idea, you grab it, which means you won't have to go "have the idea" again.

The most popular of these techniques is called mind-mapping, a name coined by Tony Buzan, a British researcher in brain functioning, to label this process of brainstorming ideas onto a graphic format. In mind-mapping, the core idea is presented in the center, with associated ideas growing out in a somewhat free-form fashion around it. For instance, if I found out that I had to move my office, I might think about computers, changing my business cards, all the connections I'd have to change, new furniture, moving the phones, purging and packing, and so on. If I captured these thoughts graphically it might start to look something like this:

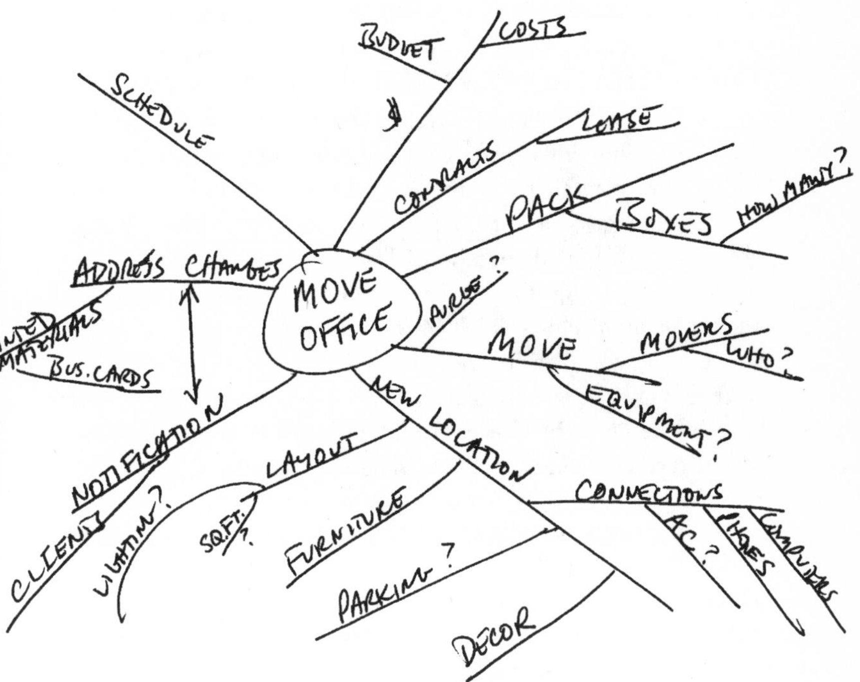

You could do this kind of mind-mapping on Post-its that could be stuck on a whiteboard, or you could input ideas into a word processor or outlining program on the computer.

Distributed Cognition

The great thing about external brainstorming is that in addition to capturing your original ideas, it can help generate many new ones that might not have occurred to you if you didn't have a mechanism to hold your thoughts and continually reflect them back to you. It's as if your mind were to say, "Look, I'm only going to give you as many ideas as you feel you can effectively use. If you're not collecting them in some trusted way, I won't give you that many. But if you're actually doing something with the ideas—even if it's just recording them for later evaluation—then here, have a bunch! And, oh wow! That reminds me of another one, and another," etc.

Nothing is more dangerous than an idea when it is the only one you have.
—Emile Chartier

Psychologists are beginning to label this and similar processes "distributed cognition." It's getting things out of your head and into objective, reviewable formats. But my English teacher in high school didn't have to know about the theory to give me the key: "David," he said, "you're going to college, and you're going to be writing papers. Write all your notes and quotes on separate three-by-five cards. Then, when you get ready to organize your thinking, just spread them all out on the floor, see the structure, and figure out what you're missing." Mr. Edmundson was teaching me a major piece of the natural planning model!

Only he who handles his ideas lightly is master of his ideas, and only he who is master of his ideas is not enslaved by them.
—Lin Yutang

Few people can hold their focus on a topic for more than a couple of minutes, without some objective structure and tool or trigger to help them. Pick a big project you have going right now and just try to think of nothing else for more than sixty seconds. This is pretty hard to do unless you have a pen and paper in hand and use those "cognitive artifacts" as the anchor for your ideas. Then you can stay with it for hours. That's why good thinking can happen while you're working on a computer document about a project, mind-mapping it on a legal pad or on a paper tablecloth in a hip restaurant, or just having a meeting about it with other people in a room that allows you to hold the context (a whiteboard with nice wet markers really helps there, too).

Brainstorming Keys

Many techniques can be used to facilitate brainstorming and out-of-the-box thinking. The basics principles, however, can be summed up as follows:

- Don't judge, challenge, evaluate, or criticize.
- Go for quantity, not quality.
- Put analysis and organization in the background.

Don't Judge, Challenge, Evaluate, or Criticize It's easy for the unnatural planning model to rear its ugly head in brainstorming, making people jump to premature evaluations and critiques of ideas. If you care even slightly about what a critic thinks, you'll censure your expressive process as you look for the "right" thing to say. There's a very subtle distinction between keeping brainstorming on target with the topic and stifling the creative process. It's also important that brainstorming be put into the overall context of the planning process, because if you think you're doing it just for its own sake, it can seem trite and inappropriately off course. If you can understand it instead as something you're doing right now, for a certain period, before you move toward a resolution at the end, you'll feel more comfortable giving this part of the process its due.

A good way to find out what something might be is to uncover all the things it's probably not.

This is not to suggest that you should shut off critical thinking, though—everything ought to be fair game at this stage. It's just wise to understand what kinds of thoughts you're having and to park them for use in the most appropriate way. The primary criterion must be expansion, not contraction.

Go for Quantity, Not Quality Going for quantity keeps your thinking expansive. Often you won't know what's a good idea until you have it. And sometimes you'll realize it's a good idea, or the germ of one, only later on. You know how shopping at a big store with lots of options lets you feel comfortable about your choice? The same holds true for project thinking. The greater the volume of thoughts you have to work with, the better the context you can create for developing options and trusting your choices.

Put Analysis and Organization in the Background Analysis and evaluation and organization of your thoughts should be given as free a rein as creative out-of-the-box thinking. But in the brainstorming phase, this critical activity should not be the driver.

Making a list can be a creative thing to do, a way to consider the people who should be on your team, the customer requirements for the software, or the components of the business plan. Just make sure to grab all that and keep going until you get into the weeding and organizing of focus that make up the next stage.

Organizing

If you've done a thorough job of emptying your head of all the things that came up in the brainstorming phase, you'll notice that a natural organization is emerging. As my high school English teacher suggested, once you get all the ideas out of your head and in front of your eyes, you'll automatically notice natural relationships and structure. This is what most people are referring to when they talk about "project plans."

Organizing usually happens when you identify components and subcomponents, sequences or events, and/or priorities. What are the things that must occur to create the final result? In what order must they occur? What is the most important element to ensure the success of the project?

This is the stage in which you can make good use of structuring tools ranging from informal bullet points, scribbled literally on the back of an envelope, to project-planning software like Microsoft Project. When a project calls for substantial objective control, you'll need some type of hierarchical outline with components and subcomponents, and/or a GANTT-type chart showing stages of the project laid out over time, with independent and dependent parts and milestones identified in relationship to the whole.

A "project plan" identifies the smaller outcomes, which can then be naturally planned.

Creative thinking doesn't stop here; it just takes another form. Once you perceive a basic structure, your mind will start trying to "fill in the blanks." Identifying three key things that you need to handle on the project, for example, may cause you to think of a fourth and a fifth when you see them all lined up.

The Basics of Organizing

The key steps here are:

- Identify the significant pieces.
- Sort by (one or more):
    - components
    - sequences
    - priorities
- Detail to the required degree.

I have never seen any two projects that needed to have exactly the same amount of structure and detail developed in order to get things off people's minds and moving successfully. But almost all projects can use some form of creative thinking from the left side of the brain, along the lines of "What's the plan?"

Next Actions

The final stage of planning comes down to decisions about the allocation and reallocation of physical resources to actually get the project moving. The question to ask here is, "What's the next action?"

As we noted in the previous chapter, this kind of grounded, reality-based thinking, combined with clarification of the desired outcome, forms the critical component of knowledge work. In my experience, creating a list of what your real projects are and consistently managing your next action for each one will constitute 90 percent of what is generally thought of as project planning. This "runway level" approach will make you "honest" about all kinds of things: Are you really serious about doing this? Who's responsible? Have you thought things through enough?

At some point, if the project is an actionable one, this next-action decision must be made.* Answering the question about what specifically you would do about something physically if you had nothing else to do will test the maturity of your thinking about the project. If you're not yet ready to answer that question, you have more to flesh out at some prior level in the natural planning sequence.

The Basics

- Decide on next actions for each of the current moving parts of the project.
- Decide on the next action in the planning process, if necessary.

Activating the "Moving Parts" A project is sufficiently planned for implementation when every next-action step has been decided on every front that can actually be moved on without some other component's having to be completed first. If the project has multiple components, each of them should be assessed appropriately by asking, "Is there something that anyone could be doing on this right now?" You could be coordinating speakers for the confer-

---

*You can also plan nonactionable projects and *not* need a next action—for example, designing your dream house. The lack of a next action by default makes it a "someday/maybe" project . . . and that's fine for anything of that nature.

ence, for instance, at the same time that you're finding the appropriate site.

In some cases there will be only one aspect that can be activated, and everything else will depend on the results of that. So there may be only one next action, which will be the linchpin for all the rest.

More to Plan? What if there's still more planning to be done before you can feel comfortable with what's next? There's still an action step—it is just a *process* action. What's the next step in the continuation of planning? Drafting more ideas. E-mailing Ana Maria and Sean to get their input. Telling your assistant to set up a planning meeting with the product team.

The habit of clarifying the next action on projects, no matter what the situation, is fundamental to you staying in relaxed control.

When the Next Action Is Someone Else's . . . If the next action is not yours, you must nevertheless clarify whose it is (this is a primary use of the "Waiting For" action list). In a group-planning situation, it isn't necessary for everyone to know what the next step is on every part of the project. Often all that's required is to allocate responsibility for parts of the project to the appropriate persons and leave it up to them to identify next actions on their particular pieces.

This next-action conversation forces organizational clarity. Issues and details emerge that don't show up until someone holds everyone's "feet to the fire" about the physical-level reality of resource allocation. It's a simple, practical discussion to foster, and one that can significantly stir the pot and identify weak links.

How Much Planning Do You Really Need to Do?

How much of this planning model do you really need to flesh out, and to what degree of detail? The simple answer is, as much as you need to get the project off your mind.

In general, the reason things are on your mind is that the

outcome and the action step(s) have not been appropriately defined, and/or reminders of them have not been put in places where you can be trusted to look for them appropriately. Additionally, you may not have developed the details, perspectives, and solutions sufficiently to trust the efficacy of your blueprint.

Most projects, given my definition of a project as an outcome requiring more than one action, need no more than a listing of their outcome and next action for you to get them off your mind. You need a new stockbroker? You just have to call a friend for a recommendation. You want to set up a printer at home? You just need to surf the Web to check out different models and prices. I estimate that 80 percent of projects are of that nature. You'll still be doing the full planning model on all of them, but only in your head, and just enough to figure out next actions and keep them going until they're complete.

If the project is still on your mind, there's more planning to do.

Another 15 percent or so of projects might require at least some external form of brainstorming—maybe a mind-map or a few notes in a word processor or PowerPoint file. That might be sufficient for planning meeting agendas, your vacation, or a speech to the local chamber of commerce.

A final 5 percent of projects might need the deliberate application of one or more of the five phases of the natural planning model. The model provides a practical recipe for unsticking things, resolving them, and moving them forward productively. Are you aware of a need for greater clarity, or greater action, on any of your projects? If so, using the model can often be the key to making effective progress.

Need More Clarity?

If greater clarity is what you need, shift your thinking *up* the natural planning scale. People are often very busy (*action*) but nonetheless experience confusion and a lack of clear direction. They need to pull out their plan, or create one (*organize*). If there's a lack of clarity at the planning level, there's probably a need for more *brainstorming* to generate a sufficient inventory of ideas to create trust in the plan. If the brainstorming session gets bogged down with fuzzy thinking, the focus should shift back to the *vision* of the outcome, ensuring that the reticular filter in the brain will open up to deliver the best how-to thinking. If the *outcome/vision* is unclear, you must return to a clean analysis of why you're engaged in the situation in the first place (*purpose*).

Need More to Be Happening?

If more action is what's needed, you need to move *down* the model. There may be enthusiasm about the *purpose* of a project but at the same time some resistance to actually fleshing out what fulfilling it in the real world might look like. These days, the task of "improving quality of work life" may be on the radar for a manager, but often he won't yet have defined a clear picture of the desired result. The thinking must go to the specifics of the *vision*. Again, ask yourself, "What would the outcome look like?"

> *Plans get you into things but you've got to work your way out.*
>
> *—Will Rogers*

If you've formulated an answer to that question, but things are still stuck, it's probably time for you to grapple with some of the "how" issues and the operational details and perspectives (*brainstorming*). I often have clients who have inherited a relatively clearly articulated project, like "Implement the new performance-review system," but who aren't moving forward because they haven't yet taken a few minutes to dump some ideas out about what that might entail.

If brainstorming gets hung up (and very often it does for more "blue sky" types), rigor may be required to do some evaluation of and decision-making about mission-critical deliverables that have to be handled (*organizing*). This is sometimes the case when an informal back-and-forth meeting that has generated lots of ideas ends without producing any decision about what actually needs to happen next on the project.

And if there *is* a plan, but the rubber still isn't hitting the road like it should, someone needs to assess each component with the focus of "What's the next action, and who's got it?" One manager, who had taken over responsibility many months in advance for organizing a major annual conference, asked me how to prevent the crisis all-nighters her team had experienced near the deadline the previous year. When she produced an outline of the various pieces of the project she'd inherited, I asked, "Which pieces could actually be moved on right now?" After identifying half a dozen, we clarified the next action on each one. It was off and running.

In the last two chapters, I have covered the basic models of how to stay maximally productive and in control, with minimal effort, at the two most basic levels of our life and work: the actions we take and the projects we enter into that generate many of those actions.

The fundamentals remain true—you must be responsible for collecting all your open loops, applying a front-end thought process to each of them, and managing the results with organization, review, and action.

You need no new skills to increase your productivity—just a new set of behaviors about when and where to apply them.

For all those situations that you have any level of commitment to complete, there is a natural planning process that goes on to get you from here to there. Leveraging that five-phase model can often make the evolution easier, faster, and more productive.

These models are simple to understand and easy to implement. Applying them creates remarkable results. You need essentially no new skills—you already know how to write things down, clarify outcomes, decide next actions, put things into categories, review it all, and make intuitive choices. *Right now* you have the ability to focus on successful results, brainstorm, organize your thinking, and get moving on your next steps.

But just knowing how to do all of those things does not produce results. Merely having the *ability* to be highly productive, relaxed, and in control doesn't make you that way. If you're like most people, you can use a coach—someone to walk you step by step through the experience and provide some guideposts and handy tricks along the way, until your new operational style is elegantly embedded.

You'll find that in part 2.

part 2

Practicing Stress-Free Productivity

4

Getting Started: Setting Up the Time, Space, and Tools

IN PART 2 we'll move from a conceptual framework and limited application of workflow mastery to full-scale implementation and best practices. Going through this program often gives people a level of relaxed control they may never have experienced before, but it usually requires the catalyst of step-by-step procedures to get there. To that end, I'll provide a logical sequence of things to do, to make it as easy as possible for you to get on board and glean the most value from these techniques.

Implementation—Whether All-Out or Casual—Is a Lot About "Tricks"

If you're not sure you're committed to an all-out implementation of these methods, let me assure you that a lot of the value people get from this material is good "tricks." Sometimes just one good trick can make it worthwhile to range through this information: I've had people tell me, for example, that the best thing they got from my two-day seminar was advice on setting up and using a tickler file. Tricks are for the not-so-smart, not-so-conscious part of us. To a great degree, the highest-performing people I know are those who have installed the best tricks in their lives. I know that's

> *It is easier to act yourself into a better way of feeling than to feel yourself into a better way of action.*
> —*O. H. Mowrer*

true of me. The smart part of us sets up things for us to do that the not-so-smart part responds to almost automatically, creating behavior that produces high-performance results. We trick ourselves into doing what we ought to be doing.

For instance, if you're a semiregular exerciser like me, you probably have your own little tricks to get you to exercise. My best trick is *costume*—the clothing I put on or take off. If I put on exercise gear, I'll start to feel like exercising; if I don't, I'm very likely to feel like doing something else.

Let's look at an example of a real productivity trick. You've probably taken work home that you *had* to bring back the next day, right? It was mission-critical that you not forget it the next morning. So where did you put it the night before? Did you put it in front of the door, or on your keys, so you'd be sure to take it with you? For this you got a higher education? What a sophisticated piece of self-management technology you've installed in your life! But actually that's just what it is. The smart part of you the night before knows that the not-so-smart part of you first thing in the morning may barely be conscious. "What's this in front of the door!? Oh, that's right, I've got to take this with me!"

What a class act. But really, it is. It's a trick I call Put It in Front of the Door. For our purposes the "door" is going to be the door of your mind, not your house. But it's the same idea.

If you were to take out your calendar right now and look closely at every single item for the next fourteen days, you'd probably come up with *at least* one "Oh-that-reminds-me-I-need-to____." If you then captured that value-added thought into some place that would trigger you to act, you'd feel better already, have a clearer head, and get more positive things done. It's not rocket science, just a good trick.

You increase your productivity and creativity exponentially when you think about the right things at the right time and have the tools to capture your value-added thinking.

If you take out a clean sheet of paper right now, along with your favorite writing instrument, and for three minutes focus solely on the most awesome project on your mind, I guarantee you'll have at least one

"Oh, yeah, I need to consider___." Then capture what shows up in your head on the piece of paper and put it where you might actually use the idea or information. You won't be one ounce smarter than you were ten minutes ago, but you'll have added value to your work and life.

Much of learning how to manage workflow in a "black belt" way is about laying out the gear and practicing the moves so that the requisite thinking happens more automatically and it's a lot easier to get engaged in the game. The suggestions that follow about getting time, space, and tools in place are all trusted methods for making things happen at a terrific new level.

If you're sincere about making a major leap forward in your personal management systems, I recommend that you pay close attention to the details and follow through on the suggestions provided below in their entirety. The whole will be greater than the sum of the parts. You'll also discover that the execution of this program will produce real progress on real things that are going on in your life right now. We'll get lots done that you want to get done, in new and efficient ways that may amaze you.

Setting Aside the Time

I recommend that you create a block of time to initialize this process and prepare a workstation with the appropriate space, furniture, and tools. If your space is properly set up and streamlined, it can reduce your unconscious resistance to dealing with your stuff and even make it *attractive* for you to sit down and crank through your input and your work. An ideal time frame for most people is two whole days, back to back. (Don't be put off by that if you don't have that long to spend, though: doing any of the activities I suggest will be useful, no matter how much or how little time you devote to them. Two days are not required to benefit from these techniques and principles—they will start to pay off almost instantly.) Implementing the full collection process can take up to six hours or more, and processing and deciding on actions for all the input you'll want to externalize and capture into your system can easily take another eight hours. Of course you can also collect and process your stuff in chunks, but it'll be much easier if you can tackle that front-end portion in one fell swoop.

The ideal time for me to work with a professional is on a weekend or holiday because the chance of outside disturbance is minimal then. If I work with someone on a typical workday, we first make sure that no meetings are scheduled and only emergency interruptions are allowed; phone calls are routed to voicemail, or logged by secretaries for review and handling during a break. I don't recommend using "after hours" for this work. It usually means seriously reduced horsepower and a big tendency to get caught up in "rabbit trails." *

For many of the executives I work with, holding the world back for two contiguous days is the hardest part of the whole process—the perceived necessity to be constantly available for meetings and communications when they're "at work" is difficult for them to let go of. That's why we often resort to weekends. If you work in an open cubicle or office, it will be even more of a challenge to isolate sufficient time blocks on a regular workday during office hours.

Dedicate two days to this process, and it will be worth many times that in terms of your productivity and mental health.

It's not that the procedure itself is so "sacred"; it's just that it takes a lot of psychic energy to collect and process such a large inventory of open loops, especially when they've been "open," "undecided," or "stuck" for way too long. Interruptions can double the time it takes to get through everything. If you can get to ground zero in one contained time period, it gives you a huge sense of control and accomplishment and frees up a reservoir of energy and creativity. Later on you can

*After hours is actually a good time to crank through a group of similar tasks that you wouldn't normally do in the course of your typical workday, like filing a big backlog of papers, organizing photographs, surfing the Web about your upcoming vacation location, or processing expense receipts.

maintain your system in shorter spurts around and "between the lines" of you regular day.

Setting Up the Space

You'll need a physical location to serve as a central cockpit of control. If you already have a desk and office space set up where you work, that's probably the best place to start. If you work from a home office, obviously *that* will be your prime location. If you already have both, you'll want to establish identical, even interchangeable systems in both places.

The basics for a work space are just a writing surface and room for an in-basket. Some people, such as a foreman in a machine shop, an intake nurse on a hospital floor, or your children's nanny, won't need much more than that. The writing surface will of course expand for most professionals, to include a phone, a computer, stacking trays, working file drawers, reference shelves. Some may feel the need for a fax, a printer, a VCR, and/or multimedia conferencing equipment. The seriously self-contained will also want gear for exercise, leisure, and hobbies.

A functional work space is critical. If you don't already have a dedicated work space and in-basket, get them now. That goes for students, homemakers, and retirees, too. Everyone must have a physical locus of control from which to deal with everything else.

If I had to set up an emergency workstation in just a few minutes, I would buy a door, put it on top of two two-drawer filing cabinets (one at each end), place three stack-baskets on it, and add a legal pad and pen. That would be my home base (if I had time to sit down, I'd also buy a stool!). Believe it or not, I've been in several executive offices that wouldn't be as functional.

If You Go to an Office, You'll Still Need a Space at Home

Don't skimp on work space at home. As you'll discover through this process, it's critical that you have at least a satellite home

You must have a focused work space—at home, at work, and if possible even in transit.

system identical to the one in your office. Many people I've worked with have been somewhat embarrassed by the degree of chaos that reigns in their homes, in contrast to their offices at work; they've gotten tremendous value from giving themselves permission to establish the same setup in both places. If you're like many of them, you'll find that a weekend spent setting up a home workstation can make a revolutionary change in your ability to organize your life.

An Office Space in Transit

If you move around much, as a business traveler or just as a person with a mobile life-style, you'll also want to set up an efficiently organized micro-office-in-transit. More than likely this will consist of a briefcase, pack, or satchel with appropriate folders and portable workstation supplies.

Many people lose opportunities to be productive because they're not equipped to take advantage of the odd moments and windows of time that open up as they move from one place to another, or when they're in off-site environments. The combination of a good processing style, the right tools, and good interconnected systems at home and at work can make traveling a highly leveraged way to get certain kinds of work done.

Don't Share Space!

It is imperative that you have your own work space—or at least your own in-basket and a physical place in which to process paper. Too many married couples I've worked with have tried to work out of a single desk at home, and it always makes light-years of difference when they expand to two workstations. Far from being the "separation" they expect, the move in fact relieves them of a subtle stress in their relationship about managing the stuff of their shared lives. One couple even decided to set up an additional mini-workstation in the kitchen for the stay-at-home mom, so she could process work while keeping an eye on their infant in the family room.

Some organizations are interested in the concept of "hoteling"—that is, having people create totally self-contained and mobile workstation capabilities so they can "plug in" anywhere in the company, at any time, and work from there. I have my doubts about how well that concept will work in practice. A friend who was involved in setting up an "office of the future" model in Washington, D.C., for the U.S. Government, claimed that hoteling tended to fall apart because of the "Mine!" factor—people wanted their *own* stuff. I suggest there's a deeper reason for the failure: there needs to be zero resistance at the less-than-conscious level for us to *use* the systems we have. Having to continually reinvent our in-basket, our filing system, and how and where we process our stuff can only be a source of incessant distraction.

You can work virtually virtually everywhere if you have a clean, compact system and know how to process your stuff rapidly and portably. But you'll still need a "home base" with a well-grooved set of tools and sufficient space for all the reference and support material that you'll want somewhere close at hand when you "land." Most people I work with need at least four file drawers for their general-reference and project-support types of paper-based materials—and it's hard to imagine that all of that could ever be totally and easily movable.

It is critical that you have your *own* work space. You want to *use* your systems, not just think about them.

Getting the Tools You'll Need

If you're committed to a full implementation of this workflow process, there are some basic supplies and equipment that you'll need to get you started. As you go along, you're likely to dance between using what you're used to and evaluating the possibilities for new and different gear to work with.

Note that good tools don't necessarily have to be expensive. Often, on the low-tech side, the more "executive" something looks, the more dysfunctional it really is.

The Basic Processing Tools

Let's assume you're starting from scratch. In addition to a desktop work space, you'll need:

- Paper-holding trays (at least three)
- A stack of plain letter-size paper
- A pen/pencil
- Post-its (3×3s)
- Paper clips
- Binder clips
- A stapler and staples
- Scotch tape
- Rubber bands
- An automatic labeler
- File folders
- A calendar
- Wastebasket/recycling bins

Paper-Holding Trays

These will serve as your in-basket and out-basket, with one or two others for work-in-progress support papers and/or your "read and review" stack. The most functional trays are the side-facing letter or legal stackable kinds, which have no "lip" on them to keep you from sliding out a single piece of paper.

Plain Paper

You'll use plain paper for the initial collection process. Believe it or not, putting one thought on one full-size sheet of paper can have enormous value. Although most people will wind up processing their notes into some sort of list organizer, a few will actually stick with the simple piece-of-paper-per-thought system. In any case, it's important to have plenty of letter-size writing paper or tablets around to make capturing ad hoc input easy.

Post-its, Clips, Stapler, Etc.

Post-its, clips, stapler, tape, and rubber bands will come in handy for routing and storing paper-based materials. We're not finished with paper yet (if you haven't noticed!), and the simple tools for managing it are essential.

Moment-to-moment collecting, thinking, processing, and organizing are challenging enough; always ensure that you have the tools to make them as easy as possible.

The Labeler

The labeler is a surprisingly critical tool in our work. Thousands of executives and professionals and homemakers I have worked with now have their own automatic labelers, and my archives are full of their comments, like, "Incredible—I wouldn't have believed what a difference it makes!" The labeler will be used to label your file folders, binder spines, and numerous other things.

At this writing, I recommend the Brother labeler—it's the most user-friendly. Get the least expensive one that sits on a desk and has an AC adapter (so you won't have to worry about batteries). Also get a large supply of cassettes of label tape—black letters on white tape (instead of clear) are much easier to read and allow you to relabel folders you might want to reuse.

You can get software and printer sheets to make computer-generated labels, but I prefer the stand-alone tool. If you have to wait to do your filing or labeling as a batch job, you'll most likely resist making files for single pieces of paper, and it'll add the formality factor, which really puts the brakes on this system.

File Folders

You'll need plenty of file folders (get letter size if you can, legal size if you must). You may also need an equal number of Pendaflex-style file-folder hangers, if your filing system requires them. Plain manila folders are fine—color-coding is a level of complexity that's hardly ever worth the effort. Your general-reference filing system should just be a simple library.

Calendar

Although you may not need a calendar just to collect your incomplete items, you'll certainly come up with actions that need to be put there, too. As I noted earlier, the calendar should be used not to hold action lists but to track the "hard landscape" of things that *have* to get done on a specific day or at a specific time.

Most professionals these days already have some sort of working calendar system in place, ranging from pocket week-at-a-glance booklets, to loose-leaf organizers with day-, week-, month-, and year-at-a-glance options, to single-user software organizers, to group-ware calendars used companywide, like Outlook or Lotus Notes.

The calendar has often been the central tool that people rely on to "get organized." It's certainly a critical component in managing particular kinds of data and reminders of the commitments that relate to specific times and days. There are many reminders and some data that you will want a calendar for, but you won't be stopping there: your calendar will need to be integrated with a much more comprehensive system that will emerge as you apply this method.

You may wonder what kind of calendar would be best for you to use, and I'll discuss that in more detail in the next chapter. For now, just keep using the one you've got. After you develop a feel for the whole systematic approach, you'll have a better reference point for deciding about graduating to a different tool.

Wastebasket/Recycling Bins

If you're like most people, you're going to toss a lot more stuff than you expect, so get ready to create a good bit of trash. Some executives I have coached have found it extremely useful to arrange for a large Dumpster to be parked immediately outside their offices the day we work together!

Do You Need an Organizer?

Whether or not you'll need an organizer will depend on a number of factors. Are you already committed to using one? How do you want to see your reminders of actions, agendas, and projects? Where and how often might you need to review them? Because your head is *not* the place in which to hold things, you'll obviously need *something* to manage your triggers externally. You could maintain everything in a purely low-tech fashion, by keeping pieces of paper in folders. Or you could even use a paper-based notebook or planner, or a digital version thereof. Or you could even employ some combination of these.

Once you know how to process your stuff and what to organize, you really just need to create and manage lists.

All of the low-tech gear listed in the previous section is used for various aspects of collecting, processing, and organizing. You'll use a tray and random paper for collecting. As you process your in-basket, you'll complete many less-than-two-minute actions that will require Post-its, a stapler, and paper clips. The magazines, articles, and long memos that are your longer-than-two-minute reading will go in another of the trays. And you'll probably have quite a bit just to file. What's left—maintaining a project inventory, logging calendar items and action and agenda reminders, and tracking the things you're waiting for—will require some form of *lists,* or reviewable groupings of similar items.

Lists can be managed simply in a low-tech way, as pieces of paper kept in a file folder (e.g., separate sheets/notes for each person you need to call in a "Calls" file), or they can be arranged in a more "mid-tech" fashion, in loose-leaf notebooks or planners (a page titled "Calls" with the names listed down the sheet). Or they can be high-tech, digital versions of paper lists (such a "Calls" category in the "To Do" section of a Palm PDA or in Microsoft Outlook "Tasks").

In addition to holding portable reference material (e.g., telephone/address info), most organizers are designed for managing lists. (Your calendar is actually a form of a list—with time- and day-specific action reminders listed chronologically.) Probably thousands of types of organizers have been on the market since the 1980s, from the early rash of pocket Day-Timers to the current flood of high-tech personal digital assistants (PDAs) and PC-based software products like Microsoft Outlook and Lotus Notes.

Should you implement the *Getting Things Done* process into what you're currently using, or should you install something new? The answer is, do whichever one will actually help you change your behavior so you'll use the tools appropriately. There are efficiency factors to consider here, too. Do you get a lot of digital information that would be easier to track with a digital tool? Do you need a paper-based calendar for all the appointments you have to make and change rapidly on the run? Do you need reminders of things like calls you have to make when it's not easy to carry file folders? And so on. There are also the aesthetic and enjoyment factors. I've done some of my best planning and updating for myself when I simply wanted some excuse to use (i.e., play with) my Palm organizer while waiting for dinner in a restaurant!

One of the best tricks for enhancing your personal productivity is having organizing tools that you love to use.

When considering whether to get and use an organizer, and if so, which one, keep in mind that all you really need to do is manage lists. You've got to be able to create a list on the run and review it easily and as regularly as you need to. Once you know what to put *on* the lists, and how to use them, the medium really doesn't matter. Just go for simplicity, speed, and fun.

The Critical Factor of a Filing System

A simple and highly functional personal reference system is critical to this process. The filing system at hand is the first thing I assess before beginning the workflow process in anyone's office. As I noted in chapter 2, the lack of a good general-reference system can be one of the greatest obstacles to imple-

If your filing system isn't fast, functional, and *fun*, you'll resist the whole process.

menting a personal management system, and for most of the executives I have personally coached, it represents one of the biggest opportunities for improvement. Many times I have driven to the local office-supply store with a client and bought a filing cabinet, a big stock of file folders, and a labeler, just so we could create an appropriate place in which to put two-thirds of the "stuff" lying around his/her desk and credenza and even on the office floors.

We're concerned here mostly with general-reference filing—as distinct from discrete filing systems devoted to contracts, financial information, or other categories of data that deserve their own place and indexing. General-reference files should hold articles, brochures, pieces of paper, notes, printouts, faxes—basically anything that you want to keep for its interesting or useful data and that doesn't fit into your specialized filing systems and won't stand up by itself on a shelf (as will large software manuals and seminar binders).

If you have a trusted secretary or assistant who maintains that system for you, so you can put a "File as X" Post-it on the document and send it "out" to him or her, great. But ask yourself if you still have some personally interesting or confidential support material that should be accessible at any moment, even when your assistant isn't around. If so, you'll still need your own system, either in your desk or right beside it somewhere.

Success Factors for Filing

I strongly suggest that you maintain your own personal, at-hand filing system. It should take you less than one minute to pick something up out of your in-basket or print it from e-mail, decide it needs no action but has some potential future value, and finish storing it in a trusted system. If it takes you longer than a minute to complete that sequence of actions, you have a significant improvement opportunity, since you probably won't file the document; you'll stack it or stuff it instead. Besides being fast, the system needs to be fun and easy, current and complete. Otherwise you'll unconsciously resist emptying your in-basket because you know there's likely to be something in there that ought to get filed, and you won't even want to look at the papers. Take heart: I've seen people go from resisting to actually *enjoying* sorting through their stacks once their personal filing system is set up and humming.

You must feel equally comfortable about filing a single piece of paper on a new topic—even a scribbled note—in its own file as you would about filing a more formal, larger document. Because it requires so much work to make and organize files, people either don't keep them or have junked-up cabinets and drawers full of all sorts of one-of-a-kind items, like a menu for the local take-out café or the current train schedule.

Whatever you need to do to get your reference system to that quick and easy standard for everything it has to hold, do it. My system works wonderfully for me and for many others who try it, and I highly recommend that you consider incorporating all of the following guidelines to really make reference filing automatic.

Keep Your General-Reference Files at Hand's Reach Filing has to be instantaneous and easy. If you have to get up every time you have some ad hoc piece of paper you want to file, you'll tend to stack it instead of filing it, and you're also likely to just resist the whole in-basket process (because you subconsciously know there's stuff in there that might need *filing*!). Many people I have coached have redesigned their office space so they have four general-reference file drawers literally in "swivel distance," instead of across their room.

One Alpha System I have one A–Z alphabetical filing system, not multiple systems. People have a tendency to want to use their files as a personal organization system, and therefore they attempt to organize them by projects or areas of focus. This magnifies geometrically the number of places something *isn't* when you forget where you filed it. One simple alpha system files everything by topic, project, person, or company, so it can be in only three or four places if you forget exactly where you put it. You can usually put at least one subset of topics on each label, like "Gardening—pots" and "Gardening—ideas." These would be filed under G.

Currently I have four file drawers for my general-reference files, and each is clearly marked on the outside—"A–E," "F–L," and so on—so I don't have to think about where something goes once it's labeled.

Every once in a while someone has such a huge amount of reference material on one topic or project that it should be put in its own discrete drawer or cabinet. But if it is less than a half a file drawer's worth, I recommended including it in the single general alphabetical system.

Have Lots of Fresh Folders I keep a giant stack of fresh, new file folders instantly at hand and reachable from where I sit to process my in-basket. Nothing is worse than having something to file and not having an abundance of folders to grab from to make the process easy. At any given time I want to have an inventory of almost half a file drawer full of unused or reusable folders. Rule of thumb: reorder when the number drops below a hundred.

Keep the Drawer Less Than Three-Quarters Full Always try to keep your file drawers less than three-quarters full. If they're stuffed, you'll unconsciously resist putting things in there, and reference materials will tend to stack up instead. If a drawer is starting to get tight, I may purge it while I'm on hold on the phone.

I know almost no one who doesn't have overstuffed file drawers. If you value your cuticles, and if you want to get rid of your unconscious resistance to filing, then you must keep the drawers loose enough that you can insert and retrieve files without effort.

Some people's reaction to this is "I'd have to buy more file cabinets!" as if that were something horrible. Help me out here. If the stuff is worth keeping, it's worth keeping so that it's easily accessible, right? And if it's not, then why are you keeping it? It's said that we're in the Information Age; if there's any validity to that, and if you're doing *anything* that hinders your usage of it . . . not smart.

You may need to create another tier of reference storage to give yourself sufficient working room with your general-reference files at hand. Material such as finished project notes and "dead" client files may still need to be kept, but can be stored off-site or at least out of your work space.

Label Your File Folders with an Auto Labeler Typeset labels change the nature of your files and your relationship to them. Labeled files feel comfortable on a boardroom table; everyone can identify them; you can easily see what they are from a distance and in your briefcase; and when you open your file drawers, you get to see what looks almost like a printed index of your files in alphabetical order. It makes it fun to open the drawer to find or insert things.

Perhaps later in this new millennium the brain scientists will give us some esoteric and complex neurological explanation for why labeled files work so effectively. Until then, trust me. Get a labeler. And get your *own*. To make the whole system work without a hitch, you'll need to have it *at hand* all the time, so you can file something whenever you want. And don't share! If you have something to file and your labeler's not there, you'll just stack the material instead of filing it. The labeler should be as basic a tool as your stapler.

Get High-Quality Mechanics File cabinets are not the place to skimp on quality. Nothing is worse than trying to open a heavy file drawer and hearing that awful *screech!* that happens when you wrestle with the roller bearings on one of those $29.95 "special sale" cabinets. You really need a file cabinet whose drawer, even when it's three-quarters full, will glide open and click shut with the smoothness and solidity of a door on a German car. I'm not kidding.

Get Rid of Hanging Files If You Can At the risk of seriously offending a lot of people who are already using hanging files, I recommend that you totally do away with the hanging-file hardware and use just plain folders standing up by themselves in the file drawer, held up by the movable metal plate in the back. Hanging folders are much less efficient because of the effort it takes to make a new file ad hoc and the formality that imposes on the filing system.

Here's an e-mail I received recently from a senior manager who actually took my advice after avoiding it for a couple of years because of his investment in the hanging hardware:

> *Your system is FANTASTIC!! I've completely redone my files at home and at work—it only took a combined four days to do it, but I've done away with Pendaflex and have gone to the manila folder system, with A–Z and nothing else. WOW! It's so much easier. My desk for some reason is a lot neater, too, without those stacks of "to be filed" stuff hanging around!*

But If You Can't . . . Many people are stuck with the hanging-file system, at least at work, because side-opening hanging-folder filing cabinets have become standard corporate issue. If you have to work with hanging files, then I recommend that you:

In the fire zone of real work, if it takes longer than sixty seconds to file something, you won't file, you'll stack.

- Label the files, not the hangers. That lets you carry the file folders for meetings and when traveling, without taking the hanger.

- Use only *one file folder per hanger.* This will keep the drawer visually neat and prevent the weirdness that results when multiple files make a hanger uneven. Having to recalibrate files in an alpha system every time a folder gets full is too much trouble.

- Keep a big supply of plain hangers and new file folders in the front of your first file drawer so you can make new files and store them in a flash.

Purge Your Files at Least Once a Year Cleaning house in your files regularly keeps them from going stale and seeming like a black hole, and it also gives you the freedom to keep anything on a whim "in case you might need it." You know everything will be reassessed within a few months anyway, and you can redecide then what's worth keeping and what isn't. As I say, I purge my files while I'm on hold on the phone (or marking time on a conference call that's dragging on and on!).

I recommend that all organizations (if they don't have one already) establish a Dumpster Day, when all employees get to come to work in sneakers and jeans, put their phones on do-not-disturb, and get current with all their stored stuff.* Dumpsters are brought in, and everyone has permission to spend the whole day in purge mode. A personal Dumpster Day is an ideal thing to put into your tickler file, either during the holidays, at year's end, or around early-spring tax-preparation time, when you might want to tie it in with archiving the previous year's financial files.

One Final Thing to Prepare . . .

You've blocked off some time, you've gotten a work area set up, and you've got the basic tools to start implementing the methodology. Now what?

If you've decided to commit a certain amount of time to setting up your workflow system, there's one more thing that you'll need to do to make it maximally effective: you must clear the decks of any other commitments for the duration of the session.

If there's someone you absolutely need to call, or something your secretary has to handle for you or you have to check with your spouse about, do it *now*. Or make an agreement with your-

---

*A great time to do this is Christmas Eve Day, or some similar near-holiday that falls on a workday. Most people are in "party mode" anyway, so it's an ideal opportunity to get funky and clean house.

self about when you *will* do it, and then put some reminder of that where you won't miss it. It's critical that your full psychic attention be available for the work at hand.

Almost without exception, when I sit down to begin coaching people, even though they've blocked out time and committed significant money to utilize me as a resource for that time, they still have things they're going to have to do before we quit for the day, and they haven't arranged for them yet in their own systems. "Oh, yeah, I've got to call this client back sometime today," they'll say, or "I have to check in with my spouse to see if he's gotten the tickets for tonight." It bespeaks a certain lack of awareness and maturity in our culture, I think, that so many sophisticated people are ignoring those levels of responsibility to their own psyche, on an ongoing operational basis.

So have you handled all that? Good. Now it's time to gather representatives of all of your open loops into one place.

5

Collection: Corralling Your "Stuff"

IN CHAPTER 2 I described the basic procedures for *collecting* your work. This chapter will lead you in more detail through the process of getting all your incompletes, all your "stuff," into one place—into "in." That's the critical first step in getting to the state of "mind like water." Just gathering a few more things than you currently have will probably create a positive feeling for you. But if you can hang in there and really do the whole collection process, 100 percent, it will change your experience dramatically and give you an important new reference point for being on top of your work.

When I coach a client through this process, the collection phase usually takes between one and six hours, though it did take all of twenty hours with one person (finally I told him, "You get the idea"). It can take longer than you think if you are committed to a full-blown capture that will include everything at work and everywhere else. That means going through every storage area and every nook and cranny in every location, including cars, boats, and other homes, if you have them.

Be assured that if you give yourself at least a couple of hours to tackle this part, you can grab the major portion of things outstanding. And you can even capture the rest by creating relevant placeholding notes—for example, "Purge and process boat storage shed" and "Deal with hall closet."

In the real world, you probably won't be able to keep your stuff 100 percent collected all of the time. If you're like most people, you'll move too fast and be engaged in too many things during the course of a week to get all your ideas and commitments captured outside your head. But it should become an ideal standard that keeps you motivated to consistently "clean house" of all the things about your work and life that have your attention.

Ready, Set . . .

There are very practical reasons to gather everything before you start *processing* it:

1 | it's helpful to have a sense of the volume of stuff you have to deal with;
2 | it lets you know where the "end of the tunnel" is; and
3 | when you're *processing* and *organizing,* you don't want to be distracted psychologically by an amorphous mass of stuff that might still be "somewhere." Once you have all the things that require your attention gathered in one place, you'll automatically be operating from a state of enhanced focus and control.

It can be daunting to capture into one location, at one time, all the things that don't belong where they are. It may even seem a little counterintuitive, because for the most part, most of that stuff was not, and is not, "that important"; that's why it's still lying around. It wasn't an urgent thing when it first showed up, and probably nothing's blown up yet because it hasn't been dealt with. It's the business card you put in your wallet of somebody you thought you might want to contact sometime. It's the little piece of techno-gear in the bottom desk drawer that you're missing a part for. It's the printer that you keep telling yourself you're going to move to a better location in your office. These are the kinds of things that nag at you but that you haven't decided either to deal with or to drop entirely from your list of open loops. But because you think there still *could* be something important in there, that "stuff" is controlling *you* and taking up more psychic energy than it deserves. Keep in mind, you can feel good about what you're not doing, only when you *know* what you're not doing.

So it's time to begin. Grab your in-basket and a half-inch stack of plain paper for your notes, and let's . . .

. . . Go!

Physical Gathering

Train yourself to notice and collect anything that doesn't belong where it is forever.

The first activity is to search your physical environment for anything that doesn't belong where it is, the way it is, permanently, and put it into your in-basket. You'll be gathering things that are incomplete, things that have some decision about potential action tied to them. They all go into "in," so they'll be available for later processing.

What Stays Where It Is

The best way to create a clean decision about whether something should go into the in-basket is to understand clearly what *shouldn't* go in. Here are the four categories of things that can remain where they are, the way they are, with no action tied to them:

- Supplies
- Reference material
- Decoration
- Equipment

Supplies . . . include anything you need to keep because you use it regularly. Stationery, business cards, stamps, staples, Post-it pads, legal pads, paper clips, ballpoint refills, batteries, forms you need to fill out from time to time, rubber bands—all of these qualify. Many people also have a "personal supplies" drawer at work containing dental floss, Kleenex, breath mints, and so on.

Reference Material . . . is anything you simply keep for information as needed, such as manuals for your software, the local take-out deli menu, or your kid's soccer schedule. This category includes your telephone and address information, any material relevant to projects, themes, and topics, and sources such as dictionaries, encyclopedias, and almanacs.

Decoration . . . means pictures of family, artwork, and fun and inspiring things pinned to your bulletin board. You also might have plaques, mementos, and/or plants.

Equipment . . . is obviously the telephone, computer, fax, printer, wastebasket, furniture, and/or VCR.

You no doubt have a lot of things that fall into these four categories—basically all your tools and your gear, which have no actions tied to them. Everything else goes into "in." But many of the things you might initially interpret as supplies, reference, decoration, or equipment could also have action associated with them because they still aren't exactly the way they need to be.

For instance, most people have, in their desk drawers and on their credenzas and bulletin boards, a lot of reference materials that either are out of date or need to be organized somewhere else. Those should go into "in." Likewise, if your supplies drawer is out of control, full of lots of dead or unorganized stuff, that's an incomplete that needs to be captured. Are the photos of your kids *current* ones? Is the artwork what you *want* on the wall? Are the mementos really something you still want to keep? Is the furniture precisely the way it should be? Is the computer set up the way you want it? Are the plants in your office alive? In other words, supplies, reference materials, decoration, and equipment *may* need to be tossed into the in-basket if they're not just where they should be, the way they should be.

Issues About Collecting

As you engage in the collecting phase, you may run into one or more of the following:

- you've got a lot more than will fit into one in-basket;
- you're likely to get derailed into purging and organizing;
- you may have some form of stuff already collected and organized; and/or
- you're likely to run across some critical things that you want to keep in front of you.

What If an Item Is Too Big to Go in the In-Basket? If you can't physically put something in the in-basket, then write a note on a piece of letter-size plain paper to represent it. For instance, if you have a poster or other piece of artwork behind the door to your office, just write "Artwork behind door" on a letter-size piece of paper and put the paper in the in-basket.

Be sure to date it, too. This has a couple of benefits. If your organization system winds up containing some of these pieces of paper representing something else, it'll be useful to know when the note was created. It's also just a great habit to date everything you hand-write, from Post-it notes to your assistant, to voice-mails you download onto a pad, to notes you take on a phone call with a client. The 3 percent of the time that this little piece of information will be extremely useful makes it worth developing the habit.

What If the Pile Is Too Big to Fit into the In-Basket? If you're like 98 percent of my clients, your initial gathering activity will collect much more than can be comfortably stacked in an in-basket. If that's the case, just create stacks around the in-basket, and maybe even on the floor underneath it. Ultimately you'll be emptying the in-stacks, as you process and organize everything. In the meantime, though, make sure that there's some obvious visual distinction between the stacks that are "in" and everything else.

Instant Dumping If it's immediately evident that something is trash, go ahead and toss it when you see it. For some of my clients, this marks the first time they have ever cleaned their center desk drawer!

If you're not sure what something is or whether it's worth keeping, go ahead and put it into "in." You'll be able to decide about it later, when you process the in-basket. What you *don't* want to do is to let yourself get wrapped up in things piece by piece, *trying* to decide this or that. You'll do that later anyway if it's in "in," and it's easier to make those kinds of choices when you're in processing mode. The objective for the collection process is to get everything into "in" *as quickly as possible* so you've appropriately retrenched and "drawn the battle lines."

Be Careful of the Purge-and-Organize Bug! Many people get hit with the purge-and-organize virus as they're going through various areas of their office (and their home). If that happens to you, it's OK, so long as you have a major open window of time to get through the whole process (like at least a whole week ahead of you). Otherwise you'll need to break it up into chunks and capture them as little projects or actions to do, with reminders in your system, like "Purge four-drawer cabinet" or "Clean office closet."

What you *don't* want to do is let yourself get caught running down a rabbit trail cleaning up some piece of your work and then not be able to get through the whole action-management implementation process. It may take longer than you think, and you want to go for the gold and finish processing all your stuff and setting up your system as soon as possible.

What About Things That Are Already on Lists and in Organizers? You may already have some lists and some sort of organization system in place. But unless you're thoroughly familiar with this workflow-processing model and have implemented it previously, I recommend that you treat those lists as items still to be processed, like everything else in "in." You'll want your system to be consistent, and it'll be necessary to evaluate everything from the same viewpoint to get it that way.

"But I Can't Lose ***That*** *Thing . . . !"* Often in the collection process someone will run across a piece of paper or a document that causes her to say, "Oh, my God! I forgot about that! I've *got* to deal with that!" It could be a phone slip with a return call she was supposed to handle two days before, or some meeting notes that remind her of an action she was supposed to take weeks ago. She doesn't want to put whatever it is into the huge stack of other stuff in her in-basket because she's afraid she might lose track of it again.

If that happens to you, first ask yourself if it's something that really *has* to be handled before you get though this initial implementation time. If so, best deal with it immediately so you get it off your mind. If not, go ahead and put it into "in." You're going to get all that processed and emptied soon anyway, so it won't be lost.

If you can't deal with the action in the moment, and you still just *have* to have the reminder right in front of you, go ahead and create an "emergency" stack somewhere close at hand. It's not an ideal solution, but it'll do. Keep in mind that some potential anxiousness is going to surface as you make your stuff more conscious to you than it's been. Create whatever supports you need.

Start with Your Desktop

Ready now? OK. Start piling those things on your desk into "in." Often there'll be numerous things right at hand that need to go in there. Many people use their whole desktop as "in"; if you're one of them, you'll have several stacks around you to begin your "in" collection with. Start at one end of your work space and move around, dealing with everything on every cubic inch. Typical items will be:

- Stacks of mail and memos
- Phone slips

- Collected business cards
- Notes from meetings

Resist the urge to say, as almost everyone does initially, "Well, I know what's in that stack, and that's where I want to leave it." That's *exactly* what hasn't worked before, and it all needs to go into the in-basket.

As you go around your desktop, ask yourself if you have any intention of changing any of the tools or equipment there. Is your phone OK? Your computer? The desk itself? If anything needs changing, write a note about it and toss it into "in."

Desk Drawers

Next tackle the desk drawers, if you have them, one at a time. Any attention on anything in there? Any actionable items? Is there anything that doesn't belong there? If the answer to any of these questions is yes, put the actionable item into "in" or write a note about it. Again, whether you use this opportunity to clean and organize the drawers or simply make a note to do it later will depend on how much time you have and how much stuff is in there.

Countertops

Continue working your way around your office, collecting everything sitting on the tops of credenzas or counters or cabinets that doesn't belong there permanently. Often there will be stacks of reading material, mail, and miscellaneous folders and support material for actions and projects. Collect it all.

Maybe there is reference material that you've already used and just left out. If that's so, and if you can return it to the file cabinet or the bookshelf in just a second, go ahead and do that. Be careful to check with yourself, though, about whether there is some potential action tied to the material before you put it away. If there is, put it into "in" so you can deal with it later in the process.

Inside the Cabinets

Now look inside the cabinets. What's in there? These are perfect areas for stashing large supplies and reference materials, and equally seductive for holding deeper levels of stuff. Any broken or out-of-date things in there? Often I'll find collectibles and nostalgia that aren't meaningful to my clients any longer. One general manager of an insurance office, for example, wound up tossing out at least a small Dumpster's worth of "recognition" awards he had accumulated over the years.

Consider whether your collectible and nostalgia items are still meaningful to you.

Again, if some of these areas are out of control and need purging and organizing, write that on a note and toss it into "in."

Floors, Walls, and Shelves

Anything on bulletin boards that needs action? Anything tacked onto the walls that doesn't belong there? Any attention on your pictures, artwork, plaques, or decorations? How about the open shelves? Any books that need to be read or donated? Any catalogs, manuals, or three-ring binders that are out of date or have some potential action associated with them? Any piles or stacks of things on the floor? Just scoot them over next to your in-basket to add to the inventory.

Equipment, Furniture, and Fixtures

Is there anything you want to do to or change about any of your office equipment or furniture or the physical space itself? Does everything work? Do you have all the lighting you need? If there are actionable items, you know what to do: make a note and put it in "in."

Other Locations

Depending on the scope of what you're addressing in this process, you may want to do some version of the same kind of gathering anywhere else you keep stuff. If you're determined to get to a really empty head, it's imperative that you do it *everywhere*.

Some executives I work with find it immensely valuable to take me home with them and have me walk them through this process there as well. Often they've allowed the "not so important" trap to ensnare them in their home life, and it has gnawed away at their energy.

Don't let the "not so important" trap gnaw away your energy at home.

Mental Gathering: The Mind-Sweep

Once you feel you've collected all the physical things in your environment that need processing, you'll want to collect anything else that may be residing in your psychic RAM. What has your attention that isn't represented by something already in your in-basket?

This is where the stack of plain paper really comes into play. I recommend that you write out each thought, each idea, each project or thing that has your attention, on a *separate sheet of paper*. You could make one long list on a pad, but given how you will later be processing each item individually, it's actually more effective to put everything on separate sheets. You will likely not keep these pieces of paper (unless you decide that low-tech is your best organizing method), but it'll be handy to have them as discrete items to deal with as you're processing.

It will probably take you between twenty minutes and an hour to clear your head onto separate notes, *after* you've gathered everything else. You'll find that things will tend to occur to you in somewhat random fashion—little things, big things, personal things, professional things, in no particular order.

In this instance, go for quantity. It's much better to overdo this process than to risk missing something. You can always toss the junk later. Your first idea may be "Save the ozone layer," and then you'll think, "I need cat food!" Grab them all. Don't be surprised if you discover you've created quite a stack of paper in "in" during this procedure.

"Trigger" List

To assist in clearing your head, you may want to review the following "Incompletion Triggers" list, item by item, to see if you've forgotten anything. Often you'll just need a jog to unearth something lurking in a corner of your mind. Remember, when something occurs to you, write it on a piece of paper and toss it into "in."

"Incompletion Triggers" List

Professional

- Projects started, not completed
- Projects that need to be started
- Commitments/promises to others
  - Boss/partners
  - Colleagues
  - Subordinates
  - Other people in organization
  - "Outside" people
    - Customers
    - Other organizations
    - Professionals
- Communications to make/get
  - Internal/External
    - Initiate or respond to:
      - Phone calls
      - Voice-mail
      - E-mail
      - Pages
      - Faxes
      - Letters
      - Memos
- Other writing to finish/submit
  - Reports
  - Evaluations/reviews
  - Proposals
  - Articles
  - Promotional materials
  - Manuals/instructions
  - Rewrites and edits
- Meetings that need to be set/requested
- Who needs to know about what decisions?
- Significant read/review
- Financial
  - Cash flow
  - Statistics
  - Budgets
  - Forecasts/projections
  - P&Ls
  - Balance sheet
  - Credit line
- Planning/organizing
  - Formal planning (goals, targets, objectives)
  - Current projects (next stages)
  - Upcoming projects

- Business/marketing plans
- Organizational initiatives
- Upcoming events
- Meetings
- Presentations
- Organizational structuring
- Changes in facilities
- Installation of new systems/equipment
- Travel

Banks
- Receivables
- Payables
- Petty cash

Administration
- Legal issues
- Insurance
- Personnel
- Policies/procedures

Customers
- Internal
- External

Marketing

Promotion

Sales
- Customer service

Systems
- Phones
- Computers
- Office equipment
- Other equipment
- Utilities
- Filing
- Storage
  - Inventories

Supplies

Office/site
- Office organization
- Furniture
- Decorations

Waiting for . . .
- Information
- Delegated tasks/projects
- Completions critical to projects
- Replies to:
  - Letters
  - Memos
  - Calls
  - Proposals
  - Requisitions
  - Reimbursements
  - Petty cash
  - Insurance
  - Ordered items
  - Items being repaired
  - Tickets
  - Decisions of others

Professional development
- Training/seminars
- Things to learn
- Things to look up
- Skills to practice/learn especially re: computers
- Tape/video training
- Résumés

Outside education

Research—need to find out about . . .

Professional wardrobe

Personal

Projects started, not completed
Projects that need to be started
Commitments/promises to others
- Spouse
- Children
- Family
- Friends
- Professionals
- Borrowed items

Projects: other organizations
- Service
- Civic
- Volunteer

Communications to make/get
- Family
- Friends
- Professional
- Initiate or respond to:
  - Phone calls
  - Letters
  - Cards

Upcoming events
- Special occasions
- Birthdays
- Anniversaries
- Weddings
- Graduations
- Holidays
- Travel
- Weekend trips
- Vacations
- Social events
- Cultural events
- Sporting events

R&D—things to do
- Places to go
- People to meet/invite
- Local attractions

Administration
- Financial
  - Bills
  - Banks
  - Investments
  - Loans
  - Taxes
- Insurance
- Legal affairs
- Filing

Waiting for . . .
- Mail order
- Repair
- Reimbursements
- Loaned items
- Medical data
- RSVPs

Home/household
- Landlords
- Property ownership
  - Legal
  - Real estate
  - Zoning
  - Taxes
  - Builders/contractors
- Heating/air-conditioning
- Plumbing
- Electricity
- Roofing
- Landscape

- Driveway
- Walls/floors/ceilings
- Decoration
- Furniture
- Utilities
- Appliances
- Lightbulbs/wiring
- Kitchen things
- Washer/dryer/vacuum
- Areas to organize/clean

Computers
- Software
- Hardware
- Connections
- CD-ROM
- E-mail/Internet
- TV
- VCR
- Music/CDs/tapes
- Cameras/film
- Phones
- Answering machine
- Sports equipment
- Closets/clothes
- Garage/storage
- Vehicle repair/maintenance
- Tools
- Luggage
- Pets

Health care
- Doctors
- Dentists
- Specialists

Hobbies
- Books/records/tapes/disks

Errands
- Hardware store
- Drugstore
- Market
- Bank
- Cleaner
- Stationer

Community
- Neighborhood
- Schools
- Local government

Civic issues

The "In" Inventory

If your head is empty of everything, personally and professionally, then your in-basket is probably quite full, and likely spilling over. In addition to the paper-based and physical items in your in-basket, your inventory of "in" should include any resident voice-mails and all the e-mails that are currently staged in the "in" area of your communication software. It should also include any items on your organizer lists for which you have not yet determined next actions.

I usually recommend that clients download their voice-mails onto paper notes and put those into their in-baskets, along with their whole organizer notebooks, which usually need significant reassessment. If you've been using something like a Palm PDA or Microsoft Outlook or Lotus Organizer for anything other than calendar and telephone/address functionality, I suggest you print out any task and to-do lists and put them, too, into your in-basket. E-mails are best left where they are, because of their volume and the efficiency factor of dealing with them within their own minisystem.

Connection is completed when you can easily see the edges to the inventory of everything that is complete.

But "In" Doesn't Stay in "In"

When you've done all that, you're ready to take the next step. You don't want to leave anything in "in" for an indefinite period of time, because then it would without fail creep back into your psyche again, since your mind would know you weren't dealing with it. Of course, one of the main factors in people's resistance to collecting stuff into "in" is the lack of a good processing and organizing methodology to handle it.

That brings us to the next chapter: "Getting 'In' to Empty."

6

Processing: Getting "In" to Empty

ASSUMING THAT YOU have collected everything that has your attention, your job now is to actually get to the bottom of "in." Getting "in" to empty doesn't mean actually *doing* all the actions and projects that you've collected. It just means identifying each item and deciding what it is, what it means, and what you're going to do with it.

When you've finished processing "in," you will have

1 | trashed what you don't need;
2 | completed any less-than-two-minute actions;
3 | handed off to others anything that can be delegated;
4 | sorted into your own organizing system reminders of actions that require more than two minutes; and
5 | identified any larger commitments (projects) you now have, based on the input.

To get an overview of this process, you may find it useful here to refer to the Workflow Diagram on page 120. The center column illustrates all the steps involved in processing and deciding your next actions.

This chapter focuses on the components in the diagram's center column, the steps from "in" to next action. You'll immediately see the natural organization that results from following this process for each of your open loops. For instance, if you pick up something from "in" and realize, "I've got to call Andrea about

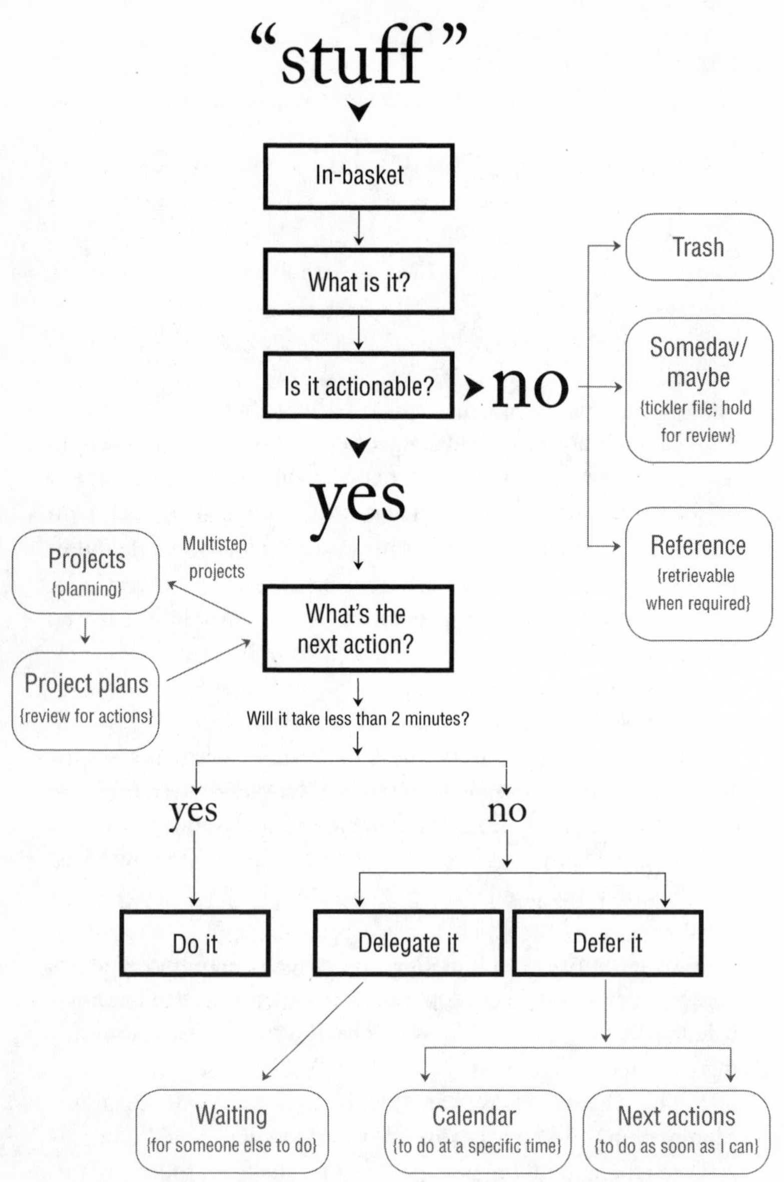

WORKFLOW DIAGRAM—PROCESSING

that, but I've got to do it on Monday, when she's in her office," then you'll defer that action immediately and enter it into your calendar for Monday.

I recommend that you read through this chapter and the next one, on organizing your actions, before you actually start processing what you've collected in "in." It may save you some steps. When I coach clients through this process, it invariably becomes a dance back and forth between the simple decision-making stage of *processing* the open loops and the trickier task of figuring out the best way to enter these decisions in a client's particular *organization* system.

Many of my coaching clients, for example, are eager to get set up personally on a PDA organizer that will synchronize with Microsoft Outlook, which their company is using for e-mail and scheduling. The first thing we have to do (after we've collected the in-basket) is make sure all their hardware and software are working. Then we clean up (print out and erase, usually) everything they have previously tried to organize in their Outlook task lists and put it all into "in." Then we establish some working categories such as "Calls," "Errands," "Agendas," "At Computer," and so on. As we begin to process the in-basket, the client can go immediately to his computer and type his action steps directly into the system he will ultimately depend on.

If you're not sure yet what you're going to be using as a personal reminder system, don't worry. You can begin very appropriately with the low-tech initial process of notes on pieces of paper. You can always upgrade your tools later, once you have your system in place.

Processing Guidelines

The best way to learn this model is by doing. But there are a few basic rules to follow:

- Process the top item first.
- Process one item at a time.
- Never put anything back into "in."

Top Item First

Even if the second item down is a personal note to you from the President of your country, and the top item is a piece of junk mail, you've got to process the junk mail first! That's an exaggeration to make a point, but the principle is an important one: everything gets processed equally. The verb "process" does not mean "spend time on." It just means "decide what the thing is and what action is required, and then dispatch it accordingly." You're going to get to the bottom of the basket as soon as you can anyway, and you don't want to avoid dealing with *anything* in there.

Process does not mean "spend time on."

Emergency Scanning Is Not Processing

Most people get to their in-basket or their e-mail and look for the most urgent, most fun, or most interesting stuff to deal with first. "Emergency scanning" is fine and necessary sometimes (I do it, too). Maybe you've just come back from an off-site meeting and have to be on a long conference call in fifteen minutes. So you check to make sure there are no land mines about to explode and to see if your client has e-mailed you back OK'ing the big proposal.

But that's not processing your in-basket; it's emergency scanning. When you're in processing mode, you must get into the habit of starting at one end and just cranking through items one at a time, in order. As soon as you break that rule, and process only what you *feel* like processing, and in whatever order, you'll invariably begin to leave things unprocessed. Then you will no longer have a functioning funnel, and it will back up all over your desk and office.

LIFO or FIFO?

Theoretically, you should flip your in-basket upside down and process first the first thing that came in. As long as you go from one end clear through to the other within a reasonable period of time, though, it won't make much difference. You're going to see it all in short order anyway. And if you're going to attempt to clear up a big backlog of e-mails staged in "in," you'll actually discover it's more efficient to process the last-in first because of all the discussion threads that accumulate on top of one another.

The in-basket is a processing station, not a storage bin.

One Item at a Time

You may find you have a tendency, while processing your in-basket, to pick something up, not know exactly what you want to do about it, and then let your eyes wander onto another item farther down the stack and get engaged with *it*. That item may be more attractive to your psyche because you *know* right away what to do with *it*—and you don't feel like thinking about what's in your hand. This is dangerous territory. What's in your hand is likely to land on a "hmppphhh" stack on the side of your desk because you become distracted by something easier, more important, or more interesting below it.

Most people also want to take a whole stack of things out of the in-basket at once, put it right in front of them, and try to crank through it. Although I empathize with the desire to "deal with a big chunk," I constantly remind clients to put back everything but the one item on top. The focus on just one thing forces the requisite attention and decision-making to get through all your stuff. And if you get interrupted (which is likely), you won't have umpteen parts of "in" scattered around outside the tray and out of control again.

The Multitasking Exception

There's a subtle exception to the one-item-at-a-time rule. Some personality types really *need* to shift their focus away from something for at least a minute in order to make a decision about it. When I see this going on with someone, I let him take two or sometimes three things out at once as he's processing. It's then easier and faster for him to make a choice about the action required.

Remember, multitasking is an exception—and it works only if you hold to the discipline of working through every item in short order, and never avoid *any* decision for longer than a minute or two.

Nothing Goes Back into "In"

There's a one-way path out of "in." This is actually what was meant by the old admonition to "handle things once," though handling things just once is in fact a bad idea. If you did that, you'd never have a list, because you would finish everything as soon as you saw it. You'd also be highly ineffective and inefficient, since most things you deal with are *not* to be acted upon the first time you become aware of them. Where the advice does hold is in eliminating the bad habit of continually picking things up out of "in," not deciding what they mean or what you're going to do about them, and then just leaving them there. A better admonition would be, "The first time you pick something up from your in-basket, decide what to do about it and where it goes. Never put it back in "in."

The Key Processing Question: "What's the Next Action?"

You've got the message. You're going to deal with one item at a time. And you're going to make a firm next-action decision about each one. This may sound easy—and it is—but it requires you to do some fast, hard thinking. Much of the time the action will not be self-evident; it will need to be determined.

On that first item, for example, do you need to call someone? Fill something out? Get information from the Web? Buy something at the store? Talk to your secretary? E-mail your boss? What? If there's an action, its specific nature will determine the next set of options. But what if you say, "There's really nothing to do with this"?

I am rather like a mosquito in a nudist camp; I know what I want to do, but I don't know where to begin.
—Stephen Bayne

What If There Is No Action?

It's likely that a portion of your in-basket will require no action. There will be three types of things in this category:

- Trash
- Items to incubate
- Reference material

Trash

If you've been following my suggestions, you'll no doubt already have tossed out a big pile of stuff. It's also likely that you will have put stacks of material into "in" that include things you don't need anymore. So don't be surprised if there's still a lot more to throw away as you process your stuff.

Processing all the things in your world will make you more conscious of what you are going to do and what you should *not* be doing. One director of a foundation I worked with discovered that he had allowed way too many e-mails (thousands!) to accumulate—e-mails that in fact he wasn't ever going to respond to anyway. He told me that using my method forced him to "go on a healthy diet" about what he would allow to hang around his world as an incompletion.

It's likely that at some point you'll come up against the question of whether or not to keep something for future reference. I have two ways of dealing with that:

- When in doubt, throw it out.
- When in doubt, keep it.

Take your pick. I think either approach is fine. You just need to trust your intuition and be realistic about your space. Most people have some angst about all of this because their systems have never really been totally functional and clear-edged before. If you make a clean distinction between what's reference and supplies and what requires action, and if your reference system is simple and workable, you can easily keep as much material as you can accommodate. Since no action is required on it, it's just a matter of physical space and logistics.

Filing experts can offer you more detailed guidelines about all this, and your CPA can provide record-retention timetables that will tell you how long you should keep what kinds of documentation. My suggestion is that you make the distinction about whether something is actionable or not. Once it's clear that no action is needed, there's room for lots of options.

Incubate

There will probably be things in your in-basket about which you will say to yourself, "There's nothing to do on this *now,* but there *might* be later." Examples of this would be:

- A flier announcing a chamber of commerce breakfast with a guest speaker you might want to hear, but it's two weeks away, and you're not sure yet if you'll be at home then or out of town on a business trip.

- An agenda for a board meeting you've been invited to attend in three weeks. No action is required on it, other than your briefing yourself a day ahead of the meeting by reading the agenda.

- An advertisement for the next Quicken software upgrade for your personal finances. Do you really need this next version? You don't know . . . you'd rather sleep on it for another week.

- An idea you had about something you might want to do for next year's annual sales meeting. There's nothing to do on this now, but you'd like to be reminded when the time comes to start planning for it.

- A note to yourself about taking a watercolor class, which you have zero time for right now.

What do you do with these kinds of things? There are two options that could work:

- Write them on a "Someday/Maybe" list.
- Put them on your calendar or in a "tickler" file.

The point of all of these incubation procedures is that they give you a way to get the items off your mind *right now* and let you feel confident that some reminder of the possible action will resurface at an appropriate time. I'll elaborate on these in more detail in the next chapter, on *organizing*. For now, just put a Post-it on such items, and label them "maybe" or "remind on October 17," and set them aside in a "pending" category you will be accumulating for later sorting.*

Reference

Many of the things you will uncover in "in" will need no action but may have value as potentially useful information about projects

---

*One of your extra stack baskets is ideal for this purpose. Use it temporarily during this initial processing to gather things to organize later. Afterward you can use it to hold pending work-in-progress papers and physical reminders of next actions.

and topics. Ideally, you have already set up a workable filing system (as described in chapter 4) for your reference and support information. As you come across material in your in-basket and e-mail that you'd like to keep for archival or support purposes, file it.

You'll probably discover that there are lots of miscellaneous kinds of things that you want to keep but have piled up in stacks or stuffed into drawers because your reference system was too formal or just plain nonexistent. Let me remind you here that a less-than-sixty-second, fun-to-use general-reference filing system within arm's reach of where you sit is a mission-critical component of full implementation of this methodology. In the "battle zone" of real life, if it's not easy, fast, and fun to file, you'll stack instead of organizing. And then it will become much more difficult to keep things processed.

Whenever you come across something you want to keep, make a label for it, put it in a file folder, and tuck that into your filing drawer. Or put a Post-it on it instructing your secretary or assistant to do the same. In my early days of coaching I used to give my clients permission to keep a "To File" pile. No longer. I discovered that if you can't get it into your system immediately, you're probably not ever going to. If you won't do it now, you likely won't do it later, either.

And If There Is an Action . . . What *Is* It?

This is the biggie. If there's something that needs to be *done* about the item in "in," then you need to decide what exactly that next action is. "Next Actions" again, means the next physical, visible activity that would be required to move the situation toward closure.

This is both easier and more difficult than it sounds.

The next action *should* be easy to figure out, but there are often some quick analyses and several planning steps that haven't occurred yet in your mind, and these have to happen before you can determine precisely what has to happen to complete the item, even if it's a fairly simple one.

Let's look at a sample list of the things that a person might typically have his attention on.

• Clean the garage
• Do my taxes
• Conference I'm going to
• Bobby's birthday
• Press release
• Performance reviews
• Management changes

Although each of these items may seem relatively clear as a task or project, determining the next action on each one will take some thought.

• Clean the garage

. . . Well, I just have to get in there and start. No, wait a minute, there's a big refrigerator in there that I need to get rid of first. I should find out if John Patrick wants it for his camp. I should . . .

• Call John re refrigerator in garage

What about . . .

• Do my taxes

. . . but I actually can't start on them until I have my last K-1 back. Can't do anything until then. So I'm . . .

• Waiting for K-1 from Acme Trust

And for the . . .

• Conference I'm going to

. . . I need to find out whether Sandra is going to prepare a press kit for us. I guess I need to . . .

• E-mail Sandra re press kits for the conference

. . . and so forth. The action steps—"Call John," "Waiting for K-1," "E-mail Sandra"—are what need to be decided about everything that is actionable in your in-basket.

The Action Step Needs to Be the Absolute Next Physical Thing to Do Remember that these are physical, visible activities. Many people think they've determined the "next action" when they get it down to "set meeting." But that's *not* the next action, because it's not descriptive of physical behavior. How do you set a meeting? Well, it could be with a phone call or an e-mail, but to whom? Decide. If you don't decide now, you'll still have to decide at some other point, and what this process is designed to do is actually get you to *finish* the thinking exercise about this item. If you haven't identified the next physical action required to kick-start it, there will be a psychological gap every time you think about it even vaguely. You'll tend to resist noticing it.

Until you know what the next physical action is, there's still more thinking required before anything can happen.

When you get to a phone or to your computer, you want to have all your thinking completed so you can use the tools you have and the location you're in to more easily get things done, having already defined what there is to do.

What if you say to yourself, "Well, the next thing I need to do is decide what to do about this?" That's a tricky one. Deciding isn't really an action, because actions take time, and deciding doesn't. There's always some physical activity that can be done to facilitate your decision-making. Ninety-nine percent of the time you just need more information before you can make a decision. That additional information can come from external

Determine what you need to *do* in order to *decide*.

sources ("Call Susan to get her input on the proposal") or from internal thinking ("Draft ideas about new reorganization"). Either way, there's still a next action to be determined in order to move the project forward.

Once You Decide What the Action Step Is

You have three options once you decide what the next action really is.

- *Do it* (if the action takes less than two minutes).
- *Delegate it* (if you're not the most appropriate person to do the action).
- *Defer it* into your organization system as an option for work to do later.

Do It

If the next action can be done in two minutes or less, do it when you first pick the item up. If the memo requires just a thirty-second reading and then a quick "yes"/"no"/other response on a Post-it back to the sender, do it now. If you can browse the catalog in just a minute or two to see if there might be anything of interest in it, browse away, and then toss it, route it, or reference it as required. If the next action on something is to leave a quick message on someone's voice-mail, make the call now.

Even if the item is not a "high priority" one, do it now if you're ever going to do it at all. The rationale for the two-minute rule is that that's more or less the point where it starts taking longer to store and track an item than to deal with it the first time it's in your hands—in other words, it's the efficiency cutoff. If the thing's not important enough to be done, *throw it away*. If it is, and if you're going to do it sometime, the efficiency factor should come into play.

Many people find that getting into the habit of following the two-minute rule creates a dramatic improvement in their productivity. One vice president of a large software company told me that it gave him an additional hour a day of quality discretionary time! He was one of those 300-e-mails-a-day high-tech executives, highly focused for most of the workday on three key initiatives. Many of those e-mails were from people who reported to him—and they needed his eyes on something, his comments and OKs, in order to move forward. But because they were not on a topic in his rifle sights, he would just stage the e-mails in "in," to get to "later." After several thousand of them piled up, he would have to go in to work and spend whole weekends trying to catch up. That would have been OK if he were twenty-six, when everything's an adrenaline rush anyway, but he was in his thirties and had young kids. Working all weekend was no longer acceptable behavior. When I coached him we went through all 800-plus e-mails he currently had in "in." It turned out that a lot could be dumped, quite a few needed to be filed as reference, and many others required less-than-two-minute replies that he whipped through. I checked with him a year later, and he was still current! He never let his e-mails mount up beyond a screenful anymore. He said it had changed the nature of his division because of the dramatic decrease in his own response time. His staff thought he was now made of Teflon!

The two-minute rule is magic.

That's a rather dramatic testimonial, but it's an indication of just how critical some of these simple processing behaviors can be, especially as the volume and speed of the input increase for you personally.

Two minutes is in fact just a guideline. If you have a long open window of time in which to process your in-basket, you can extend the cutoff for each item to five or ten minutes. If you've got to get to the bottom of all your input rapidly, in order to figure out how best to use your afternoon, then you may want to shorten the time to one minute, or even thirty seconds, so you can get through everything a little faster.

It's not a bad idea to time yourself for a few of these while you're becoming familiar with the process. Most clients I work with have difficulty estimating how long two minutes actually is, and they greatly *underestimate* how long certain actions are likely to take. For instance, if your action is to leave someone a message, and you get the real person instead of his or her voice-mail, the call will usually take quite a bit longer than two minutes.

You'll be surprised how many two-minute actions you can perform even on your most critical projects.

There's nothing you really need to track about your two-minute actions—you just do them. If, however, you take an action and don't finish the project with that one action, you'll need to clarify what's *next* on it, and manage that according to the same criteria. For instance, if you act to replace the cartridge in your favorite pen and discover that you're out of cartridge refills, you'll want to decide on the next action about getting them ("Buy refills at the store") and *do, delegate,* or *defer* it appropriately.

Adhere to the two-minute rule and see how much you get done in the process of clearing out your "in" stacks. Many people are amazed by how many two-minute actions are possible, often on some of their most critical current projects.

Let me make one more observation regarding the two-minute rule, this time as it relates to your comfort with typing e-mails. If you're in a large-volume e-mail environment, you'll greatly improve your productivity by increasing your typing speed and using the shortcut keyboard commands for your operating system and your common e-mail software. Too many sophisticated professionals are seriously hamstrung because they still hunt and peck and try to use their mouse too much. More work could be dispatched faster by combining the two-minute rule with improved computer skills. I've found that many executives aren't resisting technology, they're just resisting their keyboards!

Delegate It

If the next action is going to take longer than two minutes, ask yourself, "Am I the best person to be doing it?" If not, hand it off to the appropriate party, in a systematic format.

Delegation is not always downstream. You may decide, "This has got to get over to Customer Service," or "My boss needs to put his eyes on this next," or "I need my partner's point of view on this."

A "systematic format" could be any of the following:

- Send the appropriate party an e-mail.
- Write a note or an overnote on paper and route the item "out" to that person.
- Leave him or her a voice-mail.
- Add it as an agenda item on a list for your next real-time conversation with that person.
- Talk to him or her directly, either face-to-face or by phone.

Although any of these options can work, I would recommend them in the above order, top to bottom. E-mail is usually the fastest mode into the system; it provides an electronic record; and the receiver gets to deal with it at his or her convenience. Written notes are next because they too can get into the system immediately, and the recipient then has a physical particle to use as an organizational reminder. If you're passing on paper-based material as part of the handoff, a written communication is obviously the way to go; as with e-mail, the person you hand it off to can then deal with it on his or her own schedule. Voice-mail can be efficient, and many professionals live by it; the downside is that tracking becomes an additional requirement for both you and the recipient, and what you say is not always what gets heard. Next would be saving the communication on an agenda list or in a folder for your next regular meeting with the person. Sometimes this is necessary because of the sensitive or detailed nature of the topic, but it then must wait to get moving until that meeting occurs. The least preferable option would be to interrupt what both you and the person are doing to talk about the item. This is immediate, but it hampers workflow for both of you and has the same downside as voice-mail: no written record.

Tracking the Handoff If you do delegate an action to someone else, and if you care at all whether something happens as a result, you'll need to track it. As I will walk you through in the next chapter, about *organizing*, you'll see that a significant category to manage is "Waiting For."

As you develop your own customized system, what you eventually hand off and then track could look like a list in a planner, a file folder holding separate papers for each item, and/or a list categorized as "Waiting For" in your software. For now, if you don't have a trusted system set up already, just put a note on a piece of paper—"W/F: reply from Bob"—and put that into a "Pending" stack of notes in a separate pile or tray that may result from your processing.

What If the Ball Is Already in Someone Else's Court? In the example cited above about waiting for the last K-1 to come in so you can do your taxes, the next action is currently on someone else's plate. In such situations you will also want to track the action as a delegated item, or as a "Waiting For." On the paper that says "Do my taxes," write something like "Waiting for K-1 from Acme Trust" and put that into your "Pending" stack.

It's important that you record the date on everything you hand off to others. This, of all the categories in your personal system, is the most crucial one to keep tabs on. The few times you will actually want to refer to that information ("But I called and ordered that on March 12") will make it worth establishing this as a lifelong habit.

Defer It

It's likely that most of the next actions you determine for things in "in" will be yours to do and will take longer than two minutes to complete. A call you need to make to a customer; an e-mail you need to spend a little time thinking about and drafting to your team; a gift you need to buy for your brother at the stationery store; a piece of software you need to download from the Web and try out; a conversation you must have with your spouse about an investment you think you should make—all of these fit that description.

These actions will have to be written down somewhere and then organized in the appropriate categories so you can access them when you need to. For the moment, go ahead and put Post-its on the pieces of paper in "in," with the action written on them, and add these to the "Pending" stack of papers that have been processed.

The "Pending" Things That Are Left

If you follow the instructions in this chapter, you'll dump a mess of things, file a bunch, do a lot of two-minute actions, and hand off a number of items to other people. You'll also wind up with a stack of items that have actions associated with them that you still need to do—soon, someday, or on a specific date—and reminders of things you're waiting on from other people. This "Pending" group is made up of the actions you've delegated or deferred. It is what still needs to be organized in some fashion in your personal system, a topic I'll cover in step-by-step detail in the next chapter.

Identifying the *Projects* You Have

This last step in getting to the bottom of "in" requires a shift in perspective from the single-action details to the larger picture—your projects.

Again, I define a "project" as any outcome you're committed to achieving that will take more than one action step to complete. If you look through an inventory of actions that you have already been generating—"Call Frank about the car alarm"; "E-mail Bernadette re conference materials"—you'll no doubt recognize a number of things that are larger than the single action you've defined. There's still going to be something about "car alarm" to do after the call to Frank, and there will still be something to handle about the conference after the e-mail to Bernadette.

I hope you're able to see the very practical reason for defining projects as broadly as I do: If the action step you've identified will not complete the commitment, then you'll need some stake in the ground to keep reminding you of actions you have pending until you have closure. You need to make a list of projects. A "Projects" list may include anything from "Give holiday party" to "Divest the Widget product line" to "Finalize compensation package." The purpose of this list is not to reflect your priorities but just to ensure that you've got placeholders for all those open loops.

Right now you probably have between thirty and a hundred projects.

Whether you draw up your "Projects" list while you're initially processing your in-basket or after you've set up your action lists doesn't really matter. It just needs to be done at *some* point, and it must be maintained, as it's the key driver for reviewing where you are and where you want to be.

For now, let's make sure your organizing setup is "all systems go."

7

Organizing: Setting Up the Right Buckets

HAVING A TOTAL and seamless system of organization in place gives you tremendous power because it allows your mind to let go of lower-level thinking and graduate to intuitive focusing, undistracted by matters that haven't been dealt with appropriately. But your physical organization system must be better than your mental one in order for that to happen.

Airtight organization is required for your focus to remain on the broader horizon.

In this chapter I'll lead you through the organizing steps and tools that will be required as you process your in-basket. As you initially process "in," you'll create lists and groupings of things you want to organize and you'll invariably think of additional items to include. In other words, your organization system is not something that you'll necessarily create all at once, in a vacuum. It will evolve as you process your stuff and test out whether you have put everything in the best place for *you*.

I got it all together, but I forgot where I put it.
—Anonymous

The outer ring of the Workflow Diagram (opposite) shows the main groupings into which things will go as you decide what they are and what needs to be done about them.

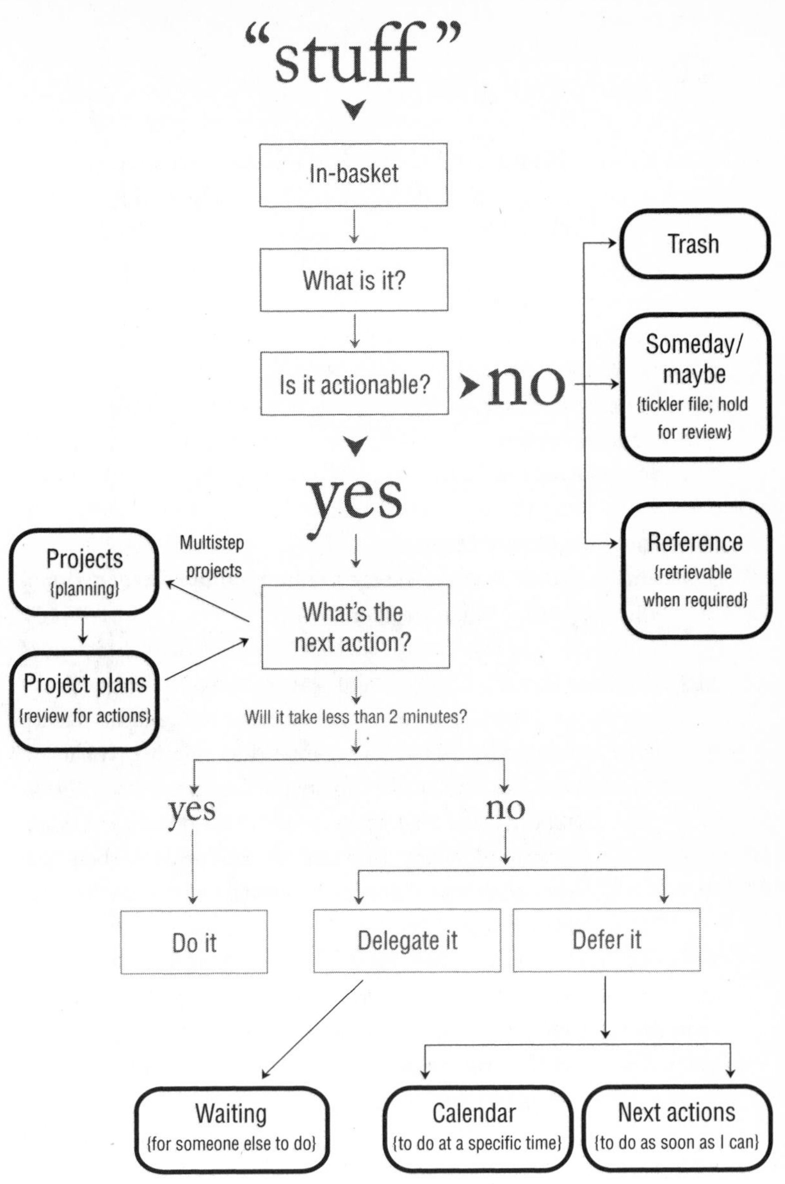

WORKFLOW DIAGRAM—ORGANIZING

The Basic Categories

There are seven primary *types* of things that you'll want to keep track of and manage from an organizational perspective:

- A "Projects" list
- Project support material
- Calendared actions and information
- "Next Actions" lists
- A "Waiting For" list
- Reference material
- A "Someday/Maybe" list

The Importance of Hard Edges

It's critical that all of these categories be kept pristinely distinct from one another. They each represent a discrete type of agreement we make with ourselves, and if they lose their edges and begin to blend, much of the value of organizing will be lost.

The categories must be kept visually, physically, and psychologically separate.

If you put reference materials in the same pile as things you still want to read, for example, you'll go numb to the stack. If you put items on your "Next Actions" lists that really need to go on the calendar, because they have to occur on specific days, then you won't trust your calendar and you'll continually have to reassess your action lists. If you have a project that you're not going to be doing anything about for some time, it must go onto your "Someday/Maybe" list so you can relate to the "Projects" list with the rigorous action-generating focus it needs. And if something you're "Waiting For" is included on one of your action lists, you'll continually get bogged down by nonproductive rethinking.

All You Really Need Is Lists and Folders

Once you know *what* you need to keep track of (covered in the previous chapter, on *Processing*), all you really need is lists and folders for reference and support materials. Your lists (which, as I've indicated, could also be items in folders) will keep track of projects and someday/maybes, as well as the actions you'll need to take on your active open loops. Folders (digital or paper-based) will be required to hold your reference material and the support information for active projects.

I would not give a fig for the simplicity on this side of complexity, but I would give my life for the simplicity on the other side of complexity.
—*Oliver Wendell Holmes*

Lots of people have been making lists for years but have never found the procedure to be particularly effective. There's rampant skepticism about systems as simple as the one I'm recommending. But most list-makers haven't put the appropriate things on their lists, or have left them incomplete, which has kept the lists themselves from being very functional. Once you know what goes *on* the lists, however, things get much easier; then you just need a way to manage them.

As I've said, you shouldn't bother to create some external structuring of the priorities on your lists that you'll then have to rearrange or rewrite as things change. Attempting to impose such scaffolding has been a big source of frustration in many people's organizing. You'll be prioritizing more intuitively as you see the whole list, against quite a number of shifting variables. The list is just a way for you to keep track of the total inventory of active things to which you have made a commitment, and to have that inventory available for review.

When I refer to a "list," keep in mind that I mean nothing more than a grouping of items with some similar characteristic. A list could look like one of three things: (1) a file folder with separate paper notes for the items within the category; (2) an actual list on a titled piece of paper (often within a loose-leaf organizer or planner); or (3) an inventory in a software program or on a digital assistant, such as Microsoft Outlook task categories or a category on a handheld PDA.

Organizing Action Reminders

If you've emptied your in-basket, you'll undoubtedly have created a stack of "Pending" reminders for yourself, representing longer-than-two-minute actions that cannot be delegated to someone else. You'll probably have anywhere from twenty to sixty or seventy or more such items. You'll also have accumulated reminders of things that you've handed off to other people, and perhaps some things that need be placed in your calendar or a "Someday/Maybe" kind of holder.

You'll want to sort all of this into groupings that make sense to you so you can review them as options for work to do when you have time. You'll also want to decide on the most appropriate way physically to organize those groups, whether as items in folders or on lists, either paper-based or digital.

The Actions That Go on Your Calendar

For the purposes of organization, as I've said, there are two basic kinds of actions: those that must be done on a certain day and/or at a particular time, and those that just need to be done as soon as you can get to them, around your other calendared items. Calendared action items can be either time-specific (e.g., "4:00–5:00 meet with Jim") or day-specific ("Call Rachel Tuesday to see if she got the proposal").

As you were processing your in-basket, you probably came across things that you put right into your calendar as they showed up. You may have realized that the next action on getting a medical checkup, for example, was to call and make the appointment, and so (since the action required two minutes or less) you actually did it when it occurred to you. Writing the appointment into your calendar as you made it would then have been common sense.

The calendar should show only the "hard landscape" around which you do the rest of your actions.

What many people *want* to do, however, based

on old habits of writing daily to-do lists, is put actions on the calendar that they think they'd really *like* to get done next Monday, say, but that then actually might not, and that might then have to be taken over to following days. *Resist this impulse.* You need to trust your calendar as sacred territory, reflecting the exact hard edges of your day's commitments, which should be noticeable at a glance while you're on the run. That'll be much easier if the only things in there are those that you absolutely *have* to get done on that day. When the calendar is relegated to its proper role in organizing, the majority of the actions that you need to do are left in the category of "as soon as possible, against all the other things I have to do."

Organizing As-Soon-As-Possible Actions by Context

Over many years I have discovered that the best way to be reminded of an "as soon as I can" action is by the particular *context* required for that action—that is, either the tool or the location or the person needed to complete it. For instance, if the action requires a computer, it should go on an "At Computer" list. If your action demands that you be out in your car driving around (such as stopping by the bank or going to the hardware store), the "Errands" list would be the appropriate place to track it. If the next step is to talk about something face-to-face with your partner Emily, putting it into an "Emily" folder or list makes the most sense.

How discrete these categories will need to be will depend on (1) how many actions you actually have to track; and (2) how often you change the contexts within which to do them.

If you are that rare person who has only twenty-five next actions, a single "Next Actions" list might suffice. It could include items as diverse as "Buy nails" and "Talk to boss about staff changes" and "Draft ideas about off-site meeting." If, however, you have fifty or a hundred next actions pending, keeping all of those on one big list would make it too difficult to see what you needed to see; each time you got any window of time to do something, you'd have to do unproductive resorting. If you happened to be on a short break at a conference, during which you might be able to make some calls, you'd have to identify the items that were calls among a big batch of unrelated items. When you went out to do odds and ends, you'd probably want to pick out your errands and make another list.

Another productivity factor that this kind of organization supports is leveraging your energy when you're in a certain mode. When you're in "phone mode," it helps to make a lot of phone calls—just crank down your "Calls" list. When your computer is up and running and you're cruising along digitally, it's useful to get as much done on-line as you can without having to shift into another kind of activity. It takes more energy than most people realize to unhook out of one set of behaviors and get into another kind of rhythm and tool set. And obviously, when a key person is sitting in front of you in your office, you'd be wise to have all the things you need to talk about with him or her immediately at hand.

The Most Common Categories of Action Reminders

You'll probably find that at least a few of the following common list headings for next actions will make sense for you:

- "Calls"
- "At Computer"
- "Errands"
- "Office Actions" or "At Office" (miscellaneous)
- "At Home"
- "Agendas" (for people and meetings)
- "Read/Review"

"Calls" This is the list of all the phone calls you need to make; you can work off it as long as you have a phone available. The more mobile you are (especially if you have a cell phone), the more useful you'll find it to have one single list of all your calls: those strange little windows of time that you wind up with when you're off-site or traveling—on a break or waiting for a plane, maybe—offer a perfect opportunity to work down your list. Hav-

ing a discrete "Calls" list makes it much easier to focus and intuitively pick the best call to make in the moment.

I suggest that you take the time to write the phone number itself alongside each item. There are many situations in which you would probably make the call if the number was already there in front of you but not if you had to look it up.

"At Computer" If you work with a computer—particularly if you move around with a laptop or have a PC at work and another one at home—it can be helpful to group all those actions that you need to do when it's on and running. This will allow you to see all your options for computer work to do, reminding you of all the e-mails you need to send, the documents you need to draft or edit, and so on.

Because I fly a lot, I even maintain an "On-Line" action list, separate from my "At Computer" one. When I'm on a plane, I can't easily connect to the Web or to my server, as many actions require. So instead of having to rethink what I can and can't do whenever I look at my "At Computer" list, I can trust that none of my "At Computer" actions require that I be connected, which frees my mind to make choices based on other criteria.

Think carefully about *where* and *how* you can and can't do *which* actions, and organize your lists accordingly.

If you have a computer only at work, you may not need a separate "At Computer" list; "Office Actions" may cover those actions because the office is the only place you can do them anyway. (Similarly, if you have a computer only at home, and it's not a laptop, you may be able to put computer-specific actions on your "At Home" list.)

"Errands" It makes a lot of sense to group together in one place reminders of all the things you need to do when you're "out and about." When you know you need to get in your car and go somewhere, it's great to be able to look at the list while you're on the road. Actions like "Get stock certificates from safety-deposit box,"

"Pick up pictures at framers," and "Buy petunias at nursery" would all go here.

This list could, of course, be nothing more elaborate than a Post-it that you keep in your planner somewhere, or a screen in an "Errands" category of the "To Do" section on your Palm organizer.

It's often helpful to track sublists within individual "Errands" items. For instance, as soon as you realize you need something from the hardware store, you might want to make "Hardware Store" the list item and then append a sublist of all the things you want to pick up there, as you think of them. On the low-tech end, you could create a "Hardware Store" Post-it; on the high-tech side, if you were using a digital list, you could attach a "note" to "Hardware Store" on your list and input the details there.

We must strive to reach that simplicity that lies beyond sophistication.
—John Gardner

Because I travel in major metropolitan areas so much, I keep *two* "Errands" lists—"Errands—Ojai" (where I live) and "Errands—Anywhere," for all those other things I can pick up even when I'm on the road. "T-connectors for irrigation" would go on "Errands—Ojai," but "Get dress socks" would go on "Errands—Anywhere."

"Office Actions"/"At Office" If you work in an office, there will be certain things that you can do only there, and a list of those will be a useful thing to have in front of you then—though obviously, if you have a phone and a computer in your office, and you have "Calls" and "At Computer" as separate lists, *they'll* be in play as well. I'd use an "Office Actions" or "At Office" list for anything that required an Internet connection available only, or even most conveniently, in the office—for example, a reminder to download a large software program from the Web would go on this list for me.

"At Home" Many actions can be done only at home, and it makes sense to keep a list specific to that context. I'm sure you've got numerous personal and around-the-house projects, and often the

next thing to do *on* them is just to *do* them. "Hang new print," "Organize CDs," and "Switch closets to winter clothes" would be typical items for this grouping.

If you have an office at home, as I do, anything that can be done only there goes on the "At Home" list. (If you work *only* at home and don't go to another office, you won't need an "Office Actions" list at all—the "At Home" list will suffice.)

"Agendas" Invariably you'll find that many of your next actions need to either occur in a real-time interaction with someone or be brought up in a committee, team, or staff meeting. You have to talk to your partner about an idea for next year; you want to check with your spouse about his schedule for the spring; you need to delegate a task to your secretary that's too complicated to explain in an e-mail. And you must make an announcement at the Monday staff meeting about the change in expense-report policies.

Standing meetings and people you deal with on an ongoing basis may need their own "Agenda" lists.

These next actions should be put on separate "Agenda" lists for each of those people and for that meeting (assuming that you attend it regularly). Professionals who keep a file folder to hold all the things they need to go over with their boss already use a version of this method. If you're conscientious about determining all your next actions, though, you may find that you'll need somewhere between three and fifteen of these kinds of lists. I recommend that separate files or lists be kept for bosses, partners, assistants, spouses, and children. You should also keep the same kind of list for your attorney, financial adviser, accountant, and/or computer consultant, as well as for anyone else with whom you might have more than one thing to go over the next time you talk on the phone.

If you participate in standing meetings—staff meetings, project meetings, board meetings, committee meetings, whatever—they, too, deserve their own files, in which you can collect things that will need to be addressed on those occasions.

Often you'll want to keep a running list of things to go over with someone you'll be interacting with only for a limited period of time. For instance, if you have a contractor doing a significant piece of work on your house or property, you can create a list for him for the duration of the project. As you're walking around the site after he's left for the day, you may notice several things you need to talk with him about, and you'll want that list to be easy to capture and to access as needed.

Given the usefulness of this type of list, your system should allow you to add "Agendas" ad hoc, as needed, quickly and simply. For example, inserting a page for a person or a meeting within an "Agenda" section in a loose-leaf notebook planner takes only seconds, as does adding a dedicated "Memo" in a PDA's "Agenda" category.

"Read/Review" You will no doubt have discovered in your in-basket a number of things for which your next action is to *read*. I hope you will have held to the two-minute rule and dispatched a number of those quick-skim items already—tossing, filing, or routing them forward as appropriate.

To-read items that you know will demand more than two minutes of your time are usually best managed in a separate physical stack-basket labeled "Read/Review." This is still a "list" by my definition, but one that's more efficiently dealt with by grouping the documents and magazines themselves in a tray and/or portable folder.

For many people, the "Read/Review" stack can get quite large. That's why it's critical that the pile be reserved only for those longer-than-two-minute things that you actually *want to read when you have time*. That can be daunting enough in itself, but things get *seriously* out of control and psychologically numbing when the edges of this category are not clearly defined. A pristine delineation will at least make you conscious of the inventory, and if you're like most people, having some type of self-regulating mechanism will help you become more aware of what you want to keep and what you should just get rid of.

It's practical to have that stack of reading material at hand and easy to grab on the run when you're on your way to a meeting that may be late starting, a seminar that may have a window of time when nothing is going on, or a dentist appointment that may keep you waiting to get your teeth cleaned. Those are all great opportunities to crank through that kind of reading. People who don't have their "Read/Review" material organized can waste a lot of time, since life is full of weird little windows when it could be processed.

Those who make the worst use of their time are the first to complain of its shortness.
—Jean de La Bruysre

Organizing "Waiting For"

Like reminders of the actions *you* need to do, reminders of all the things that you're waiting to get back from or get done by others have to be sorted and grouped. You won't necessarily be tracking discrete action steps here, but more often final deliverables or projects that others are responsible for, such as the tickets you've ordered from the theater, the scanner that's coming for the office, the OK on the proposal from your client, and so on. When the next action on something is up to someone else, you don't need an *action* reminder, just a trigger about what you're waiting for from whom. Your role is to review that list as often as you need to and assess whether you ought to be *taking* an action such as checking the status or lighting a fire under the project.

You'll probably find it works best to keep this "Waiting For" list close at hand, in the same system as your own "Next Actions" reminder lists. The responsibility for the next step may bounce back and forth many times before a project is finished. For example, you may need to make a call to a vendor to request a proposal for a piece of work (on your "Calls" list.) Having made the call, you then wait for the vendor to get back to you with the proposal (the proposal goes to your "Waiting For" list). When the proposal comes in, you have to review it (it lands in your "Read/Review" stack-basket). Once you've gone over it, you send it to your boss for her approval (now it's back on your "Waiting For" list). And so on.*

You'll get a great feeling when you know that your "Waiting For" list is the complete inventory of everything you care about that other people are supposed to be doing.

Using the Original Item as Its Own Action Reminder

The most efficient way to track your action reminders is to add them to lists or folders as they occur to you. The originating trigger won't be needed after you have processed it. You might take notes in the meeting with your boss, but you can toss those after you've pulled out any projects and actions associated with them. While some people try to archive voice-mails that they still need to "do something about," that's not the most effective way to manage the reminders embedded in them.

Keep actionable e-mails and paper separated from all the rest.

There are some exceptions to this rule, however. Certain kinds of input will most efficiently serve as their own reminders of required actions, rather than your having to write something about them on a list. This is particularly true for some paper-based materials and some e-mails.

Managing Paper-Based Workflow

Some things are their own best reminders of work to be done. The category of "Read/Review" articles, publications, and documents is the most common example. It would obviously be overkill to write "Review *Fortune* magazine" on some action list when you could just as easily toss the magazine itself into your "Read/Review" basket to act as the trigger.

---

*Digital list managers (like the Palm's) or low-tech papers in separate folders have an advantage here over lists on paper because they let you easily move an item from one category to another as the action changes, without your having to rewrite anything.

Another example: people who find it easier to deal with bills by paying them all at one time and in one location will want to keep their bills in a folder or stack-basket labeled "Bills to Pay" (or, more generically, "Financial to Process"). Similarly, receipts for expense reporting should be either dealt with at the time they're generated or kept in their own "Receipts to Process" envelope or folder.*

The specific nature of your work, your input, and your workstation may make it more efficient to organize other categories using only the original paper itself. A customer-service professional, for instance, may deal with numerous requests that show up in a standard written form, and in that case maintaining a basket or file containing only those actionable items is the best way to manage them.

Whether it makes more sense to write reminders on a list or to use the originating documents in a basket or folder will depend to a great extent on logistics. Could you use those reminders somewhere other than at your desk? If so, the portability of the material should be considered. If you couldn't possibly *do* that work anywhere but at your desk, then managing reminders of it solely at your workstation is the better choice.

Whichever option you select, the reminders should be in visibly discrete categories based upon the next action required. If the next action on a service order is to make a call, it should be in a "Calls" group; if the action step is to review information and input it into the computer, it should be labeled "At Computer." Most undermining of the effectiveness of many workflow systems I see is the fact that all the documents of one type (e.g., service requests) are kept in a single tray, even though different kinds of actions may be required on each one. One request needs a phone

---

*This approach can be dangerous, however, if you don't put those "Bills to Pay" or "Receipts to Process" in front of your face as consistently as you should. Just having them "organized" isn't sufficient to get them off your mind—you've also got to review them appropriately.

call, another needs data reviewed, and still another is waiting for someone to get back with some information—but they're all sorted together. This arrangement can cause a person's mind to go numb to the stack because of all the decisions that are still pending about the next-action level of doing.

My personal system is highly portable, with almost everything kept on lists, but I still maintain two categories of paper-based reminders. I travel with a "Read/Review" plastic file folder and another one labeled "Data Entry." In the latter I put anything for which the next action is simply to input data into my computer (business cards that need to get into my telephone/address list, quotes for my "Quotes" database, articles about restaurants I want to put on my "Travel—Cities" sublists, etc.).

Managing E-mail-Based Workflow

Like some paper-based materials, e-mails that need action are sometimes best as their own reminders—in this case within the tracked e-mail system itself. This is especially likely to be true if you get a lot of e-mail and spend a lot of your work time with your e-mail software booted up. E-mails that you need to act on may then be stored within the system instead of having their embedded actions written out on a list.

Many of my clients have found it helpful to set up two or three unique folders on their e-mail navigator bars. True, most folders in e-mail should be used for reference or archived materials, but it's also possible to set up a workable system that will keep your actionable messages discretely organized, outside of the "in" area itself (which is where most people keep them).

I recommend that you create one folder for any longer-than-two-minute e-mails that you need to act on (again, you should be able to dispatch many messages right off the bat by following the two-minute rule). The folder name should begin with a prefix letter or symbol so that (1) it looks different from your reference folders and (2) it sits at the top of your folders in the navigator bar. Use something like the "@" sign in Microsoft or the dash ("–") in

Lotus, which sort into their systems at the top. Your resulting "@ACTION" folder will hold those e-mails that you need to do something about.

Next you can create a folder titled "@WAITING FOR," which will show up in the same place as the "@ACTION" folder. Then, as you receive e-mails that indicate that someone is going to do something that you care about tracking, you can drag them over into the "@WAITING FOR" file. It can also hold reminders for anything that you delegate via e-mail: when you forward something, or use e-mail to make a request or delegate an action, just save a copy into the "@WAITING FOR" file.*

Some applications (such as Lotus Notes) allow you to file a copy of an e-mail into one of your folders as you send it (with a "Send and File" button). Others (e.g., Outlook) will simultaneously save only into your universal "Sent Mail" folder. In the latter case, what seems to work best for many is to copy ("cc" or "bcc") themselves when they delegate via e-mail, and then to pull that copy into their "@WAITING FOR" folder. (It's relatively easy to program Outlook to automatically send any e-mail that you "cc" to yourself into a designated folder, which would replicate the process just described.)

Getting E-mail "In" to "Empty" The method detailed above will enable you to actually get everything out of your e-mail in-basket, which will be a huge boon to your clarity about and control of your day-to-day work. You'll reclaim "in" as "in," so anything residing there will be like a message on your answering machine—a blinking light telling you you need to process something! Most people use their e-mail "in" for staging still-undecided actionable things and reference, a practice that rapidly numbs the mind: they know they've got to reassess everything *every*

---

*Microsoft Outlook allows users to copy or move e-mails into its "Tasks" context, which, if organized according to my recommended categories, could work equally well.

It requires much less energy to maintain e-mail at a zero base than at a thousand base.

time they glance at the screen. If you never had more than a screenful of e-mails, this approach might be reasonably functional, but with the volume most professionals are dealing with these days, that doesn't apply.

Again, getting "in" empty doesn't mean you've handled everything. It means that you've DELETED what you could, FILED what you wanted to keep but don't need to act on, DONE the less-than-two-minute responses, and moved into your reminder folders all the things you're waiting for and all your actionable e-mails. *Now* you can open the "@ACTION" file and review the e-mails that you've determined you need to spend time on. Isn't that process easier to relate to than fumbling through multiple screens, fearing all the while that you may miss something that'll blow up on you?

A Caution About Dispersing Reminders of Your Actions

"Out of sight, out of mind" is not really out of mind.

There's an obvious danger in putting reminders of things you need to do somewhere out of sight. The function of an organization system is primarily to supply the reminders you need to see *when* you need to see them, so you can trust your choices about what you're doing (and what you're not doing). Before you leave the office for the day, the actionable e-mails that you still have pending must be reviewed individually, just like your "Calls" or "At Computer" lists. In essence, "@ACTION" is an extension of your "At Computer" list and should be handled in exactly the same fashion. Your paper-based "Pending" workflow must likewise be assessed like a list if the paper materials are being used as your only reminders.

Distributing action triggers in a folder, on lists, and/or in an e-mail system is perfectly OK, *as long as you review all of the categories to which you've entrusted your triggers equally, as required.* You don't want things lurking in the recesses of your systems and not being used for their intended purpose: reminding you.

In order to hang out with friends or take a long, aimless walk and truly have nothing on your mind, you've got to know where all your actionable items are located, what they are, and that they will wait. And you need to be able to do that in a few seconds, not days.

Organizing Project Reminders

Creating and maintaining one list of all your projects (that is, again, every commitment or desired outcome that may require more than one action step to complete) can be a profound experience! You probably have more of them than you think. If you haven't done so already, I recommend that initially you make a "Projects" list in a very simple format, similar to the ones you've used for your lists of actions: it can be a category in a digital organizer, a page in a loose-leaf planner, or even a single file folder labeled "PROJECTS," with either a master list or separate sheets of paper for each one.

The "Projects" List(s)

The "Projects" list is not meant to hold plans or details about your projects themselves, nor should you try to keep it arranged by priority or size or urgency—it's just a comprehensive index of your open loops. You actually won't be working off of the "Projects" list during your day-to-day activities; for the most part, your action lists and any ad hoc tasks that come up will constitute your tactical in-the-moment focus. Remember, you can't *do* a project, you can only do the action steps it requires.

A complete and current "Projects" list is the major operational tool for moving from tree-hugging to forest management.

The real value of the "Projects" list lies in the complete review it can provide (at least once a week), allowing you to ensure that you have action steps defined for all of your projects, and that nothing is slipping through the cracks. A quick glance at this list from time to time will enhance your underlying sense of control. You'll also know that you have an inventory available to you (and to others) whenever it seems advisable to evaluate workload(s).

One List, or Subdivided?

Most people find that one list is the best way to go because it serves as a master inventory rather than as a daily prioritizing guideline. The organizing system merely provides placeholders for all your open loops and options so your mind can more easily make the necessary intuitive, moment-to-moment strategic decisions.

Frankly, it doesn't matter how many different lists of projects you have, so long as you look at the contents of *all* of them as often as you need to, since for the most part you'll do that in one fell swoop during your Weekly Review.

Some Common Ways to Subsort Projects

There are some situations in which it makes good sense to subsort a "Projects" list. Let's look at these one by one.

Personal/Professional Many people feel more comfortable seeing their lists divided up between personal and professional projects. If you're among them, be advised that your "Personal" list will need to be reviewed as judiciously as your "Professional" one, and not just saved for weekends. Many actions on personal things will need to be handled on weekdays, exactly like everything else. And often some of the greatest pressures on professionals stem from the personal aspects of their lives that they are letting slip.

Delegated Projects If you're a senior manager or executive, you probably have several projects that you are directly responsible for but have handed off to people who report to you. While you could, of course, put them on your "Waiting For" list, it might make better sense to create a "Projects—Delegated" list to track them: your task will be simply to review the list regularly enough to ensure that everything on it is moving along appropriately.

Specific Types of Projects Some professionals have as part of their work several different projects of the same *type,* which in some instances it may be valuable to group together as a sublist of "Projects." For example, I maintain a separate category called "Projects to Deliver," a chronological listing of all the upcoming seminars, coaching, and consulting assignments I've committed to. These events are "projects" like the rest, in that I need to keep noting whether things are moving along on and in place for them until they're completed. But I find it helpful to see them all organized on one list, in the order in which they are coming up on my calendar, apart from my other projects.

If you are a real estate agent, sell consulting services, or develop proposals for a relatively small number of prospective clients in any profession, you will likely find it useful to see all of your outstanding "sales relationships in progress" in one view. This could be a separate list in your planner called "Client Projects in Development," or if you already have file folders for each in-progress project, it may suffice to group them all in one file stand on your credenza. Just realize that this approach will work only if it represents a complete set of all of those situations that require action, and only if you review them regularly along with the rest of your projects, keeping them current and conscious.

What About Subprojects?

Some of your projects will likely have major *sub*projects, each of which could in theory be seen as a whole project. If you're moving into a new house, for instance, and are upgrading and changing much of the property, you may have a list of actionable items like "Finalize landscaping," "Renovate kitchen," "Rewire basement," and so on, all of which could in themselves be considered separate projects. Do you make all of this one entry on your "Projects" list—say, "Finish new home renovations"—or do you write up each of the subprojects as an individual line item?

Actually, it won't matter, as long as you review all the components of the project as frequently as you need to to stay productive. No external tool or organizing format is going to be perfect for sorting both horizontally across and vertically down through all your projects; you'll still have to be aware of the whole in some cohesive way (such as via your Weekly Review). If you make the large project your one listing on your "Projects" list, you'll want to keep a list of the subprojects and/or the project plan itself as "project support material" to be reviewed when you come to that major item. I would recommend doing it this way if big pieces of the project are *dependent* on other pieces getting done first. In that scenario you might have subprojects with no next actions attached to them because they are in a sense "waiting for" other things to happen before they can move forward. For instance, you might not be able to start on "Renovate kitchen" until you finish "Rewire basement." However, you might be able to proceed on "Finalize landscaping" independent of either of the other subprojects. You would therefore want a next action to be continually current on "Rewire basement" *and* "Finalize landscaping."

Don't be too concerned about which way is best. If you're not sure, I'd vote for putting your Big Projects on the "Projects" list and holding the subpieces in your project support material, making sure to include them in your Weekly Review. If that arrangement doesn't feel quite right, try including the *active* and independent subprojects as separate entries on your master list.

How you list projects and subprojects is up to you; just be sure you know where to find all the moving parts.

There's no perfect system for tracking all your projects and subprojects the same way. You just need to know you *have* projects and, if they have associated components, where to find the appropriate reminders for them.

Project Support Materials

Project support materials are not project actions, and they're not project reminders. They're resources to support your actions and thinking about your projects.

Don't Use Support Material for Reminding Typically, people use stacks of papers and thickly stuffed file folders *as reminders* that (1) they've *got* a project, and (2) they've got to do something about it. They're essentially making support materials serve as action reminders. The problem is that next actions and "Waiting For" items on these projects have usually not been determined and are psychologically still embedded in the stacks and the folders—giving them the aura of just more "stuff" that repels its (un)organizer instead of attracting him or her to action. When you're on the run, in the heat of the activities of the day, files like that are the last thing you'll want to pick up and peruse for actions. You'll actually go numb to the files and the piles because they don't prompt you to do anything and they simply create more anxiety.

If you're in this kind of situation, you must first add the project itself to your "Projects" list, as a reminder that there's an outcome to be achieved. Then the action steps and "Waiting For" items must be put onto their appropriate action reminder lists. Finally, when it's time to actually *do* an action, like making a call to someone about the project, you can pull out all the materials you think you might need to have as support during the conversation.

To reiterate, you *don't* want to use support materials as your primary reminders of what to do—that should be relegated to your action lists. If, however, the materials contain project plans and overviews in addition to ad hoc archival and reference information, you may want to keep them a little more visibly accessible than you do the pure reference materials in your filing cabinet. The latter place is fine for support stuff, too, so long as you have the discipline to pull out the file drawer and take a look at the plan every time you do your Weekly Review. If not, you're better off storing those kinds of project support files in a standing file holder or a separate "Pending" stack-basket on your desk or credenza.

To return to the previous example of moving into a new house, you could have a folder labeled "New House" containing all the plans and details and notes about the landscaping and the kitchen and the basement. In your Weekly Review, when you came to "Finish new home renovations" on your "Projects" list, you'd pull out the "New House" file and thumb through all your notes to ensure that you weren't missing any possible next actions. Those actions would then get done, delegated, or deferred onto your action lists, and the folder would be refiled until you needed it again for doing the actions or for your next Weekly Review.

Many people who interact with prospects and clients have attempted to use client folders and/or contact-management software such as Act! to "manage the account." The problem here is that some material is just facts or historical data that needs to be stored as background for when you might be able to use it, and some of what must be tracked is the actions required to move the relationships forward. The latter can be more effectively organized within your action-lists system. Client information is just that, and it can be folded into a general-reference file on the client or stored within a client-focused library. (I use Act! for the single great feature it offers of allowing me to cross-reference general company information and significant interactions with key people within the company. It's just a good client-centered database.) If I need to call a client, I don't want that reminder embedded anywhere but on my "Calls" list.

Organizing Ad Hoc Project Thinking

In chapter 3, I suggested that you will often have ideas that you'll want to keep about projects but that are not necessarily next actions. Those ideas fall into the broad category of "project support materials," and may be anything from a notion about something you might want to do on your next vacation to a clarification of some major components in a project plan. These thoughts could come as you're driving down the freeway listening to a news story on the radio, or reading a relevant article. What do you do with that kind of material?

There is no need ever to lose an idea about a project, theme, or topic.

My recommendation here is that you consider where you're keeping tabs on the project or topic itself, how you might add information to it in that format, and where you might store any more extensive data associated with it. Most professionals will have several options for how to handle support materials, including attaching notes to a list item, organizing digital information in e-mail and/or databases, and maintaining paper-based files and notes in notebooks.

Attached Notes Most organizing software allows you to attach a digital "note" to a list or calendar entry. If you're keeping a "Projects" list within the software, you can go to the project you had a thought about, open or attach a "note" to it, and type in your idea. This is an excellent way to capture "back-of-the-envelope" project thinking. If your "Projects" list is paper-based, you can attach a Post-it note next to the item on your master list or, if you're a low-tech type, on the item's separate sheet. In any case, you'll need to remember to look at the attachment when you review your project, to make use of the data.

E-mail and Databases E-mails that might contain good information related to your projects can be held in a dedicated e-mail folder (just follow the instructions on pages 152–53 for "@ACTION" and call it something like "@PROJECTS"). You may also find it worthwhile, if you don't have one already, to set up a more rigorous kind of digital database for organizing your thinking on a project or topic. If your company uses Lotus Notes, for example, you can create a project database either for your own private use on your PC or to be shared with others in your network.* It's worth looking into some of the other types of free-form databases that are on the market, too—even just for your own use. It's great to be able to cut and paste from the Web or from e-mails and drop data under a topic somewhere or type in your own thoughts. Be sure, also, to explore the technology and tools that you already have—just learning how to use all the lists and attachments in something like the Palm organizer may provide you with sufficient "back-of-the-envelope" capability.

Paper-Based Files Having a separate file folder devoted to each project makes a lot of sense when you're accumulating paper-based materials; it may be low-tech, but it's an elegant solution nonetheless. Simplicity and ease of handling make for a good general-reference filing system—one that lets you feel comfortable about creating a folder for scraps of paper from a meeting.

Pages in Notebooks A great advantage of paper-based loose-leaf notebooks is that you can dedicate a whole page or group of pages to an individual project. For years I maintained a midsize notebook with a "Projects" list in front and a "Project Support" section toward the back, where I always had some blank pages to capture any random thinking or plans and details about projects on my list.

Each of the methods described above can be effective in organizing project thinking. The key is that you must consistently look for any action steps inherent in your project notes, and review the notes themselves as often as you think is necessary, given the nature of the project.

You'll also want to clear out many of your notes once they

---

*Many Lotus Notes users don't even realize they can do this, but in fact it's one of the program's most powerful features. If you have Notes, check with your resident IT resource person and have him or her request system permission and show you how.

become inactive or unreal, to keep the whole system from catching the "stale" virus. I've found a lot of value in capturing these types of thoughts, more for the way it consistently helps my thinking process than because I end up using every idea (most I don't!). But I try to make sure not to let my old thoughts stay around too long, pretending they're useful when they're not.

Organizing Nonactionable Data

Interestingly, one of the biggest problems with most people's personal management systems is that they blend a few actionable things with a large amount of data and material that has value but no action attached. Having good, consistent structures with which to manage the nonactionable items in our work and lives is as important as managing our action and project reminders. When the nonactionable items aren't properly managed, they clog up the whole process.

Unactionable items fall into two large categories: reference materials and reminders of things that need no action now but might at a later date.

Reference Materials

Much of what comes across your desk and into your life in general is reference material. There's no action required, but it's information that you want to keep, for a variety of reasons. Your major decisions will be how much to keep, how much room to dedicate to it, what form it should be stored in, and where. Much of that will be a personal or organizational judgment call based upon legal or logistical concerns or personal preferences. The only time you should have attention on your reference material is when you need to change your system in some way because you have too much or too little information, given your needs or preferences.

The problem most people have psychologically with all their stuff is that it's still "stuff"—that is, they haven't decided what's actionable and what's not. Once you've made a clean distinction about which is which, what's left as reference should have no pull or incompletion associated with it—it's just your library. Your only decision then is how big a library you want. When you've fully implemented this action-management methodology, you can be as big a packrat as your space (physical and digital) will allow. As I've increased the size of the hard disk in my computer, I've kept that much more e-mail in my archives. The more the merrier, as far as I'm concerned, since increasing the volume of pure reference material adds no psychic weight.

The Variety of Reference Systems

There are a number of ways to organize reference material, and many types of tools to use. What follows is a brief discussion of some of the most common.

- General-reference filing—paper and e-mail
- Large-category filing
- Rolodexes and contact managers
- Libraries and archives

Your filing system should be a simple library of data, easily retrievable—not your reminder for actions, projects, priorities, or prospects.

General-Reference Filing As I've said, a good filing system is critical for processing and organizing your stuff. It's also a must for dealing with the sometimes huge volume of paper-based materials that are valuable for you for one reason or another. Ideally you will already have set up a general-reference filing system as you were processing "in." You need to feel comfortable storing even a single piece of paper that you might want to refer to later, and your system must be informal and accessible enough that it's a snap to file it away in your alphabetized general-reference system, right at hand where you work. If you're not set up that way yet, look back at chapter 4 for help on this topic.

Most people seem to wind up with 200 to 400 paper-based general-reference files and 30 to 100 e-mail reference folders.

Large-Category Filing Any topic that requires more than fifty file folders should probably be given its own section or drawer, with its own alpha-sorted system. For instance, if you're managing a corporate merger and need to keep hold of a lot of the paperwork, you may want to dedicate two or three whole file cabinets to all the documentation required in the due-diligence process. If gardening or sailing or cooking is your passion, you may need at least a whole file drawer for those designated hobbies.

Bear in mind that if your "area of focus" has support material that could blend into other "areas of focus," you may run into the dilemma of whether to store the information in general reference or in the specialized reference files. When you read a great article about wood fencing and want to keep it, does that go in your "Garden" cabinet or in the general system with other information about home-related projects? As a general rule, it's best to stick with one general-reference system except for a very limited number of discrete topics.

Rolodexes and Contact Managers Much of the information that you need to keep is directly related to people in your network. You need to track contact information of all sorts—home and office phone numbers and addresses, cell-phone numbers, fax numbers, e-mail addresses, and so on. In addition, if you find it useful, you may want to maintain information about birthdays, names of friends' and colleagues' family members, hobbies, favorite wines and foods, and the like. In a more rigorous professional vein, you may need or want to track hire dates, performance-review dates, goals and objectives, and other potentially relevant data for staff development purposes.

The telephone/address section of most of the organizers sold in the last fifty years is probably (along with the calendar) their most commonly used component. Everyone needs to keep track of phone numbers. It's instructive to note that this is purely and simply reference material. No action is required—this is just information that you might need to access in the future.

So there's no big mystery about how to organize it, aside from the logistics for your individual needs. Again, the only problem comes up when people try to make their Rolodexes serve as tools for reminding them about things they need to *do*. That doesn't work. As long as all the actions relative to people you know have been identified and tracked in your action reminder lists, there's no role for telephone and address systems to fill other than being a neutral address book.

The only issue then becomes how much information you need to keep and where and in what equipment you need to keep it in order to have it accessible when you want it. Nothing's perfect in that regard, but as the small digital tools become easier to use and connect to larger databases, you'll be able to have more information at hand with the same or less effort.

Libraries and Archives: Personalized Levels Information that might be useful lives at many levels. You could probably find out pretty much *anything* if you were willing to dig deep enough. The question of how much to keep, how close, and in what form, will be a changing reality, given the variables of your needs and your particular comfort levels with data. Relative to your personal organization and productivity, this is not a core issue, so long as all of your projects and actions are in a control system that you work with regularly. Reference material in all its forms then becomes nothing more or less than material to capture and create access to according to your particular proclivities and requirements.

If material is purely for reference, the only issue is whether it's worth the time and space required to keep it.

Some degree of consistency will always make things easier. What kinds of things do you need with you all the time? Those must go into your ubiquitous planner or PDA. What do you need specifically for meetings or off-site events? That should be put into your briefcase, pack, satchel, or purse. What might you need when you're working in your office? That should be put into your personal filing system or your networked computer. What about rare situations relative to your job? Material needed for those could be archived in departmental files or off-site storage. What could you find anytime you might need it, on the Web? You don't need to do anything with that information, unless you need it when you're away from a Web connection, in which case you should print the data out when you're online and store it in a file you can take with you.

Do you see how that personal organization of reference material is simply a logistical issue? Distinguishing actionable things from nonactionable ones is the key success factor in this arena. Once you've done that, you have total freedom to manage and organize as much or as little reference material as you want. It's a highly individual decision that ought to be based on the ratio of the value received to the time and effort required to capture and maintain it.

Someday/Maybes

The last thing to deal with in your organization system is how to track things that you may want to reassess in the future. These could range from a special trip you might want to take one day, to books you might want to read, to projects you might want to tackle in the next fiscal year, to skills and talents you might want to develop. For a full implementation of this model you'll need some sort of "back burner" or "on hold" component.

Someday/Maybe's are not throwaway items. They may be some of the most interesting and creative things you'll ever get involved with.

There are several ways to stage things for later review, all of which will work to get them off your current radar and your mind. You can put the items on various versions of "Someday/Maybe" lists or trigger them on your calendar or in a paper-based "tickler" system.

"Someday/Maybe" List

It's highly likely that if you did a complete mind-sweep when you were collecting things out of your psychic RAM, you came up with some things you're not *sure* you want to commit to. "Learn Spanish," "Get Marcie a horse," "Climb Mt. Washington," and "Build a guest cottage" are typical projects that fall into this category.

If you haven't already done it, I recommend that you create a "Someday/Maybe" list in whatever organizing system you've chosen. Then give yourself permission to populate that list with all the items of that type that have occurred to you so far. You'll probably discover that simply having the list and starting to fill it out will cause you to come up with all kinds of creative ideas.

You may also be surprised to find that some of the things you write on the list will actually come to pass, almost without your making any conscious effort to make them happen. If you acknowledge the power of the imagination to foster changes in perception and performance, it's easy to see how having a "Someday/Maybe" list out in front of your conscious mind could potentially add many wonderful adventures to your life and work. We're likely to seize opportunities when they arise if we've already identified and captured them as a possibility. That has certainly been my own experience: learning to play the flute and how to sail big boats both started in this category for me. In addition to your in-basket, there are two rich sources to tap for your "Someday/Maybe" list: your creative imagination and your list of current projects.

Make an Inventory of Your Creative Imaginings What are the things you really might want to do someday if you have the time, money, and inclination? Write them on your have "Someday/Maybe" list. Typical categories include:

- Things to get or build for your home
- Hobbies to take up

- Skills to learn
- Creative expressions to explore
- Clothes and accessories to buy
- Toys (gear!) to acquire
- Trips to take
- Organizations to join
- Service projects to contribute to
- Things to see and do

Reassess Your Current Projects Now's a good time to review your "Projects" list from a more elevated perspective (that is, the standpoint of your job and goals) and consider whether you might transfer some of your current commitments to "Someday/Maybe." If on reflection you realize that an optional project doesn't have a chance of getting your attention for the next months or more, move it to this list.

> *What lies in our power to do, lies in our power not to do.*
>
> *—Aristotle*

Special Categories of "Someday/Maybe"

More than likely you have some special interests that involve lots of possible things to do. It can be fun to collect these on lists. For instance:

- Food—recipes, menus, restaurants, wines
- Children—things to do with them
- Books to read
- CDs to buy
- Videos to buy/rent
- Cultural events to attend
- Gift ideas
- Garden ideas
- Web sites to surf
- Weekend trips to take
- Meeting ideas
- Party ideas

• Ideas—Misc. (meaning you don't know where else to put them!)

These kinds of lists can be a cross between reference and "Someday/Maybe"—reference because you can just collect and add to lists of good wines or restaurants or books, to consult as you like; "Someday/Maybe" because you might want to review the listed items on a regular basis to remind yourself to try one or more of them at some point.

In any case, this is another great reason to have an organizing system that makes it easy to capture things that may add value and variety and interest to your life—without clogging your mind and work space with undecided, unfinished business.

The Danger of "Hold and Review" Files and Piles

Many people have created some sort of "Hold and Review" pile or file (or whole drawer) that vaguely fits within the category of "Someday/Maybe." They tell themselves, "When I have time, I may like to get to this," and a "Hold and Review" file seems a convenient place to put it. I personally don't recommend this particular kind of subsystem, because in virtually every case I have come across, the client "held" but didn't "review," and there was numbness and resistance about the stack. The value of "someday/maybe" disappears if you don't put your conscious awareness back on it with some consistency.

Also, there's a big difference between something that's managed well, as a "Someday/Maybe" list, and something that's just a catchall bucket for "stuff." Usually much of that stuff needs to be tossed, some of it needs to go into "Read/Review," some needs to be filed as reference, some belongs on the calendar or in a tickler file (see page 173) for review in a month or perhaps at the beginning of the next quarter, and some actually has next actions on it. Many times, after appropriately processing someone's "Hold and Review" drawer or file, I've discovered there was nothing left in it!

Using the Calendar for Future Options

Your calendar can be a very handy place to park reminders of things you *might* want to consider doing in the future. Most of the people I've coached were not nearly as comfortable with their calendars as they could have been; otherwise they probably would have found many more things to put in there.

One of the three uses of a calendar is for *day-specific information*. This category can include a number of things, but one of the most creative ways to utilize this function is to enter things that you want to take off your mind and reassess at some later date. Here are a few of the myriad things you should consider inserting:

- Triggers for activating projects
- Events you might want to participate in
- Decision catalysts

Triggers for Activating Projects If you have a project that you don't really need to think about now but that deserves a flag at some point in the future, you can pick an appropriate date and put a reminder about the project in your calendar for that day. It should go in some day-specific (versus time-specific) calendar slot for the things you want to be reminded of on that day; then when the day arrives, you see the reminder and insert the item as an active project on your "Projects" list. Typical candidates for this treatment are:

- Special events with a certain lead time for handling (product launches, fund-raising drives, etc.)
- Regular events that you need to prepare for, such as budget reviews, annual conferences, planning events, or meetings (e.g., when should you add next year's "annual sales conference" to your "Projects" list?)
- Key dates for significant people that you might want to do something about (birthdays, anniversaries, holiday gift-giving, etc.)

Events You Might Want to Participate In You probably get notices constantly about seminars, conferences, speeches, and social and cultural events that you may want to decide about attending as the time gets closer. So figure out when that "closer" time is and put a trigger in your calendar on the appropriate date—for example:

"Chamber of Commerce breakfast tomorrow?"
"Tigers season tickets go on sale today"
"PBS special on Australia tonight 8:00 P.M."
"Church BBQ next Saturday"

If you can think of any jogs like these that you'd like to put into your system, do it right now.

Decision Catalysts Once in a while there may be a significant decision that you need to make but can't (or don't want to) make right away. That's fine, as long as you've concluded that the additional information you need has to come from an *internal* rather than an *external* source (e.g., you need to sleep on it). (Obviously, external data you need in order to make a decision should go on your "Next Actions" or "Waiting For" lists.) But in order to move to a level of OK-ness about *not* deciding, you'd better put out a safety net that you can trust to get you to focus on the issue appropriately in the future. A calendar reminder can serve that purpose.*

It's OK to decide not to decide—as long as you have a decide-not-to-decide system.

Some typical decision areas in this category include:

- Hire/fire
- Merge/acquire/sell/divest
- Change job/career

*If you're using a group-accessible calendar, you must maintain discretion about these kinds of triggers. Digital calendars usually have "private" categorization functions you can use for entries you don't necessarily want everyone to see.

This is a big topic to devote so little space to, I know, but go ahead and ask yourself, "Is there any major decision for which I should create a future trigger, so I can feel comfortable just 'hanging out' with it for now?" If there is, put some reminder in your calendar to revisit the issue.

The "Tickler" File

One elegant way to manage nonactionable items that may need an action in the future is the "tickler" file.* A three-dimensional version of a calendar, it allows you to hold *physical* reminders of things that you want to see or remember—not now, but in the future. It can be an extremely functional tool, allowing you to in effect set up your own post office and "mail" things to yourself for receipt on a designated future date. I myself have used a tickler file for years and can't imagine being without it.

Essentially the tickler is a simple file-folder system that allows you to distribute paper and other physical reminders in such a way that whatever you want to see on a particular date in the future "automatically" shows up that day in your in-basket.

If you have a secretary or assistant, you can entrust at least a part of this task to him or her, assuming that he/she has some working version of this or a similar system. Typical examples would be:

- "Hand me this agenda the morning of the day I have the meeting."
- "Give this back to me on Monday to rethink, since it applies to a meeting on Wednesday."
- "Remind me about the Hong Kong trip two weeks ahead, and we'll plan the logistics."

Then every day of the week, that day's folder is pulled and reviewed.

---

*Also referred to as a "suspense," "bring forward," or "follow-up" file.

While you can (and probably should) utilize staff to handle as much of this as is appropriate, I recommend that, if you can integrate it into your life-style, you maintain your own tickler file. There are many useful functions it can perform, at least some of which you may want to avail yourself of outside the pale of your assistant's responsibilities. I use my tickler file to manage my travel tickets and confirmations; paper-based travel directions, agendas, and maps; reminders of event notifications that come in the mail; information about "might-want-to-buy" kinds of things I want to reconsider in the future; and so forth.

Bottom line: the tickler file demands only a one-second-per-day new behavior to make it work, and it has a payoff value logarithmically greater than the personal investment.

Setting Up a Tickler File You need forty-three folders—thirty-one daily files labeled "1" through "31," and twelve more labeled with the names of the months of the year. The daily files are kept in front, beginning with the file for tomorrow's date (if today is October 5, then the first file would be "6"). The succeeding daily files represent the days of the rest of the month ("6" through "31"). Behind the "31" file is the monthly file for the next month ("November"), and behind that are the daily files "1" though "5." Following that are the rest of the monthly files ("December" through "October"). The next daily file is emptied into your in-basket every day, and then the folder is refiled at the back of the dailies (at which point, instead of October 6, it represents *November* 6). In the same way, when the next monthly file reaches the front (on October 31 after you empty the daily file, the "November" file will be the next one, with the daily files "1" through "31" behind it), it's emptied into the in-basket and refiled at the back of the monthlies to represent November a year from now. This is a "perpetual" file, meaning that at any given time it contains files for the next thirty-one days and the next twelve months.

The big advantage of using file folders for your tickler system is that they allow you to store actual documents (the form that needs

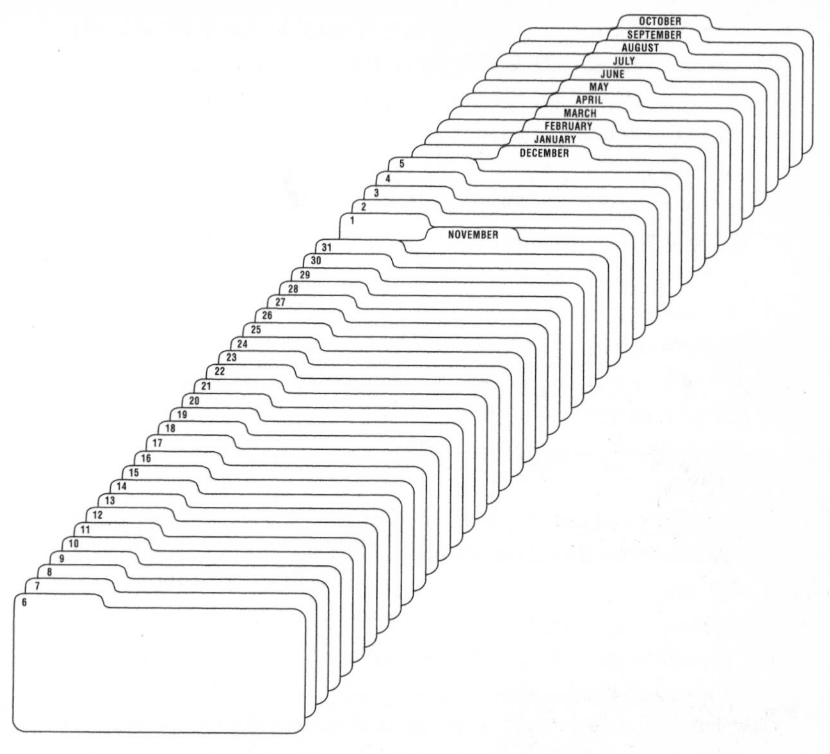

FILE-FOLDER-STYLE SAMPLE SETUP (OCTOBER 5)

to be filled out on a certain day, the memo that needs to be reviewed then, the telephone note that needs action on a specific date, etc.).

In order for the system to work, you must update it every day. If you forget to empty the daily file, you won't trust the system to handle important data, and you'll have to manage those things some other way. If you leave town (or don't access the file on the weekend), you must be sure to check the folders for the days you'll be away, *before* you go.

Checklists: Creative Reminders

The last topic in personal system organization that deserves some attention is the care and feeding of checklists, those *recipes of potential ingredients* for projects, events, and areas of value, interest, and responsibility.

The most creative checklists are often generated at the back end of a good consulting process with a team or company. Good ones also show up as areas of focus for training staff or hiring into job slots.

When I'm clearing in-baskets with clients and reviewing other things they're concerned about, we often run across little "Memos to Self" like:

- Exercise more regularly.
- Make sure we have evaluation forms for each training.
- Spend more quality time with my kids.
- Do more proactive planning for the division.
- Maintain good morale with my team.
- Ensure we are in alignment with corporate strategy.
- Keep the client billing process up to date.

What should you do with these "fuzzier" kinds of internal commitments and areas of attention?

First, Clarify Inherent Projects and Actions

For much of this kind of "stuff," there is still a project and/or an action that needs to be defined. "Exercise more regularly" *really* translates for many people into "Set up regular exercise program" (project) and "Call Sally for suggestions about personal trainers" (real action step). In such cases, *inherent* projects and actions still need to be clarified and organized into a personal system.

But there *are* some things that don't quite fit into that category.

Blueprinting Key Areas of Work and Responsibility

Objectives like "Maintain good physical conditioning" or "Physical health and vitality" may still need to be built into some sort of overview checklist that will be reviewed regularly. You have multiple layers of outcomes and standards playing on your psyche and your choices at any point in time, and knowing what those are, at all the different levels, is always a good idea.

I suggested earlier that there are at least six levels of your "work" that could be defined, and that each level deserves its own acknowledgment and evaluation. A complete inventory of everything you hold important and are committed to on each of those levels would represent an awesome checklist. It might include:

- Career goals
- Service
- Family
- Relationships
- Community
- Health and energy
- Financial resources
- Creative expression

And then moving down a level, within your job, you might want some reminders of your key areas of responsibility, your staff, your values, and so on. A list of these might contain points like:

- Team morale
- Processes
- Timelines
- Staff issues
- Workload
- Communication

All of these items could in turn be included on the lists in your personal system, as reminders to you, as needed, to keep the ship on course, on an even keel.

The More Novel the Situation, the More Control Is Required

The degree to which any of us needs to maintain checklists and external controls is directly related to our unfamiliarity with the area of responsibility. If you've been doing what you're doing for a long time, and there's no pressure on you to change in that area, you probably need minimal external personal organization to stay on cruise control. You know when things must happen, and how to make them happen, and your system is fine, status quo. Often, though, that's not the case.

Many times you'll want some sort of checklist to help you maintain a focus until you're more familiar with what you're doing. If your CEO suddenly disappeared, for example, and you had instantly to fill his shoes, you'd need some overviews and outlines in front of you for a while to ensure that you had all the mission-critical aspects of the job handled. And if you've just been hired into a new position, with new responsibilities that are relatively unfamiliar to you, you'll want a framework of control and structure, if only for the first few months.

There have been times when I needed to make a list of areas that I had to handle, temporarily, until things were under control. For instance, when my wife and I decided to create a brand-new structure for a business we'd been involved with for many years, I took on areas of responsibility I'd never had to deal with before—namely, accounting, computers, marketing, legal, and administration. For several months I needed to keep a checklist of those responsibilities in front of me to ensure that I filled in the blanks everywhere and managed the transition as well as I could. After the business got onto "cruise control" to some degree, I no longer needed that list.

Checklists can be highly useful to let you know what you *don't* need to be concerned about.

Checklists at All Levels

Be open to creating any kind of checklist as the urge strikes you. The possibilities are endless—from "Core Life Values" to "Things to Take Camping." Making lists, ad hoc, as they occur to you, is one of the most powerful yet subtlest and simplest procedures that you can install in your life.

To spark your creative thinking, here's a list of some of the topics of checklists I've seen and used over the years:

- Personal Affirmations (i.e., personal value statements)
- Job Areas of Responsibility (key responsibility areas)
- Travel Checklist (everything to take on or do before a trip)
- Weekly Review (everything to review and/or update on a weekly basis)
- Training Program Components (all the things to handle when putting on an event, front to back)
- Clients
- Conference Checklist (everything to handle when putting on a conference)
- Focus Areas (key life roles and responsibilities)
- Key People in My Life/Work (relationships to assess regularly for completion and opportunity development)
- Organization Chart (key people and areas of output to manage and maintain)
- Personal Development (things to evaluate regularly to ensure personal balance and progress)

Get comfortable with checklists, both ad hoc and more permanent. Be ready to create and eliminate them as required. Appropriately used, they can be a tremendous asset in personal productivity.

If in fact you have now *collected* everything that represents an open loop in your life and work, *processed* each one of those items in terms of what it means to you and what actions are required, and *organized* the results into a complete system that holds a current and complete overview—large and small—of all your present and "someday" projects, then you're ready for the next phase of implementation in the art of stress-free productivity—the review process.

8

Reviewing: Keeping Your System Functional

THE PURPOSE OF this whole method of workflow management is *not* to let your brain become lax, but rather to enable it to move toward more elegant and productive activity. In order to earn that freedom, however, your brain must engage on some consistent basis with all your commitments and activities. You must be assured that you're doing what you need to be doing, and that it's OK to be *not* doing what you're not doing. Reviewing your system on a regular basis and keeping it current and functional are prerequisites for that kind of control.

If you have a list of calls you must make, for example, the minute that list is not totally current with *all* the calls you need to make, your brain will not trust the system, and it won't get relief from its lower-level mental tasks. It will have to take back the job of remembering, processing, and reminding, which, as you should know by now, it doesn't do very effectively.

All of this means your system cannot be static. In order to support appropriate action choices, it must be kept up to date. And it should trigger consistent and appropriate evaluation of your life and work at several horizons.

There are two major issues that need to be handled at this point:

- What do you look at in all this, and when?
- What do you need to do, and how often, to ensure that all of it works as a consistent system, freeing you to think and manage at a higher level?

A real review process will lead to enhanced and proactive new thinking in key areas of your life and work. Such thinking emerges from both focused concentration and serendipitous brainstorming, which will be triggered and galvanized by a consistent personal review of your inventory of actions and projects.

What to Look At, When

Your personal system and behaviors need to be established in such a way that you can see all the action options you need to see, *when* you need to see them. This is really just common sense, but few people actually have their processes and their organization honed to the point where they are as functional as they could be.

When you have access to a phone and any discretionary time, you ought to at least glance at the list of all the phone calls you need to make, and then either direct yourself to the best one to handle or give yourself permission to feel OK about not bothering with any of them. When you're about to go in for a discussion with your boss or your partner, take a moment to review the outstanding agendas you have with him or her, so you'll know that you're using your time most effectively. When you need to pick up something at the dry cleaner's, first quickly review all the other errands that you might be able to do en route.

A few seconds a day is usually all you need for review, as long as you're looking at the right things at the right time.

People often ask me, "How much time do you spend looking at your system?" My answer is simply, "As much time as I need to to feel comfortable about what I'm doing." In actuality it's an accumulation of two seconds here, three seconds there. What most people don't realize is that my lists are in one sense my office. Just as you might have Post-its and stacks of phone slips at your workstation, so do I on my "Next Actions" lists. Assuming that you've completely collected, processed, and organized your stuff, you'll most likely take only a few brief moments here and there to access your system for day-to-day reminders.

Looking at Your Calendar First

Your most frequent review will probably be of your daily calendar, and your daily tickler folder if you're maintaining one, to see the "hard landscape" and assess what has to get done. You need to know the time-and-space parameters first. Knowing that you have wall-to-wall meetings from 8:00 A.M. through 6:00 P.M., for example, with barely a half-hour break for lunch, will help you make necessary decisions about any other activities.

. . . Then Your Action Lists

After you review all your day- and time-specific commitments and handle whatever you need to about them, your next most frequent area for review will be the lists of all the actions you could possibly do in your current context. If you're in your office, for instance, you'll look at your lists of calls, computer actions, and in-office things to do. This doesn't necessarily mean you will actually be *doing* anything on those lists; you'll just evaluate them against the flow of other work coming at you to ensure that you make the best choices about what to deal with. You need to feel confident that you're not missing anything critical.

Frankly, if your calendar is trustworthy and your action lists are current, they may be the only things in the system you'll need to refer to more than every couple of days. There have been many days when I didn't need to look at *any* of my lists, in fact, because it was clear from the front end—my calendar—what I *wouldn't* be able to do.

The Right Review in the Right Context

You may need to access any one of your lists at any time. When you and your spouse are decompressing at the end of the day, and you want to be sure you'll take care of the "business" the two of you manage together about home and family, you'll want to look at your accumulated agendas for him or her. On the other hand, if your boss pops in for a face-to-face conversation about current realities and priorities, it will be highly functional for you to have your "Projects" list up to date and your "Agenda" list for him or her right at hand.

Updating Your System

The real trick to ensuring the trustworthiness of the whole organization system lies in regularly refreshing your psyche and your system from a more elevated perspective. That's impossible to do, however, if your lists fall too far behind your reality. You won't be able to fool yourself about this: if your system is out of date, your brain will be forced to fully engage again at the lower level of remembering.

To make knowledge productive, we will have to learn to see both forest and tree. We will have to learn to connect.
—Peter F. Drucker

This is perhaps the biggest challenge of all. Once you've tasted what it's like to have a clear head and feel in control of everything that's going on, can you do what you need to to maintain that as an operational standard? The many years I've spent researching and implementing this methodology with countless people have proved to me that the magic key to the sustainability of the process is the Weekly Review.

The Power of the Weekly Review

If you're like me and most other people, no matter how good your intentions may be, you're going to have the world come at you faster than you can keep up. Many of us seem to have it in our natures consistently to entangle ourselves in more than we have the ability to handle. We book ourselves back to back in meetings all day, go to after-hours events that generate ideas and commitments we need to deal with, and get embroiled in engagements and projects that have the potential to spin our creative intelligence into cosmic orbits.

That whirlwind of activity is precisely what makes the Weekly Review so valuable. It builds in some capturing, reevaluation, and reprocessing time to keep you in balance. There is simply no way to do this necessary regrouping while you're trying to get everyday work done.

You will invariably take in more opportunities than your system can process on a daily basis.

The Weekly Review will also sharpen your intuitive focus on your important projects as you deal with the flood of new input and potential distractions coming at you the rest of the week. You're going to have to learn to say no—faster, and to more things—in order to stay afloat and comfortable. Having some dedicated time in which to at least get up to the project level of thinking goes a long way toward making that easier.

What Is the Weekly Review?

Very simply, the Weekly Review is whatever you need to do to get your head empty again. It's going through the five phases of workflow management—collecting, processing, organizing, and reviewing all your outstanding involvements—until you can honestly say, "I absolutely know right now everything I'm not doing but could be doing if I decided to."

From a nitty-gritty, practical standpoint, here is the drill that can get you there:

Loose Papers Pull out all miscellaneous scraps of paper, business cards, receipts, and so on that have crept into the crevices of your desk, clothing, and accessories. Put it all into your in-basket for processing.

Process Your Notes Review any journal entries, meeting notes, or miscellaneous notes scribbled on notebook paper. List action items, projects, waiting-fors, calendar events, and someday/maybes, as appropriate. File any reference notes and materials. Stage your "Read/Renew" material. Be ruthless with yourself, processing all notes and thoughts relative to interactions, projects, new initiatives, and input that have come your way since your last download, and purging those not needed.

Previous Calendar Data Review past calendar dates in detail for remaining action items, reference information, and so on, and transfer that data into the active system. Be able to archive your last week's calendar with nothing left uncaptured.

Upcoming Calendar Look at future calendar events (long- and short-term). Capture actions about arrangements and preparations for any upcoming events.

Empty Your Head Put in writing (in appropriate categories) any new projects, action items, waiting-fors, someday/maybes, and so forth that you haven't yet captured.

Review "Projects" (and Larger Outcome) Lists Evaluate the status of projects, goals, and outcomes one by one, ensuring that at least one current kick-start action for each is in your system.

Review "Next Actions" Lists Mark off completed actions. Review for reminders of further action steps to capture.

Review "Waiting For" List Record appropriate actions for any needed follow-up. Check off received items.

Review Any Relevant Checklists Is there anything you haven't done that you need to do?

Review "Someday/Maybe" List Check for any projects that may have become active and transfer them to "Projects." Delete items no longer of interest.

Review "Pending" and Support Files Browse through all work-in-progress support material to trigger new actions, completions, and waiting-fors.

Be Creative and Courageous Are there any new, wonderful, hare-brained, creative, thought-provoking, risk-taking ideas you can add to your system?

This review process is common sense, but few of us do it as well as we could, and that means as regularly as we should to keep a clear mind and a sense of relaxed control.

"Point of view" is that quintessentially human solution to information overload, an intuitive process of reducing things to an essential relevant and manageable minimum. . . . In a world of hyperabundant content, point of view will become the scarcest of resources.

—Paul Saffo

The Right Time and Place for the Review

The Weekly Review is so critical that it behooves you to establish good habits, environments, and tools to support it. Once your comfort zone has been established for the kind of relaxed control that *Getting Things Done* is all about, you won't have to worry too much about making yourself do your review—you'll *have* to to get back to your personal standards again.

Until then, do whatever you need to, once a week, to trick yourself into backing away from the daily grind for a couple of hours—not to zone out, but to rise up at least to "10,000 feet" and catch up.

If you have the luxury of an office or work space that can be somewhat isolated from the people and interactions of the day, and if you have anything resembling a typical Monday-to-Friday workweek, I recommend that you block out two hours early every Friday afternoon for the review. Three factors make this an ideal time:

- The events of the week are likely to be still fresh enough for you to be able to do a complete postmortem ("Oh, yeah, I need to make sure I get back to her about . . .").

- When you (invariably) uncover actions that require reaching people at work, you'll still have time to do that before they leave for the weekend.
- It's great to clear your psychic decks so you can go into the weekend ready for refreshment and recreation, with nothing on your mind.

You may be the kind of person, however, who doesn't have normal weekends. I, for example, often have as much to do on Saturday and Sunday as on Wednesday. But I do have the luxury(?) of frequent long plane trips, which provide an ideal opportunity for me to catch up. A good friend and client of mine, an executive in the world's largest aerospace company, has his own Sunday-night ritual of relaxing in his home office and processing the hundreds of notes he's generated during his week of back-to-back meetings.

Whatever your life-style, you need a weekly regrouping ritual. You likely have something like this (or close to it) already. If so, leverage the habit by adding into it a higher-altitude review process.

The people who find it hardest to make time for this review are those who have constantly on-demand work and home environments, with zero built-in time or space for regrouping. The most stressed professionals I have met are the ones who have to be mission-critically reactive at work (e.g., high-level equities traders and chiefs of staff) and then go home to a couple of under-ten-year-old children and a spouse who also works. The more fortunate of them have a one-hour train commute.

If you recognize yourself in that picture, your greatest challenge will be to build in a consistent process of regrouping, when your world is not directly in your face. You'll need to either accept the requirement of an after-hours time at your desk on a Friday night or establish a relaxed but at-work kind of location and time at home.

Executive Operational Review Time I've coached many executives to block out two hours on their calendars on Fridays. For them the biggest problem is how to balance quality thinking and catch-up time with the urgent demands of mission-critical interactions. This is a tough call. The most senior and savvy of them, however, know the value of sacrificing the seemingly urgent for the truly important, and they create their islands of time for some version of this process.

Your best thoughts about work won't happen while you're *at* work.

Even the executives who have integrated a consistent reflective time for their work, though, often seem to give short shrift to the more mundane review and catch-up process at the "10,000-foot" level. Between wall-to-wall meetings and ambling around your koi pond with a chardonnay at sunset, there's got to be a slightly elevated level of reflection and regrouping required for operational control and focus. If you think you have all your open loops fully identified, clarified, assessed, and actionalized, you're probably kidding yourself.

Thinking is the very essence of, and the most difficult thing to do in, business and in life. Empire builders spend hour-after-hour on mental work . . . while others party. If you're not consciously aware of putting forth the effort to exert self-guided integrated thinking . . . then you're giving in to laziness and no longer control your life.

—*David Kekich*

The "Bigger Picture" Reviews

Yes, at some point you must clarify the larger outcomes, the long-term goals, the visions and principles that ultimately drive and test your decisions.

What are your key goals and objectives in your work? What should you have in place a year or three years from now? How is your career going? Is this the life-style that is most fulfilling to you? Are you doing what you really want or need to do, from a deeper and longer-term perspective?

The explicit focus of this book is not at those "30,000-" to "50,000+-foot" levels. Urging you to operate from a higher perspective is, however, its *implicit* purpose—to assist you in making your total life expression more fulfilling and better aligned with the bigger game we're all about. As you increase the speed and agility with which you clear the "runway" and "10,000-foot" levels of your life and work, be sure to revisit the other levels you're engaged in, now and then, to maintain a truly clear head.

How often you ought to challenge yourself with that type of wide-ranging review is something only you can know. The principle I must affirm at this juncture is this:

You need to assess your life and work at the appropriate horizons, making the appropriate decisions, at the appropriate intervals, in order to really come clean.

Which brings us to the ultimate point and challenge of all this personal collecting, processing, organizing, and reviewing methodology: It's 9:22 A.M. Wednesday morning—what do you do?

9

Doing: Making the Best Action Choices

WHEN IT COMES to your real-time, plow-through, get-it-done workday, how do you decide what to do at any given point?

As I've said, my simple answer is, trust your heart. Or your spirit. Or, if you're allergic to those kinds of words, try these: your gut, the seat of your pants, your intuition.

Ultimately and always you must trust your intuition. There are many things you can do, however, that can increase that trust.

That doesn't mean you throw your life to the winds—unless, of course, it does. I actually went down that route myself with some vengeance at one point in my life, and I can attest that the lessons were valuable, if not necessarily necessary.*

As outlined in chapter 2 (pages 48-53), I have found three priority frameworks to be enormously helpful in the context of deciding actions:

- The four-criteria model for choosing actions in the moment
- The threefold model for evaluating daily work
- The six-level model for reviewing your own work

*There are various ways to give it all up. You can ignore the physical world and its realities and trust in the universe. I did that, and it was a powerful experience. And one I wouldn't wish on anyone. Surrendering to your inner awareness, however, and its intelligence and practicality in the worlds you live in, is the higher ground. Trusting yourself and the source of your intelligence is a more elegant version of freedom and personal productivity.

These happen to be shown in reverse hierarchical order—that is, the reverse of the typical strategic top-down perspective. In keeping with the nature of the *Getting Things Done* methodology, I have found it useful to once again work from the bottom up, meaning I'll start with the most mundane levels.

The Four-Criteria Model for Choosing Actions in the Moment

Remember that you make your action choices based on the following four criteria, in order:

1 | Context
2 | Time available
3 | Energy available
4 | Priority

Let's examine each of these in the light of how you can best structure your systems and behaviors to take advantage of its dynamics.

Context

At any point in time, the first thing to consider is, what could you possibly do, where you are, with the tools you have? Do you have a phone? Do you have access to the person you need to talk with face-to-face about three agenda items? Are you at the store where you need to buy something? If you can't do the action because you're not in the appropriate location or don't have the appropriate tool, don't worry about it.

As I've said, you should always organize your action reminders by context—"Calls," "At Home," "At Computer," "Errands," "Agenda for Joe," "Agenda for Staff Meeting," and so on. Since context is the first criterion that comes into play in your choice of actions, context-sorted lists prevent unnecessary reassessments about what to do. If you have a bunch of things to do on one to-do list, but you actually can't do many of them in the same context, you force yourself to continually keep reconsidering *all* of them.

If you're stuck in traffic, and the only actions you can take are calls on your cell phone, you want to be able to pull out just your "Calls" list. Your action lists should fold in or out, based on what you could possibly do at any time.

A second real benefit accrues from organizing all your actions by the *physical* context needed: that in itself forces you to make the all-important determination about the next physical action on your stuff. All of my action lists are set up this way, so I have to decide on the very next physical action before I can know which list to put an item on (is this something that requires the computer? a phone? being in a store?). People who give themselves a "Misc." action list (i.e., one not specific to a context) often let themselves slide in the next-action decision, too.

I frequently encourage clients to structure their list categories early on as they're processing their in-baskets, because that automatically grounds their projects in the real things that need to get done to get them moving.

Time Available

The second factor in choosing an action is how much time you have before you have to do something else. If your meeting is starting in ten minutes, you'll most likely select a different action to do right now than you would if the next couple of hours were clear.

Obviously, it's good to know how much time you have at hand (hence the emphasis on calendar and watch). A total-life action-reminder inventory will give you maximum information about what you need to do, and make it much easier to match your actions to the windows you have. In other words, if you have ten minutes before that next meeting, find a ten-minute thing to do. If your lists have only the "big" or "important" things on them, no item listed may be possible to handle in a ten-minute period. If you're going to have to do those shorter action things anyway, the most productive way to get them done is to utilize the little "weird time" windows that occur throughout the day.

Energy Available

We all have times when we think more effectively, and times when we should not be thinking at all.
—Daniel Cohen

Although you can increase your energy level at times by changing your context and redirecting your focus, you can do only so much. The tail end of a day taken up mostly by a marathon budget-planning session is probably not the best time to call a prospective client or start drafting a performance-review policy. It might be better to call the airline to change a reservation, process some expense receipts, or skim a trade journal.

Just as having all your next-action options available allows you to take advantage of various time slots, knowing about everything you're going to need to process and do at some point will allow you to match productive activity with your vitality level.

I recommend that you always keep an inventory of things that need to be done that require very little mental or creative horsepower. When you're in one of those low-energy states, do them. Casual reading (magazines, articles, and catalogs), telephone/address data that need to be inputted onto your computer, file purging, backing up your laptop, even just watering your plants and filling your stapler—these are some of the myriad things that you've got to deal with sometime anyway.

There is no reason not to be highly productive, even when you're not in top form.

This is one of the best reasons for having very clean edges to your personal management system: it makes it easy to continue doing productive activity when you're not in top form. If you're in a low-energy mode and your reading material is disorganized, your receipts are all over the place, your filing system is chaotic, and your in-basket is dysfunctional, it just seems like too much work to do to find and organize the tasks at hand; so you simply avoid doing anything at all and then you feel even *worse*. One of the best ways to increase your energy is to close some of your loops. So always be sure to have some easy loops to close, right at hand.

These first three criteria for choosing action (context, time, and energy) bespeak the need for a complete next-action reminder system. Sometimes you won't be in a mode to do that kind of thinking; it needs to have already been done. If it is, you can operate much more "in your zone" and choose from delineated actions that fit the situation.

Priority

Given the context you're in and the time and energy you have, the obvious next criterion for action choice is relative priority: "Out of all my remaining options, what is the most important thing for me to do?"

"How do I decide my priorities?" is a question I frequently hear from people I'm working with. It springs from their experience of having more on their plate to do than they can comfortably handle. They know that some hard choices have to be made, and that some things may not get done at all.

It is impossible to feel good about your choices unless you are clear about what your work really is.

At the end of the day, in order to feel good about what you didn't get done, you must have made some conscious decisions about your responsibilities, goals, and values. That process invariably includes an often complex interplay with the goals, values, and directions of your organization and of the other significant people in your life, and with the importance of those relationships to you.

The Threefold Model for Evaluating Daily Work

Setting priorities assumes that some things will be more important than others, but important relative to what? In this context, the answer is, to your work—that is, the job you have accepted from yourself and/or from others. This is where the next two frameworks need to be brought to bear in your thinking. They're about defining your work. Keep in mind that though much of this methodology will be within the arena of your professional focus, I'm using "work" in the universal sense, to mean anything you have a commitment to making happen, personally as well as professionally.

These days, daily work activity itself presents a relatively new type of challenge to most professionals, something that it's helpful to understand as we endeavor to build the most productive systems. As I explained earlier, during the course of the workday, at any point in time, you'll be engaged in one of three types of activities:

- Doing predefined work
- Doing work as it shows up
- Defining your work

You may be doing things on your action lists, doing things as they come up, or processing incoming inputs to determine what work that needs to be done, either then or later, from your lists.

This is common sense. But many people let themselves get wrapped around the second activity—dealing with things that show up ad hoc—much too easily, and let the other two slide, to their detriment.

Let's say it's 10:26 A.M. Monday, and you're in your office. You've just ended a half-hour unexpected phone call with a prospective client. You have three pages of scribbled notes from the conversation. There's a meeting scheduled with your staff at eleven, about half an hour from now. You were out late last night with your spouse's parents and are still a little frayed around the edges (you told your father-in-law you'd get back to him about . . . what?). Your assistant just laid six telephone messages in front of you. You have a major strategic-planning session coming up in two days, for which you have yet to formulate your ideas. The oil light in your car came on as you drove to work this morning. And your boss hinted as you passed her earlier in the hall that she'd like your thoughts on the memo she e-mailed you yesterday, before this afternoon's three o'clock meeting.

Are your systems set up to maximally support dealing with this reality, at 10:26 on Monday morning? If you're still keeping things in your head, and if you're still trying to capture only the "critical" stuff on your lists, I suggest that the answer is no.

It is often easier to get wrapped up in the urgent demands of the moment than to deal with your in-basket, e-mail, and the rest of your open loops.

I've noticed that people are actually more comfortable dealing with surprises and crises than they are taking control of processing, organizing, reviewing, and assessing that part of their work that is *not* as self-evident. It's easy to get sucked into "busy" and "urgent" mode, especially when you have a lot of unprocessed and relatively out-of-control work on your desk, in your e-mail, and on your mind.

In fact, much of our life and work just shows up in the moment, and it usually becomes the priority when it does. It's indeed true for most professionals that the nature of their job requires them to be instantly available to handle new work as it appears in many forms. For instance, you need to pay attention to your boss when he shows up and wants a few minutes of your time. You get a request from a senior executive that suddenly takes precedence over anything else you thought you needed to do today. You find out about a serious problem with fulfilling a major customer's order, and you have to take care of it right away.

These are all understandable judgment calls. But the angst

begins to mount when the other actions on your lists are not reviewed and renegotiated by you or between you and everyone else. The constant sacrifices of not doing the work you have defined on your lists can be tolerated only if you *know* what you're not doing. That requires regular processing of your in-basket (defining your work) and consistent review of complete lists of all your predetermined work.

If choosing to do work that just showed up instead of doing work you predefined is a conscious choice, based on your best call, that's playing the game the best way you can. Most people, however, have major improvements to make in how they clarify, manage, and renegotiate their total inventory of projects and actions. If you let yourself get caught up in the urgencies of the moment, without feeling comfortable about what you're *not* dealing with, the result is frustration and anxiety. Too often the stress and lowered effectiveness are blamed on the "surprises." If you know what you're doing, and what you're *not* doing, surprises are just another opportunity to be creative and excel.

In addition, when the in-basket and the action lists get ignored for too long, random things lying in them tend to surface as emergencies later on, adding more ad hoc work-as-it-shows-up to fuel the fire.

Many people use the inevitablity of an almost infinite stream of immediately evident things to do as a way to avoid the responsibilities of defining their work and managing their total inventory. It's easy to get seduced into not-quite-so-critical stuff that is right at hand, especially if your in-basket and your personal organization are out of control. Too often "managing by wandering around" is an excuse for getting away from amorphous piles of stuff.

This is where the need for knowledge-work athletics really shows up. Most people did not grow up in a world where defining the edges of work and managing huge numbers of open loops were required. But when you've developed the skill and habits of processing input rapidly into a rigorously defined system, it becomes much easier to trust your judgment calls about the dance of what to do, what to stop doing, and what to do instead.

The Moment-to-Moment Balancing Act

At the black-belt level, you can shift like lightning from one foot to the other and back again. While you're processing your in-basket, for example, your assistant comes in to tell you about a situation that needs immediate attention. No sweat—your tray is still there, with everything still to be processed in one stack, ready to be picked up again when you can get back to it. While you're on hold on the phone, you can be reviewing your action lists and getting a sense of what you're going to do when the call is done. While you wait for a meeting to start, you can work down the "Read/Review" stack you've brought with you. And when the conversation you weren't expecting with your boss shrinks the time you have before your next meeting to twelve minutes, you can easily find a way to use that window to good advantage.

To ignore the unexpected (even if it were possible) would be to live without opportunity, spontaneity, and the rich moments of which "life" is made.

—Stephen Covey

You can do only one of these work activities at a time. If you stop to talk to someone in his or her office, you're not working off your lists or processing incoming stuff. The challenge is to feel confident about what you have decided to do.

So how do you decide? This again will involve your intuitive judgments—how important is the unexpected work, against all the rest? How long can you let your in-basket go unprocessed and all your stuff unreviewed and trust that you're making good decisions about what to do?

People often complain about the interruptions that prevent them from doing their work. But interruptions are unavoidable in life. When you become elegant at dispatching what's coming in and are organized enough to take advantage of the "weird time" windows that show up, you can switch between one task and the other rapidly. You can be processing e-mails while you're on hold

Do ad hoc work as it shows up, not because it is the path of least resistance, but because it is the thing you need to do, vis-à-vis all the rest.

on a conference call. But you must learn to dance among many tasks to keep a healthy balance of your workflow. Your choices will still have to be calibrated against your own clarity about the nature and goals of your work.

Your ability to deal with surprise is your competitive edge. But at a certain point, if you're not catching up and getting things under control, staying busy with only the work at hand will undermine your effectiveness. And ultimately, in order to know whether you should stop what you're doing and do something else, you'll need to have to have a good sense of what your job requires and how that fits into the other contexts of your life. The only way you can have that is to evaluate your life and work appropriately at multiple horizons.

The Six-Level Model for Reviewing Your Own Work

The six levels of work as we saw in chapter 2 (pages 51–53) may be thought of in terms of altitude:

- 50,000+ feet: Life
- 40,000 feet: Three- to five-year visions
- 30,000 feet: One- to two-year goals
- 20,000 feet: Areas of responsibility
- 10,000 feet: Current projects
- Runway: Current actions

It makes sense that each of these levels should enhance and align with the ones above it. In other words, your priorities will sit in a hierarchy from the top down. Ultimately, if the phone call you're supposed to make clashes with your life purpose or values, to be in sync with yourself you won't make it. If your job structure doesn't match up with where you need to be a year from now, you should rethink how you've framed your areas of focus and responsibilities, if you want to get where you're going most efficiently.

Let's look at that first example from the bottom up. The phone call you need to make (action) is about the deal you're working on (project), which would increase sales (responsibility). This particular deal would give you the opportunity to move up in the sales force (job goal) because of the new market your company wants to penetrate (organization vision). And that would get you closer to the way you want to be living, both financially and professionally (life).

Your work is to discover your work and then with all your heart to give yourself to it.
—Buddha

Or, from the other direction, you've decided that you want to be your own boss and unlock some of your unique assets and talents in a particular area that resonates with you (life). So you create a business for yourself (vision), with some short-term key operational objectives (job goal). That gives you some critical roles you need to fulfill to get it rolling (responsibility), with some immediate outcomes to achieve (projects). On each of those projects you'll have things you need to do, as soon as you can do them (next actions).

The healthiest approach for relaxed control and inspired productivity is to manage all the levels in a balanced fashion. At any of these levels, it's critical to identify all the open loops, all the incompletions, and all the commitments that you have right now, as best you can. Without an acceptance and an objective assessment of what's true in the present, it's always difficult to cast off for new shores. What's on your answering machine? What are your projects relative to your kids? What are you responsible for in the office? What's pushing on you to change or attracting you to create in the next months or years? These are all open loops in your psyche, though often it takes deeper and more introspective processes to identify the bigger goals and subtler inclinations.

There is magic in being in the present in your life. I'm always

The best place to succeed is where you are with what you have.
—Charles Schwab

amazed at the power of clear observation simply about what's going on, what's true. Finding out the exact details of your personal finances, clarifying the historical data about the company you're buying, or getting the facts about who really said what to whom in an interpersonal conflict can be constructive, if not downright healing.

Getting things done, and feeling good about it, means being willing to recognize, acknowledge, and appropriately manage all the things that have your consciousness engaged. Mastering the art of stress-free productivity requires it.

Working from the Bottom Up

In order to create productive alignment in your life, you could quite reasonably start with a clarification from the top down. Decide why you're on the planet. Figure out what kind of life and work and life-style would best allow you to fulfill that contract. What kind of job and personal relationships would support that direction? What key things would you need to put in place and make happen right now, and what could you do physically as soon as possible, to kick-start each of those?

You're never lacking in opportunities to clarify your priorities at any level. Pay attention to which horizon is calling you.

In truth, you can approach your priorities from any level, at any time. I always have something that I could do constructively to enhance my awareness and focus on each level. I'm never lacking in more visions to elaborate, goals to reassess, projects to identify or create, or actions to decide on. The trick is to learn to pay attention to the ones you need to at the appropriate time, to keep you and your systems in balance.

Because everything will ultimately be driven by the priorities of the level above it, any formulation of your priorities would obviously most efficiently begin at the top. For example, if you spend time prioritizing your work and then later discover that it's not the work you think you ought to be doing, you may have "wasted" time and energy that could have been better spent defining the next job you really want. The problem is that without a sense of control at the implementation levels (current projects and actions), and without inner trust in your own ability to manage those levels appropriately, trying to manage yourself from the top down often creates frustration.

Trying to manage from the top down, when the bottom is out of control, may be the *least* effective approach.

From a practical perspective, I suggest going from the bottom up instead. I've coached people from both directions, and in terms of lasting value, I can honestly say that getting someone in control of the details of his or her current physical world, and then elevating the focus from there, has never missed.

The primary reason to work from this bottom-up direction is that it clears the psychic decks to begin with, allowing your creative attention to focus on the more meaningful and elusive visions that you may need to challenge yourself to identify. Also, this particular method has a high degree of flexibility and freedom, and it includes a thinking and organizing practice that is universal and effective no matter what it's focused on. That makes it worth learning, no matter what the actual content you're dealing with at the moment may be. Change your mind, and this process will help you adjust with maximum speed. And knowing that you have that ability will give you permission to play a bigger game. It's truly empowering.

While the "50,000-foot level" is obviously the most important context within which to set priorities, experience has shown me that when we understand and implement *all* the levels of work in which we are engaged, especially the runway and 10,000-foot levels, we gain greater freedom and resources to do the bigger work that we're all about. Although a bottom-up approach is not a key conceptual priority, from a practical perspective it's a critical factor in achieving a balanced, productive, and comfortable life.

Runway The first thing to do is make sure your action lists are complete, which in itself can be quite a task. Those who focus on gathering and objectifying all of those items discover that there are many they've forgotten, misplaced, or just not recognized.

Aside from your calendar, if you don't have at least fifty next actions and waiting-fors, including all the agendas for people and meetings, I would be skeptical about whether you really had *all* of them. If you've followed through rigorously with the steps and suggestions in part 2, though, you may have them already. If not, and you do want to get this level up-to-date, set aside some time to work through chapters 4 through 6 in real implementation mode.

When you've finished getting this level of control current, you'll automatically have a more grounded sense of immediate priorities, which is almost impossible to achieve otherwise.

Taking the inventory of your current work at all levels will automatically produce greater focus, alignment, and sense of priorities.

10,000 Feet Finalize your "Projects" list. Does it truly capture all the commitments you have that will require more than one action to get done? That will define the boundaries of the kind of week-to-week operational world you're in and allow you to relax your thinking for longer intervals.

If you make a complete list of all of the things you want to have happen in your life and work at this level, you'll discover that there are actions you need to do that you hadn't realized. Just creating this objective inventory will give you a firmer basis on which to make decisions about what to do when you have discretionary time. Invariably when people get their "Projects" list up-to-date, they discover there are several things that could be done readily to move things they care about forward.

Very few people have this clear data defined and available to themselves in some objective form. Before any discussion about what should be done this afternoon can take place, this information must be at hand.

Again, if you've been putting into practice the methodology of *Getting Things Done,* your "Projects" list will be where it needs to be. For most of our coaching clients, it takes ten to fifteen hours of collecting, processing, and organizing to get to the point of trusting the thoroughness of their inventory.

20,000 Feet This is the level of "current job responsibilities." What are the "hats" you wear? Professionally, this would relate to your current position and work. Personally, it would include the roles you've taken on in your family, in your community, and of course with yourself as a functioning person.

You may have some of these roles already defined and written out. If you've recently taken a new position and there's an agreement or contract about your areas of responsibility, that would certainly be a good start. If you've done any kind of personal goal-setting and values-clarifying exercises in the past and still have any materials you created then, add those to the mix.

Next I recommend that you make and keep a list called "Areas of Focus." You might like to separate this into "Professional" and "Personal" sublists, in which case you'll want to use them both equally for a consistent review. This is one of the most useful checklists you can create for your own self-management. It won't require the kind of once-a-week recalibration that the "Projects" list will; more likely it will have meaning on a longer recursion cycle. Depending on the speed of change in some of the more important areas of your life and work, this should be used as a trigger for potential new projects every one to three months.

If you're not totally sure what your job is, it will always feel overwhelming.

You probably have somewhere between four and seven key areas of responsibility in your work, and a similar number personally. Your job may include things like staff development, systems design, long-range planning, administrative support, marketing, and scheduling, or responsibility for facilities, fulfillment, quality control, asset management, and so on. If you're your own business, your attention will be on many more areas than if you have a very specialized function in a large organization. The rest of your life might entail areas of focus such as parenting, partnering, church, health, community service, home management, financial management, self-development, creative expression, and so forth.

The operational purpose of the "Areas of Focus" list is to ensure that you have all your projects and next actions defined, so you can manage your responsibilities appropriately. If you were to create an accounting of those and evaluate them objectively, in terms of what you're doing and should be doing, you'll undoubtedly uncover projects you need to add to your "Projects" list. You may, in reviewing the list, decide that some areas are just fine and are being taken care of. Then again, you may realize that something has been "bugging" you in one area and that a project should be created to shore it up. "Areas of Focus" is really just a more abstract and refined version of the "Triggers" list we covered earlier.

Every client I have coached in the last twenty years has uncovered at least one important gap at this level of discussion. For instance, a common "hat" a manager or executive wears is "staff development." Upon reflection, most realize they need to add a project or two in that area, such as "Upgrade our performance-review process."

A discussion of "priorities" would have to incorporate all of these levels of current agreements between yourself and others. If you get this "job description" checklist in play and keep it current, you'll probably be more relaxed and in control than most people in our culture. It will certainly go a long way toward moving you from hope to trust as you make the necessary on-the-run choices about what to do.

30,000 to 50,000+ Feet Whereas the three lower levels have mostly to do with the current state of things—your actions, projects, and areas of responsibility—from here up the factors of the future and your direction and intentions are primary. There is still an inventory to take at these plateaus, but it's more about "What is true right now about where I've decided I'm going and how I'm going to get there?" This can range from one-year goals in your job ("30,000 feet") to a three-year vision for your career and personal net worth ("40,000 feet") to intuiting your life purpose and how to maximize its expression ("50,000+ feet").

When you're not sure where you're going, you'll never know when enough is enough.

I'm blending the three uppermost levels together here because situations often can't easily be pigeonholed into one or another of these categories. Also, since *Getting Things Done* is more about the art of implementation than about how to define goals and vision, I won't offer a rigorous examination here. But by its very nature this investigation can broach potentially deep and complex arenas, which could include business strategy, organization development, career planning, and life direction and values.

For our purposes, the focus is on capturing what motivators exist for you in current reality that determine the inventory of what your work actually is, right now. Whether your directions and goals should be changed—based on deeper thinking, analysis, and intuition—could be another discussion. Even so, there are probably some things you can identify right now that can help you get current in your own thinking about your work and what's important in it.

If you were to intuitively frame a picture of what you think you might be doing twelve to eighteen months from now, or what the nature of your job will look like at that point, what would that trigger? At this level, which is subtler, there may be things personally you need to let go of, and people and systems that may need to be developed to allow the transition. And as the job itself is a moving target, given the shifting sands of the professional world these days, there may need to be projects defined to ensure viability of the outputs in your area.

In the personal arena, this is where you would want to consider things like: "My career is going to stagnate unless I assert my own goals more specifically to my boss (or my boss's boss)." Or "What new things are my children going to be doing next year, and what do I need to do differently because of that?" Or "What preparation do I need to ensure that I can deal with this health problem we've just uncovered?"

Through a longer scope you might assess: How is your career going? How is your personal life moving along? What is your organization doing relative to changes in the environment, and what impact does that have on you? These are the one-to-five-year-horizon questions that, when I ask them, elicit different and important kinds of answers from everyone.

Not long ago I coached someone in a large international bank who, after a few months of implementing this methodology and getting control of his day-to-day inventory of work, decided the time was right to invest in his own start-up high-tech firm. The thought had been too intimidating for him to address initially, but working from the "runway level" up made it much more accessible and a natural consequence of thinking at this horizon.

If you're involved in anything that has a future of longer than a year (marriage, kids, a career, a company, an art form), you would do well to think about what you might need to be doing to manage things along that vector.

Questions to ask yourself here are:

- What are the longer-term goals and objectives in my organization, and what projects do I need to have in place related to them to fulfill my responsibilities?

- What longer-term goals and objectives have I set for myself, and what projects do I need to have in place to make them happen?

- What other significant things are happening that could affect my options about what you I'm doing?

Here are some examples of the kinds of issues that show up at this level of conversation:

- The changing nature of your job, given the shifting priorities of the company. Instead of managing the production of your own training programs in-house, you're going to outsource them to vendors.

- The direction in which you feel you need to move in your career. You see yourself doing a different kind of job a year from now, and you need to make a transition out of the one you have while exploring the options for a transfer or promotion.

- The organization direction, given globalization and expansion. You see a lot of major international travel looming on the horizon for you, and given your life-style preferences, you need to consider how to readjust your career plans.

- Life-style preferences and changing needs. As your kids get older, your need to be at home with them is diminishing, and your interest in investment and retirement planning is growing.

At the topmost level of thinking, you'll need to ask some of the ultimate questions. Why does your company exist? Why do *you* exist? What is the core DNA of your existence, personally and/or organizationally, that drives your choices. This is the "big picture" stuff with which hundreds of books and gurus and models are devoted to helping you grapple.

"Why?": this is the great question with which we all struggle.

You can have all the other levels of your life and work shipshape, defined, and organized to a T. Still, if you're the slightest bit off course in terms of what at the deepest level you want or are called to be doing, you're going to be uncomfortable.

Getting Priority Thinking Off Your Mind

Take at least a few minutes, if you haven't already done so, to jot down some informal notes about things that occurred to you while you've been reading this chapter. Whatever popped into your mind at these more elevated levels of your inner radar, write it down and get it out of your head.

Then process those notes. Decide whether what you wrote down is something you really want to move on or not. If not, throw the note away, or put it on a "Someday/Maybe" list or in a folder called "Dreams and Goals I Might Get Around to at Some Point." Perhaps you want to continue accumulating more of this kind of future thinking and would like to do the exercise with more formality—for example, by drafting a new business plan with your partners, designing and writing out your idea of a dream life with your spouse, creating a more specific career map for the next three years for yourself, or just getting a personal coach who can lead you through those discussions and thought processes. If so, put that outcome on your "Projects" list, and decide the next action. Then do it, hand it off to get done, or put the action reminder on the appropriate list.

With that done, you may want to turn your focus to developmental thinking about specific projects that have been identified but not fleshed out as fully as you'd like. You'll want to ensure that you're set up for that kind of "vertical" processing.

10

Getting Projects Under Control

CHAPTERS 4 THROUGH 9 have given you all the tricks and methods you need to clear your head and make intuitive choices about what to do when. That's the horizontal level—what needs your attention and action across the horizontal landscape of your life. The last piece of the puzzle is the vertical level—the digging deep and pie-in-the-sky thinking that can leverage your creative brainpower. That gets us back to refining and energizing our project planning.

The Need for More Informal Planning

After years of working with thousands of professionals down in the trenches, I can safely say that virtually all of us could be doing more planning, more informally and more often, about our projects and our lives. And if we did, it would relieve a lot of pressure on our psyches and produce an enormous amount of creative output with minimal effort.

I've discovered that the biggest improvement opportunity in planning does not consist of techniques for the highly elaborate and complex kinds of project organizing that professional project managers sometimes use (like GANTT charts). Most of the people who need those already have them, or at least have access to the training and software required to learn about them. The real need is to capture and utilize more of the creative, proactive thinking we do—or *could* do.

The major reason for the lack of this kind of effective value-added thinking is the dearth of systems for managing the potentially infinite amount of detail that could show up as a result. This is why my approach tends to be bottom-up. If you feel out of control with your current actionable commitments, you'll resist focused planning. An unconscious pushback occurs. As you begin to apply these methods, however, you may find that they free up enormous creative and constructive thinking. If you have systems and habits ready to leverage your ideas, your productivity can expand exponentially.

The middle of every successful project looks like a disaster.
—Rosabeth Moss Cantor

In chapter 3, I covered in some detail the five phases of project planning that take something from the idea stage into physical reality.

What follows is a compilation of practical tips and techniques to facilitate the natural, informal planning processes I recommend. Although these suggestions are all based on common sense, they're not followed nearly as frequently as they could be. Put them to use whenever and as often as you can, instead of saving up your thinking for big formal meetings.

You need to set up systems and tricks that get you to think about your projects and situations more frequently, more easily, and in more depth.

Which Projects Should You Be Planning?

Most of the outcomes you have identified for your "Projects" list will not need any kind of front-end planning, other than the sort you do in your head, quickly and naturally, to come up with a next action on them. The only planning needed for "Get car inspected," for example, would be to decide to check the phone book for the nearest inspection location and call and set up a time.

There are two types of projects, however, that deserve at least some sort of planning activity: (1) those that still have your attention even after you've determined their next actions, and (2) those about which potentially useful ideas and supportive detail just show up.

The first type—the projects that you know have other things about them that must be decided on and organized—will need a more detailed approach than just identifying a next action. For these you'll need a more specific application of one or more of the other four phases of the natural planning model: purpose and principles, vision/outcome, brainstorming, and/or organizing.

The second type—the projects for which ideas just show up, ad hoc, on a beach or in a car or in a meeting—need to have an appropriate place into which these associated ideas can be captured. Then they can reside there for later use as needed.

Projects That Need Next Actions About Planning

There are probably a few projects you can think of right now, off the top of your head, that you know you want to get more objectified, fleshed out, and under control. Perhaps you have an important meeting coming up and you know you have to prepare an agenda and materials for it. Or you've just inherited the job of coordinating the annual associates' conference, and you've got to get it organized as soon as possible so you can start delegating significant pieces. Or you've got to clarify a job description for a new position on your team to give to Human Resources. If you haven't done it already, get a next action *now* that will start the planning process for each of these, and put it on the appropriate action list. Then proceed with further planning steps.

Typical Planning Steps

The most common types of planning-oriented actions will be your own brainstorming and organizing, setting up meetings, and gathering information.

Brainstorming Some of the projects that have your attention right now will require you to do your own free-form thinking; this is especially true of those for which you were not clear about what the next action would be when you made that decision. These should all have a next action, such as "Draft ideas re X."

You need to decide where and how you want to do that action, in order to know which action list to put it on. Do you do this kind of thinking best on a computer, or by hand-writing your thoughts on paper? I may choose either medium, depending on what my intuition tells me. For me this next action would go either on my "At Computer" list or on "Anywhere" (because I can draw mind-maps wherever I am, as long as I have pen and paper).

Organizing You may have some projects for which you have already collected notes and miscellaneous support materials, and you just need to sort through them and get them into a more structured form. In this case, your next action would likely be "Organize Project X notes." If you have to be in your office to do that (because that's where the files are, and you don't want to carry them around), that action should go on your "At Office" action list. If you're carrying the project notes around with you in a folder, or in a portable organizer or on a laptop, then the "Organize . . . " action would go on an "Anywhere" or "Misc." action list if you're going to do it by hand, or on "At Computer" if you're going to use a word processor, outliner, or project-planning software.

One of the greatest blocks to organizational productivity is the lack of decision by a senior person about the necessity of a meeting, and with whom, to move an important issue forward.

Setting Up Meetings Often, progress will be made on project thinking when you set up a meeting with the people you'd like to have involved in the brainstorming. That usually means sending an e-mail to the whole group or to an assistant to get it calendared, or making a phone call to the first person to nail down a time.

Gathering Information Sometimes the next task on project thinking is to gather more data. Maybe you need to talk to someone to get his or her input ("Call Bill re his thoughts on the managers' meeting"). Or you need to look through the files you just inherited from last year's conference ("Review Associate Conference archive files"). Or you want to surf the Web to get a sense of what's happening "out there" on a new topic you're exploring ("R&D search firms for sales executives").

Random Project Thinking

Don't lose any ideas about projects that could potentially be useful. Many times you'll think of something you don't want to forget when you're a place that has nothing to do with the project. You're driving to the store, for example, and you think of a great way that you might want to start off the next staff meeting. Or you're stirring the spaghetti sauce in the kitchen and it occurs to you that you might want to give out nice tote bags to participants in the upcoming conference. Or you're watching the evening news when you suddenly remember another key person you might want to include in the advisory council you're putting together.

If these aren't specifically next actions that can go directly on your action lists, you'll still need to capture and organize them somewhere that makes sense. Of course the most critical tools for ensuring that nothing gets lost is your collection system—your in-basket, pad, and paper (or equivalents) at work and at home, and in a portable version (an index card) while you're out and about. You need to hold all your ideas until you later decide what to do with them.

Tools and Structures That Support Project Thinking

No matter at what level project ideas show up, it's great to have good tools always close at hand for capturing them as they occur. Once they've been captured, it's useful to have access to them whenever you need to refer to them.

Thinking Tools

One of the great secrets to getting ideas and increasing your productivity is utilizing the function-follows-form phenomenon—great tools can trigger good thinking. (I've come up with some of my most productive thoughts when playing with my Palm organizer in an airport, waiting for a flight!)

Luck affects everything. Let your hook always be cast; in the stream where you least expect it there will be a fish.
—*Ovid*

If you aren't writing anything down, it's extremely difficult to stay focused on anything for more than a few minutes, especially if you're by yourself. But when you utilize physical tools to keep your thinking anchored, you can stay engaged constructively for hours.

Writing Instruments

Keep good writing tools around all the time so you never have any unconscious resistance to thinking due to not having anything to capture it with. If I don't have something to write with, I can sense that I'm not as comfortable letting myself think about projects and situations.

Function often follows form. Give yourself a context for capturing thoughts, and thoughts will occur that you don't yet know you have.

Conversely, I have done some great thinking and planning at times just because I wanted to use my nice-looking, smooth-writing ballpoint pen! You may not be inspired by cool gear like I am, but if you are, do yourself a favor and invest in quality writing tools.

I also suggest that you keep nice ballpoint pens at the stations where you're likely to want to take notes—particularly near the phones around your house.

Paper and Pads

In addition to writing tools, you should always have functional pads of paper close at hand. Legal pads work well because you can easily tear off pages with ideas and notes and toss them into your in-basket until you get a chance to process them. Also you will often want to keep some of your informal mind-maps, and you can put those separate pieces of paper in appropriate file folders without having to rewrite them.

Where is your closest pad? Keep it closer.

Easels and Whiteboards

If you have room for them, whiteboards and/or easel pads are very functional thinking tools to use from time to time. They give you plenty of space on which to jot down ideas, and it can be useful to keep them up in front of you for while, as you incubate on a topic. Whiteboards are great to have on a wall in your office and in meeting rooms, and the bigger the better. If you have children, I recommend that you install one in their bedrooms (I wish I'd grown up with the encouragement to have as many ideas as I could!). Be sure to keep plenty of fresh markers on hand; it's frustrating to want to start writing on a whiteboard and find that all the markers are dry and useless.

How do I know what I think, until I hear what I say?
—E. M. Forster

Whenever two or more people are gathered for a meeting, someone should start writing somewhere where the other(s) can see. Even if you erase your thoughts after a few minutes, just the act of writing them down facilitates a constructive thinking process like nothing else. (I've found it immensely helpful at times to draw informal diagrams and notes on paper tablecloths, place mats, or even napkins in restaurants, if I didn't have my own pad of paper at hand.)

The Computer

Many times I like to think on my laptop, in my word processor. There are so many things I might want to do later on with my thinking, and it feels terrific to already have it in some digital form for later editing and cutting and pasting into various other applications. Once I've booted up and the screen is ready in front of me, I find that thinking just automatically starts to happen. This is another good reason to ensure that your typing and keyboard skills are sufficient to make engaging with the computer at least easy, if not downright fun.

Leverage your computer as a think station.

The Support Structures

In addition to good tools ubiquitously at hand, it is productive to have accessible formats into which project thinking can be captured. Much as a pen and paper in front of you supports brainstorming, having good tools and places for organizing project details facilitates the more linear planning that many projects need.

Create File Folders or Loose-Leaf Pages as Needed

A good general-reference filing system, right at hand and easy to use, is not only critical to manage the general workflow process, but highly functional for project thinking as well. Often a project begins to emerge when it's triggered by relevant data, notes, and miscellaneous materials, and for this reason, you'll want to create a folder for a topic as soon as you have something to put in it. If your filing system is too formal (or nonexistent), you'll probably miss many opportunities to generate a project focus sufficiently early. As soon as you return from that first meeting with your initial notes about a topic that has just emerged on the horizon, create a file and store them in it right away (after you have gleaned any next actions, of course).

Many times, in coaching clients, I find that the mere act of creating a file for a topic into which we can organize random notes and potentially relevant materials gives them a significantly improved sense of control. It's a way of physically, visibly, and psychologically getting their "arms around it."

If you like to work with a loose-leaf notebook or planner, it's good to keep an inventory of fresh note paper or graph paper that you can use to set up a page on a theme or project as it shows up. While some projects may later deserve a whole tabbed section or even an entire notebook of their own, they don't start out that way. And most of your projects may need only a page or two to hold the few ideas you need to track.

If you don't have a good system for filing bad ideas, you probably don't have one for filing good ones, either.

Software Tools

Software is in one sense a dark black hole to explore in search of good "project management" tools. For the most part, the applications that are specifically designed for project organizing are way too complex, with too much horsepower to really be functional for 98 percent of what most people need to manage. They're appropriate only for the very small percentage of the professional world that actually needs them. The rest of us usually find bits and pieces of applications more informal and project-friendly. As I've noted, I have never seen any two projects that needed the same amount of detailing and structure to get them under control. So it would be difficult to create any one application that would suffice for the majority.

Digital Outlining Most of what anyone needs to structure his or her thinking about projects can be found in any kind of application that has a simple hierarchical outlining function. I used to use a Symantec program called Grandview, and now I often use Microsoft Word for just this kind of project planning. Here's a piece of an outline I created for one of our own planning sessions:

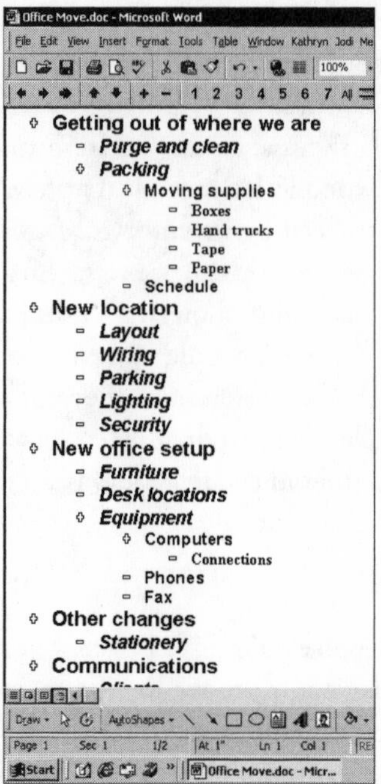

The great thing about outlining applications is that they can be as complex or as simple as required. There are numerous software programs that provide this kind of basic hierarchical structuring. The trick is to find one that you feel comfortable with, so you can rapidly get familiar with how to insert headings and subheadings and move them around as needed. Until you can stop focusing on how to use the program, you'll resist booting it up and using it to think and organize.

It doesn't really matter where you put this kind of thinking, so long as it's easily accessible so you can input and review it as needed.

Brainstorming Applications Several applications have been developed specifically to facilitate the brainstorming process. "Inspiration" was one, based on the mind-mapping techniques of

Tony Buzan. It had some useful features, but me, I've gone back to paper and cool pen for the kind of rapid, informal thinking I usually need to do.

The problem with digitizing brainstorming is that for the most part we don't need to save what we brainstorm in the *way* we brainstormed it—the critical thing is the conclusions we develop from that raw thinking. The slick brainstorming-capture tools, like electronic whiteboards and digital handwriting-copying gear, ultimately will probably not be as successful as the manufacturers hoped. We don't need to save creative thinking so much as we do the structures we generate from it. There are significant differences among collecting and processing and organizing, and different tools are usually required for them. You might as well dump ideas into a word processor.

Project-Planning Applications As I've mentioned, most project-planning software is too rigorous for the majority of the project thinking and planning we need to do. Over the years I've seen these programs more often tried and discontinued than utilized as a consistent tool. When they're used successfully, they're usually highly customized to fit very specific requirements for the company or the industry.

I anticipate that less structured and more functional applications will emerge in the coming years, based on the ways we naturally think and plan. Until then, best stick with some good and simple outliner.

Attaching Digital Notes

If you are using a digital organizer, much of the project planning you need to capture outside your head can in fact be satisfactorily managed in an attached note field. If you have the project itself as an item on a list on a Palm, or as a task in Microsoft Outlook, you can open the accompanying "Note" section and jot ideas, bullet points, and subcomponents of the project. Just ensure that you review the attachment appropriately to make it useful.

How Do I Apply All This in My World?

Just as your "Next Actions" lists need to be up-to-date, so, too, does your "Projects" list. That done, give yourself a block of time, ideally between one and three hours, to handle as much of the "vertical" thinking about each project as you can.

Clear the deck, create a context, and do some creative project thinking. You'll then be way ahead of most people.

At the very least, right now or as soon as possible, take those few of your projects that you have the most attention on or interest in right now and do some thinking and collecting and organizing on them, using whatever tools seem most appropriate.

Focus on each one, one at a time, top to bottom. As you do, ask yourself, "What about this do I want to know, capture, or remember?"

You may just want to mind-map some thoughts on a piece of paper, make a file, and toss the paper into it. You may come up with some simple bullet-point headings to attach as a "note" in your software organizer. Or you could create a Word file and start an outline on it.

Let our advance worrying become advance thinking and planning.
—*Winston Churchill*

The key is to get comfortable with having and using your ideas. And to acquire the habit of focusing your energy constructively, on intended outcomes and open loops, before you have to.

part

3

The Power of the Key Principles

11

The Power of the Collection Habit

THERE'S MUCH MORE to these simple techniques and models than may appear at first glance. Indeed, they offer a systematic method to keep your mind distraction-free, ensuring a high level of efficiency and effectiveness in your work. That in itself would be sufficient reason to implement these practices.

But there are even greater implications for the fundamental principles at work here. What follows in the next three chapters is an accounting of my experience, over the last twenty years, of the subtler and often more profound effects that can transpire from the implementation of these basic principles. The longer-term results can have a significant impact on you as an individual, and they can positively affect larger organizational cultures as well.

When people with whom you interact notice that without fail you receive, process, and organize in an airtight manner the exchanges and agreements they have with you, they begin to trust you in a unique way. Such is the power of capturing placeholders for anything that is incomplete or unprocessed in your life. It noticeably enhances your mental well-being and improves the quality of your communications and relationships, both personally and professionally.

The Personal Benefit

How did it feel to go through the collecting and downloading activity? Most people say it feels so bad, and yet feels so good. How can that be?

If you're like most people who go through the full collection process, you probably felt some form of anxiety. Descriptive terms like "overwhelmed," "panic," "frustration," "fatigue," and "disgust" tend to come up when I ask seminar participants to describe their emotions in going through a minor version of this procedure. And is there anything you think you've procrastinated on in that stack? If so, you have guilt automatically associated with it—"I could have, should have, ought to have (before now) done this."

At the same time, did you experience any sense of release, or relief, or control as you were did the drill? Most people say yes, indeed. How does that happen? Totally opposite emotional states showing up as you're doing a single exercise, almost at the same time—anxiety and relief; overwhelmed and in control. What's going on here?

When you understand the source of your negative feelings about all your stuff, you'll discover, as I did, the way to get rid of them. And if you experienced any positive feelings from collecting your stuff, you actually began the process of eliminating the negativity yourself.

The Source of the Negative Feelings

Where do the not-so-good feelings come from? Too much to do? No, there's always too much to do. If you felt bad simply because there was more to do than you could do, you'd never get rid of that feeling. Having too much to do is not the source of the negative feeling. It comes from a different place.

How have you felt when someone broke an agreement with

you? Told you they would meet you Thursday at 4:00 P.M. and never showed or called? How did that feel? Frustrating, I imagine. The price people pay when they break agreements in the world is the disintegration of trust in the relationship—a negative consequence.

But what are all those things in your in-basket? Agreements you've made with yourself. Your negative feelings are simply the result of breaking those agreements—they're the symptoms of disintegrated *self*-trust. If you tell yourself to draft a strategic plan, when you don't do it, you'll feel bad. Tell yourself to get organized, and if you fail to, welcome to guilt and frustration. Resolve to spend more time with your kids and don't—voilà! anxious and overwhelmed.

The sense of anxiety and guilt doesn't come from having too much to do; it's the automatic result of breaking agreements with yourself.

How Do You Prevent Broken Agreements with Yourself?

If the negative feelings come from broken agreements, you have three options for dealing with them and eliminating the negative consequences:

- Don't make the agreement.
- Complete the agreement.
- Renegotiate the agreement.

All of these can work to get rid of the unpleasant feelings.

Don't Make the Agreement

It probably felt pretty good to take a bunch of your old stuff, decide that you weren't going to do anything with it, and just toss it into the trash. One way to handle an incompletion in your world is to just say no!

You'd lighten up if you would just lower your standards. If you didn't care so much about things being up to a certain level—your parenting, your school system, your team's morale, the software code—you'd have fewer things to do.*

I doubt you're going to lower your standards. But once you really understand what it means, you'll probably make fewer agreements. I know I did. I used to make a lot of them, just to win people's approval. When I realized the price I was paying on the back end for not keeping those agreements, I became a lot more conscious about the ones I made. One insurance executive I worked with described the major benefit he derived from implementing this system: "Previously I would just tell everyone, 'Sure, I'll do it,' because I didn't know how much I really had to do. Now that I've got the inventory clear and complete, just to maintain my integrity I have had to say, 'No, I can't do that, I'm sorry.' The amazing thing is that instead of being upset with my refusal, everyone was impressed by my discipline!"

Maintaining an objective inventory of your work makes it much easier to say no with integrity.

Another client, an entrepreneur in the personal coaching business, recently told me that making an inventory of his work had eliminated a huge amount of worry and stress from his life. The discipline of putting everything he had his attention on into his in-basket caused him to reconsider what he really wanted to do *anything* about. If he wasn't willing to toss a note about it into "in," he just let it go!

I consider that very mature thinking. One of the best things about this whole method is that when you really take the responsibility to capture and track what's on your mind, you'll think twice about making commitments internally that you don't really need or want to make. Not being aware of all you have to do is

---

*It has been a popular concept in the self-help world that focusing on your values will simplify your life. I contend the opposite: the overwhelming amount of things that people have to do comes *from* their values. Values are critical elements for meaning and direction. But don't kid yourself—the more you focus on them, the more things you're likely to feel responsible for taking on. Your values may make it easier for you to make decisions, but don't think they'll make things any simpler.

much like having a credit card for which you don't know the balance or the limit—it's a lot easier to be irresponsible.

Complete the Agreement

Of course, another way to get rid of the negative feelings about your stuff is to just finish it and be able to mark it off as done. You actually love to do things, as long as you get the feeling that you've completed something. If you've begun to complete less-than-two-minute actions as they surface in your life, I'm sure you can attest to the psychological benefit. Most of my clients feel fantastic after just a couple of hours of processing their piles, just because of how many things they accomplish using the two-minute rule.

Out of the strain of the doing, into the peace of the done.
—Julia Louis Woodruff

One of your better weekends may be spent just finishing up a lot of little errands and tasks that have accumulated around your house and in your personal life. Invariably when you capture all the open loops, little and big, and see them on a list in front of you, some part of you will be inspired (or creatively disgusted or intimidated enough) to go knock them off the list.

We all seem to be starved for a win. It's great to satisfy that by giving yourself doable tasks you can start and finish easily.

Have you ever completed something that wasn't initially on a list, so you wrote it down and checked it off? Then you know what I mean.

There's another issue here, however. How would you feel if your list and your stack were totally—and successfully—completed? You'd probably be bouncing off the ceiling, full of creative energy. Of course, within three days, guess what you'd have? Right—another list, and probably an even bigger one! You'd feel so good about finishing all your stuff you'd likely take on bigger, more ambitious things to do.

It's a lot easier to complete agreements when you know what they are.

Not only that, but if you have a boss, what do you think he or she is going to do, after noticing the high levels of competency and productivity you're demonstrating? Right again—give you more things to do! It's the catch-22 of professional development: the better you get, the better you'd *better* get.

So, since you're not going to significantly lower your standards, or stop creating more things to do, you'd better get comfortable with the third option, if you want to keep from stressing yourself out.

Renegotiate Your Agreement

Suppose I'd told you I would meet you Thursday at 4:00 P.M., but after I made the appointment, my world changed. Now, given my new priorities, I decide I'm *not* going to meet you Thursday at four. But instead of simply not showing up, what had I better do, to maintain the integrity of the relationship? Correct—call and change the agreement. A renegotiated agreement is not a broken one.

It is the act of forgiveness that opens up the only possible way to think creatively about the future at all.

—Father Desmond Wilson

Do you understand yet why getting all your stuff out of your head and in front of you makes you feel better? Because you automatically renegotiate your agreements with yourself when you look at them, think about them, and either act on them that very moment or say, "No, not now." Here's the problem: it's impossible to renegotiate agreements with yourself that you can't remember you made!

The fact that you can't remember an agreement you made with yourself doesn't mean that you're not holding yourself liable for it. Ask any psychologist how much of a sense of past and future that part of your psyche has, the part that was storing the list you dumped: zero. It's all present tense in there. That means that as soon as you tell yourself that you should do something, if you file it only in your short-term memory, there's a part of you that thinks you should be doing it *all the time*. And *that* means that as soon as you've given yourself two things to do, and filed them only in your head, you've created instant and automatic stress and failure, because you can't do them both at the same time.

If you're like most people, you've probably got some storage area at home—maybe a garage that you told yourself a while back (maybe even six years ago!) you ought to clean and organize. If so, there's a part of you that likely thinks you should've been cleaning your garage twenty-four hours a day for the past six years! No wonder people are so tired! And have you heard that little voice inside your own mental committee every time you walk by your garage? "Why are we walking by the garage?! Aren't we supposed to be cleaning it!?" Because you can't stand that whining, nagging part of yourself, you never even go in the garage anymore if you can help it. If you want to shut that voice up, you have three options for dealing with your agreement with yourself:

1 | Lower your standards about your garage (you may have done that already). "So I have a crappy garage . . . who cares?"
2 | Keep the agreement—clean the garage.
3 | At least put "Clean garage" on a "Someday/Maybe" list. Then, when you review that list weekly and you see that item, you can tell yourself, "Not this week." The next time you walk by your garage, you won't hear a thing internally, other than "Ha! Not this week."

I'm quite sincere about this. It seems that there's a part of our psyche that doesn't know the difference between an agreement about cleaning the garage and an agreement about buying a company. In there, they're both just agreements—kept or broken. If you're holding something only internally, it will be a broken agreement if you're not moving on it in the moment.

The Radical Departure from Traditional Time Management

This method is significantly different from traditional time-management training. Most of those models leave you with the impression that if something you tell yourself to do isn't that important, then it's not that important—to track, manage, or deal with. But in my experience that's inaccurate, at least in terms of how a less-than-conscious part of us operates. It *is* how our conscious mind operates, however, so every agreement must be made conscious. That means it must be captured, objectified, and reviewed regularly in full conscious awareness so that you can put it where it belongs in your self-management arena. If that doesn't happen, it will actually take up a lot more psychic energy than it deserves.

In my experience, anything that is held only in "psychic RAM" will take up either more or less attention than it deserves. The reason to collect everything is not that everything is equally important, it's that it's *not.* Incompletions, uncollected, take on a dull sameness in the sense of the pressure they create and the attention they tie up.

How Much Collection Is Required?

You'll feel better collecting *anything* that you haven't collected yet. When you say to yourself, "Oh, that's right, I need to get butter next time I'm at the store," and you write it on your grocery list, you'll feel better. When you remember, "I've got to call my banker about the trust fund," and you write that down someplace where you know you'll see it when you're at a phone, you'll feel better. But there will be a light-year's difference when you know you have it *all.*

When will you know how much you have left in your head to collect? Only when there's nothing left. If some part of you is even vaguely aware that you don't have it all, you can't really know what percentage you have collected. How will you know when there's nothing left? When nothing else shows up as a reminder in your mind.

This doesn't mean that your mind will be empty. If you're conscious, your mind will always be focusing on something. But if it's focusing on only one thing at a time, without distraction, you'll be in your "zone."

I suggest that you use your mind to think *about* things, rather than think *of* them. You want to be *adding* value as you think about projects and people, not simply reminding yourself they exist. To fully realize that more productive place, you will need to capture it all. It takes focus and a change of habit to train yourself to recognize and download even the smallest agreements with yourself as they're created in your mind. Doing the collection process as fully as you can, and then incorporating the behavior of capturing all the new things as they emerge, will be empowering and productive.

When Relationships and Organizations Have the Collection Habit

What happens when everyone involved on a team—in a marriage, in a department, on a staff, in a family, in a company—can be trusted not to let anything slip through the cracks? Frankly, once you've achieved that, you'll hardly think about whether people are dropping the ball anymore—there will be much bigger things to occupy your attention.

But if communication gaps are still an issue, there's likely some layer of frustration and a general nervousness in the culture. Most people feel that without constant baby-sitting and handholding, things could disappear in the system and then blow up at any time. They don't realize that they're feeling this because they've been in this situation so consistently that they relate to it as if it were a permanent law, like gravity. It doesn't have to be that way.

I have noticed this for years. Good people who haven't incorporated these behaviors come into my environment, and they stick out like a sore thumb. I've lived with the standards of clear psychic RAM and hard, clean edges on in-baskets for more than two decades now. When a note sits idle in someone's in-basket unprocessed, or when he or she nods "yes, I will" in a conversation but doesn't write anything down, my "uh-oh" bell rings. This is unacceptable behavior in my world. There are much bigger fish to fry than worrying about leaks in the system.

Bailing water in a leaky boat diverts energy from rowing the boat.

I need to trust that any request or relevant information I put on a voice-mail, in an e-mail, in a conversation, or in a written note will get into the other person's system and that it will be processed and organized, soon, and available for his or her review as an option for action. If the recipient is managing voice-mails but not e-mail and paper, I have now been hamstrung to use only his or her trusted medium. That should be unacceptable behavior in any organization that cares about whether things happen with the least amount of effort.

When change is required, there must be trust that the initiatives for that change will be dealt with appropriately. Any intact system will ultimately be only as good as its weakest link, and often that Achilles' heel is a key person's dulled responsiveness to communications in the system.

I especially notice this when I walk around organizations where in-baskets are either nonexistent, or overflowing and obviously long unprocessed. These cultures usually suffer from serious "interruptitis" because they can't trust putting communications into the system.

Where cultures do have solid systems, down through the level of paper, the clarity is palpable. It's hardly even a conscious concern, and everyone's attention is more focused. The same is true in families that have instituted in-baskets—for the parents, the children, the nanny, the housekeeper, or anyone else with whom family members frequently interact. People often grimace when I tell them that my wife, Kathryn, and I put things in each other's in-baskets, even when we're sitting within a few feet of each other; to them it seems "cold and mechanical." Aside from being an act of politeness intended to avoid interrupting the other's work in progress, the practice actually fosters more warmth and freedom between us, because mechanical things are being handled in the system instead of tying up our attention in the relationship.

Unfortunately, you can't legislate personal systems. Everyone must have his or her own way to deal with what he or she has to deal with. You can, however, hold people accountable for outcomes, and for tracking and managing everything that comes their way. And you can give them the information in this book. Then, at least, they'll have no excuse for letting something fall through the cracks.

Organizations must create a culture in which it is acceptable that everyone has more to do than he or she can do, and in which it is sage to renegotiate agreements about what everyone is *not* doing.

This doesn't mean that everyone has to do everything. I hope I have described a way to relate to our relatively new knowledge-based world that gives room for everyone to have a lot more to do than he or she *can* do. The critical issue will be to facilitate a constant renegotiation process with all involved, so they feel OK about what they're not doing. That's real knowledge work, at a more sophisticated level. But there's little hope of getting there without having bulletproof collection systems in play. Remember, you can't renegotiate an agreement with yourself that you can't remember you made. And you certainly can't renegotiate agreements with others that you've lost track of.

When groups of people collectively adopt the 100 percent collection standard, they have a tight ship to sail. It doesn't mean they're sailing in the right direction, or even that they're on the right ship; it just means that the one they're on, in the direction it's going, is doing that with the most efficient energy it can.

12

The Power of the Next-Action Decision

I HAVE A personal mission to make "What's the next action?" part of the global thought process. I envision a world in which no meeting or discussion will end, and no interaction cease, without a clear determination of whether or not some action is needed—and if it is, what it will be, or at least who has responsibility for it. I envision organizations adopting a standard that anything that lands in anyone's "ten acres" will be evaluated for action required, and the resulting decisions managed appropriately. Imagine the freedom that would allow to focus attention on bigger issues and opportunities.

When a culture adopts "What's the next action?" as a standard operating query, there's an automatic increase in energy, productivity, clarity, and focus.

Over the years I have noticed an extraordinary shift in energy and productivity whenever individuals and groups installed "What's the next action?" as a fundamental and consistently asked question. As simple as the query seems, it is still somewhat rare to find it fully operational where it needs to be.

One of the greatest challenges you may encounter is that once you have gotten used to "What's the next action?" for yourself and those around you, interacting with people who aren't asking it can be highly frustrating. It clarifies things so quickly that dealing with people and environments that don't use it can seem nightmarish.

We are all accountable to define what, if anything, we are committed to make happen as we engage with ourselves and others. And at some point, for any outcome that we have an internal commitment to complete, we must make the decision about the next physical action required. There's a great difference, however, between making that decision when things show up and doing it when they *blow* up.

The Source of the Technique

I learned this simple but extraordinary next-action technique twenty years ago from a longtime friend and management-consulting mentor of mine, Dean Acheson (no relation to the former secretary of state). Dean had spent many prior years consulting with executives and researching what was required to free the psychic logjams of many of them about projects and situations they were involved in. One day he just started picking up each individual piece of paper on an executive's desk and forcing him to decide what the very next thing was that he had to do to move it forward. The results were so immediate and so profound for the executive that Dean continued for years to perfect a methodology using that same question to process the in-basket. Since then both of us have trained and coached thousands of people with this key concept, and it remains a foolproof technique. It never fails to greatly improve both the productivity and the peace of mind of the user to determine what the next physical action is that will move something forward.

Creating the Option of Doing

How could something so simple be so powerful—"What's the next action?"

To help answer that question, I invite you to revisit for a moment your mind-sweep list (see page 113). Or at least to think about all the projects that are probably sitting around in your psyche. Do you have a sense that they haven't been moving along as consistently and productively as they could be? You'll probably admit that yes, indeed, a few have been a little bit "stuck."

If you haven't known for sure whether you needed to make a call, send an e-mail, look up something, or buy an item at the store as the very next thing to move on, it hasn't been getting done. What's ironic is that it would likely require only about ten seconds of thinking to figure out what the next action would be for almost everything on your list. But it's ten seconds of thinking that most people haven't done about most things on their list.

For example, a client will have something like "tires" on a list.

I then ask, "What's that about?"

He responds, "Well, I need new tires on my car."

"So what's the next action?"

At that point the client usually wrinkles up his forehead, ponders for a few moments, and expresses his conclusion: "Well, I need to call a tire store and get some prices."

That's about how much time is required to decide what the "doing" would look like on almost everything. It's just the few seconds of focused thinking that most people have not yet done about most of their stuff.

It will probably be true, too, that the person who needs tires on his car has had that on his radar for quite a while. It's also likely that he's been at a phone hundreds of times, often with enough time and/or energy only to make just such a call. Why didn't he make it? Because in that state of mind, the last thing in the world he felt like doing was considering all his projects, including getting tires, and what their next actions were. In those moments he didn't feel like thinking at all.

What he needed was to have already figured those things out. If he gets that next-action thinking done, then, when he happens to have fifteen minutes before a meeting, with a phone at hand, and his energy at about 4.2 out of 10, he can look at the list of options of things to do and be delighted to see "Call tire store for prices" on it. "That's something I can do and complete successfully!" he'll think, and then he'll actually be motivated to make the call, just to experience the "win" of completing something useful in the time and energy window he's in. In this context he'd be incapable of starting a large proposal draft for a client, but he has sufficient resources for punching phone numbers and getting simple information quickly. It's highly probable that at some point soon he'll look at the new set of tires on his car and feel on top of the world.

The secret of getting ahead is getting started. The secret of getting started is breaking your complex overwhelming tasks into small manageable tasks, and then starting on the first one.
—Mark Twain

Defining what real doing looks like, on the most basic level, and organizing placeholder reminders that we can trust, are master keys to productivity enhancement.

These are learnable techniques, and ones that we can continue to get better at.

Often even the simplest things are stuck because we haven't made a final decision yet about the next action. People in my seminars often have things on their lists like "Get a tune-up for the car." Is "Get a tune-up" a next action? Not unless you're walking out with wrench in hand, dressed for grease.

"So, what's the next action?"

"Uh, I need to take the car to the garage. Oh, yeah, I need to find out if the garage can take it. I guess I need to call the garage and make the appointment."

"Do you have the number?"

"Darn, no . . . I don't have the number for the garage. Fred recommended that garage to me, and I don't have the number. I knew something was missing in the equation."

Without a next action, there remains a potentially infinite gap between current reality and what you need to do.

And that's often what happens with so many things for so many people. We glance at the project, and some part of us thinks, "I don't quite have all the pieces between here and there." We know something is missing, but we're not sure what it is exactly, so we quit.

"So, what's the next action?"

"I need to get the number. I guess I could get it from Fred."

"Do you have Fred's number?"

"I have Fred's number!"

So the next action really is "Call Fred for the number of the garage."

Did you notice how many steps had to be tracked back before we actually got to the real next action on this project? That's typical. Most people have many things just like that on their lists.

Why Bright People Procrastinate the Most

It's really the smartest people who have the highest number of undecided things in their lives and on their lists. Why is that? Think of how our bodies respond to the images we hold in our minds. It appears that the nervous system can't tell the difference between a well-imagined thought and reality.

To prove this to yourself, picture yourself walking into a supermarket and going over to the brightly lit fruit-and-vegetable section. Are you there? OK, now go to the citrus bins—oranges, grapefruits, lemons. Now see the big pile of yellow lemons. There's a cutting board and a knife next to them. Take one of those big yellow lemons and cut it in half. Smell that citrus smell! It's really juicy, and there's lemon juice trickling onto the board. Now take a half lemon and cut *that* in half, so you have a quarter lemon wedge in your hands. OK, now—remember how you did this as a kid?—put that quarter of a lemon in your mouth and bite into it! Scrunch!

Bright people have the capability of freaking out faster and more dramatically than anyone else.

If you played along with me, you probably noticed that the saliva content in your mouth increased at least a bit. Your body was actually trying to process citric acid! And it was just in your mind.

If your body responds to the pictures you give it, how are you likely to feel physically when you think about, say, doing your taxes? Are you sending yourself "easy," "let's go," completion, success, and "I'm a winner!" pictures? Probably not. For just that reason, what kinds of people would logically be the most resistant to being reminded about a project like that—that is, who would procrastinate the most? Of course, it would be the most creative, sensitive, and intelligent people! Because their sensitivity gives them the capability of producing in their minds lurid nightmare scenarios about what might be involved in doing the project, and all the negative consequences that might occur if it weren't done perfectly! They just freak out in an instant and quit!

I am an old man and have known a great many troubles, but most of them never happened.
—Mark Twain

Who doesn't procrastinate? Often it's the insensitive oafs who just take something and start plodding forward, unaware of all the things that could go wrong. Everyone else tends to get hung up about all kinds of things.

Do my taxes? Oh, no! It's not going to be that easy. It's going to be different this year, I'm sure. I saw the forms—they look different. There are probably new rules I'm going to have to figure out. I might have to read all that damn material. Long form, short form, medium form? File together, file separate? We'll probably want to claim deductions, but if we do we'll have to back them up, and that means we'll need all the receipts. Oh, my God—I don't know if we really have all the receipts we'd need and what if we didn't have all the receipts but we claimed the deductions anyway and we got audited? Audited? Oh, no—the IRS—JAIL!!

And so a lot of people put themselves in jail, just glancing at their 1040 tax forms. Because they're so smart, sensitive, and creative. In my many years of coaching individuals, this pattern has been borne out more times than I can count—usually it's the brightest and most sophisticated folks who have the most stuck piles, in their offices, homes, and heads. Most of the executives I work with have at least several big, complex, and amorphous projects stacked either on a credenza or on a mental shelf. There always seem to be hobgoblin thoughts lurking inside them—"If we don't look at or think about the projects, maybe they'll stay quiet!"

Ceasing negative imaging will always cause your energy to increase.

So what's the solution? There's always having a drink. Numb it out. Dumb it down. Notice what happens to many people when they get a little alcohol on the brain. It should drop their energy immediately, because it's a depressant; often, though, the energy lifts, at least initially. Why? The alcohol *is* depressing something—it's shutting down the negative self-talk and uncomfortable visions that are going on in these folks' minds. Of course my energy will increase if I stop depressing myself with overwhelming pictures of not handling something successfully. But the numb-out solutions are temporary at best. The "stuff" doesn't go away. And unfortunately, when we numb ourselves out, we can't do it selectively—the source of inspiration and enthusiasm and personal energy also seems to get numbed.

Intelligent Dumbing Down

There is another solution: intelligently dumbing down your brain by figuring out the next action. You'll invariably feel a relieving of pressure about anything you have a commitment to change or do, when you decide on the very next physical action required to move it forward. Nothing, essentially, will change in the world. But shifting your focus to something that your mind perceives as a doable, completeable task will create a real increase in positive energy, direction, and motivation. If you truly captured all the things that have your attention during the mind-sweep, go through the list again now and decide on the single very next action to take on every one of them. Notice what happens to your energy.

No matter how big and tough a problem may be, get rid of confusion by taking one little step toward solution. Do something.
—George F. Nordenholt

You are either attracted or repelled by the things on your lists; there isn't any neutral territory. You are either positively drawn toward completing the action or reluctant to think about what it is and resistant to getting involved in it. Often it's simply the next-action decision that makes the difference between the two extremes.

In following up with people who have taken my seminars or been coached by my colleagues or me, I've discovered that one of the subtler ways many of them fall off the wagon is in letting their action lists grow back into lists of tasks or subprojects instead of discrete next actions. They're still ahead of most people because they're actually writing things down, but they often find themselves stuck, and procrastinating, because they've allowed their action lists to harbor items like:

> Everything on your lists and in your stacks is either attractive or repulsive to you—there's no neutral ground when it comes to your stuff.

"Meeting with the banquet committee"
"Johnny's birthday"
"Receptionist"
"Slide presentation"

In other words, things have morphed back into "stuff"-ness instead of staying at the action level. There are no clear next actions here, and anyone keeping a list filled with items like this would send his or her brain into overload every time he/she looked at it.

Is this extra work? Is figuring out the next action on your commitments additional effort to expend that you don't need to? No, of course not. If you need to get your car tuned, for instance, you're going to have to figure out that next action at some point anyway. The problem is that most people wait to do it until the next action is "Call the Auto Club for tow truck!!"

> *You can only cure retail but you can prevent wholesale.*
> —*Brock Chisolm*

So when do you think most people really make a lot of their next-action decisions about their stuff—when it shows up, or when it blows up? And do you think there might be a difference in the quality of their lives if they handled this knowledge work on the front end instead of the back? Which do you think is the more efficient way to move through life—deciding next actions on your projects as soon as they appear on your radar screen and then efficiently grouping them into categories of actions that you get done in certain uniform contexts, or avoiding thinking about what exactly needs to be done until it *has* to be done, then nickel-and-diming your activities as you try to catch up and put out the fires?

Avoiding action decisions until the pressure of the last minute creates huge inefficiencies and unnecessary stress.

That may sound exaggerated, but when I ask groups of people to estimate when most of the action decisions are made in their companies, with few exceptions they say, "When things blow up." One global corporate client surveyed its population about sources of stress in its culture, and the number one complaint was the last-minute crisis work consistently promoted by team leaders who failed to make appropriate decisions on the front end.

The Value of a Next-Action Decision-Making Standard

I have had several sophisticated senior executives tell me that installing "What's the next action?" as an operational standard in their organizations was transformative in terms of measurable performance output. It changed their culture permanently and significantly for the better.

Why? Because the question forces clarity, accountability, productivity, and empowerment.

Clarity

Too many discussions end with only a vague sense that people know what they have decided and are going to do. But without a clear conclusion that there *is* a next action, much less what it is or who's got it, more often than not a lot of "stuff" gets left up in the air.

I am frequently asked to facilitate meetings. I've learned the hard way that no matter where we are in the conversation, twenty minutes before the agreed end-time of the discussion I must force the question: "So what's the next action here?" In my experience, there is usually twenty minutes' worth of clarifying (and sometimes tough decisions) still required to come up with an answer.

This is radical common sense—radical because it often compels discussion at deeper levels than people are comfortable with. "Are we serious about this?" "Do we really know what we're doing here?" "Are we really ready to allocate precious time and resources to this?" It's very easy to avoid these more relevant levels of thinking. What prevents those issues from slipping away into amorphous "stuff" is forcing the decision about the next action. Some further conversation, exploration, deliberation, and negotiation are often needed to put the topic to rest. The world is too unpredictable these days to permit assumptions about outcomes: we need to take responsibility for moving things to clarity.

> *Talk does not cook rice.*
> *—Chinese proverb*

You have to have some experience of this to really know what I mean here. If you do, you're probably saying to yourself, "Yes!" If you're not sure what I'm talking about, I suggest that in your next meeting with anyone, you end the conversation with the question, "So what's the next action here?" Then notice what happens.

Accountability

The dark side of "collaborative cultures" is the allergy they foster to holding anyone responsible for having the ball. "Mine or yours?" is unfortunately not in the common vocabulary of many such organizations. There is a sense that that would be impolite. "We're all in this together" is a worthy sentiment, but seldom a reality in the hard-nosed day-to-day world of work. Too many meetings end with a vague feeling among the players that something ought to happen, and the hope that it's not their personal job to make it so.

The way *I* see it, what's truly impolite is allowing people to walk away from discussions unclear. Real "togetherness" of a group is reflected by the responsibility that all take for defining the real things to do and the specific people assigned to do them, so everyone is freed of the angst of still-undecided actions.

Again, if you've been there, you'll know what I'm talking about. If you haven't, test it out—take a small risk and ask "So what's the next action on this?" at the end of each discussion point in your next staff meeting, or in your next "family conversation" around the dinner table.

Productivity

Organizations naturally become more productive when they model and train front-end next-action decision-making. For all the reasons mentioned above, determining the required physical allocation of resources necessary to make something happen as soon as the outcome has been clarified will produce more results sooner, and with less effort.

There are risks and costs to a program of action, but they are far less than the long-range risks and costs of comfortable inaction.

—John F. Kennedy

Learning to break through the barriers of the sophisticated creative thinking that can freeze activity—that is, the entangled psychic webs we spin—is a superior skill. "Productivity" has been touted for decades as a desirable thing to improve in organizations. Anything that can help maximize output will do that. But in the world of knowledge work, all the computers and telecom improvements and leadership seminars on the planet will make no difference in this regard unless the individuals involved increase their operational responsiveness. And that requires thinking about something that lands in your world *before* you have to.

One of the biggest productivity leaks I have seen in some organizations is the lack of next actions determined for "long-term" projects. "Long-term" does not mean "Someday/Maybe."

Those projects with distant goal lines are still to be done as soon as possible; "long-term" simply means, "more action steps until it's done," not "no need to decide next actions because the day of reckoning is so far away." When every project and open loop in an organization is being monitored, it's a whole new ball game.

Productivity will improve only when individuals increase their operational responsiveness. And in knowledge work, that means clarifying actions on the front end instead of the back.

Empowerment

Perhaps the greatest benefit of adopting the next-action approach is that it dramatically increases your ability to make things happen, with a concomitant rise in your self-esteem and constructive outlook.

People are constantly doing things, but usually only when they have to, under fire from themselves or others. They get no sense of winning, or of being in control, or of cooperating among themselves and with their world. People are starving for those experiences.

The daily behaviors that define the things that are incomplete and the moves that are needed to complete them must change. Getting things going of your own accord, before you're forced to by external pressure and internal stress, builds a firm foundation of self-worth that will spread into every aspect of your life. You are the captain of your own ship; the more you act from that perspective, the better things will go for you.

Asking "What's the next action?" undermines the victim mentality. It presupposes that there is a possibility of change, and that there is something you can do to make it happen. That is the assumed affirmation in the behavior. And these kinds of "assumed affirmations" often work more fundamentally to build a positive self-image than can repeating "I am a powerful, effective person, making things happen in my life!" a thousand times.

Is there too much complaining in your culture? The next time someone moans about something, try asking, "So what's the next action?" People will complain only about something that they assume could be better than it currently is. The action question forces the issue. If it can be changed, there's some action that will change it. If it can't, it must be considered part of the landscape to be incorporated in strategy and tactics. Complaining is a sign that someone isn't willing to risk moving on a changeable situation, or won't consider the immutable circumstance in his or her plans. This is a temporary and hollow form of self-validation.

People are always blaming their circumstances for what they are. I don't believe in circumstances. The people who get on in this world are the people who get up and look for the circumstances they want, and, if they can't find them, make them.
—*George Bernard Shaw*

Although my colleagues and I rarely promote our work in this way, I notice people really empowering themselves every day as we coach them in applying the next-action technique. The light in their eyes and the lightness in their step increase, and a positive spark shows up in their thinking and demeanor. We are all already powerful, but deciding on and effectively managing the physical actions required to move things forward seems to exercise that power in ways that call forward the more positive aspects of our nature.

When you start to make things happen, you really begin to believe that you can make things happen. And *that* makes things happen.

13

The Power of Outcome Focusing

THE POWER OF directing our mental and imaginative processes to create change has been studied and promoted in thousands of contexts—from the early "positive thinking" books to recent discoveries in advanced neurophysiology.

My own interest has been in applying of the principle in terms of practical reality: Does it help get things done? And if so, how do we best utilize it in managing the work of our lives? Can we really use this information in ways that allow us to produce what we want to have happen with less effort? The answer has been a resounding yes.

Focus and the Fast Track

Over the years I have seen the application of the method presented in this book create profound results for people in their day-to-day worlds. As you begin to use it habitually as your primary means of addressing all situations—from processing e-mails, to buying a house or a company, to structuring meetings or having conversations with your kids—your personal productivity can go through the roof.

Many of the professionals I have worked with who integrated this method now find themselves experiencing enhanced or even new jobs and careers. These processes really work in the arena of the ordinary things we must deal with daily—the stuff of our work. When you demonstrate to yourself and to others an increasing ability to get things done "in the trenches," you probably won't stay in the same trench for very long.* It's been inspiring for me to learn and coach others how to deal with the immediate realities down where the rubber hits the road—and how to tie in the power of positive imagery to practical experiences in all our daily lives.

The "fast track" alluded to in the section heading above is a bit of misnomer. For some, slowing down, getting out of the squirrel cage, and taking care of themselves may be the major change precipitated by this methodology. The bottom line is it makes you more conscious, more focused, and more capable of implementing the changes and results you want, whatever they are.

"Create a way to regularly spend more time with my daughter" is as specific a project as any, and equally demanding of a next action to be determined. Having the vague, gnawing sense that you "should" do something about your relationship with your daughter, and not actually doing anything, can be a killer. I often work with clients who are willing to acknowledge the real things of their lives at this level as "incompletes"—to write them down, define real projects about them, and ensure that next actions are decided on—until the finish line is crossed. That is real productivity, perhaps in its most awesome manifestation.

The Significance of Applied Outcome Thinking

What I want to emphasize now is how learning to process the details of our work and lives with this clear and consistent system

---

*Of course, the people who are *most* attracted to implementing *Getting Things Done* are usually already on a self-development track and don't assume that they'll be doing the same thing a year from now that they're doing now, anyway. But they love the fact that this method gets them there faster and more easily.

can affect others and ourselves in significant ways we may not expect.

As I've said, employing next-action decision-making results in clarity, productivity, accountability, and empowerment. Exactly the same results happen when you hold yourself to the discipline of identifying the real results you want and, more specifically, the projects you need to define in order to produce them.

Defining specific projects and next actions that address real quality-of-life issues is productivity at its best.

It's all connected. You can't really define the right action until you know the outcome, and your outcome is disconnected from reality if you're not clear about what you need to do physically to make it happen. You can get at it from either direction, and you must, to get things done.

As an expert in whole-brain learning and good friend of mine, Steven Snyder, put it, "There are only two problems in life: (1) you know what you want, and you don't know how to get it; and/or (2) you don't know what you want." If that's true (and I think it is) then there are only two solutions:

- Make it up.
- Make it happen.

This can be construed from the models of yin/yang, right brain/left brain, creator/destroyer—or whatever equivalent works best for you. The truth is, our energy as human beings seems to have a dualistic and teleological reality—we create and identify with things that aren't real yet on all the levels we experience; and when we do, we recognize how to restructure our current world to morph it into the new one, and experience an impetus to make it so.

We are constantly creating and fulfilling.

Things that have your attention need your *in*tention engaged. "What does this mean to me?" "Why is it here?" "What do I want to have be true about this?" ("What's the successful

Life affords no higher pleasure than that of surmounting difficulties, passing from one step of success to another, forming new wishes and seeing them gratified.
—Dr. Samuel Johnson

outcome?") Everything you experience as incomplete must have a reference point for "complete."

Once you've decide that there is something to be changed and a mold to fill, you ask yourself, "How do I now make this happen?" and/or "What resources do I need to allocate to make it happen?" ("What's the next action?").

Your life and work are made up of outcomes and actions. When your operational behavior is grooved to organize everything that comes your way, at all levels, based upon those dynamics, a deep alignment occurs, and wondrous things emerge. You become highly productive. You make things up, and you make them happen.

The Magic of Mastering the Mundane

My clients often wonder how I can sit with them in their offices, often for hours on end, as they empty the drawers of their desks and painstakingly go through the minutiae of stuff that they have let accumulate in their minds and their physical space. Aside from the common embarrassment they feel about the volume of their irresponsibly dealt-with details, they assume I should be bored to tears. Quite the contrary. Much to my own surprise, I find it to be some of the most engaging work I do with people. I know the release and relief and freedom that sit on the other side of dealing with these things. I know that we all need practice and support and a strong, clear focus to get through them, until we have the built-in standards and behaviors we need to engage with them as they demand. I know how significant a change these people may experience in their relationships with their bosses, their partners, their spouses, their kids, and themselves over the next few hours and (we hope) days and years.

It's not boring. It's some of the best work we do.

Multilevel Outcome Management

The challenge is to marry high-level idealistic focus to the mundane activity of life. In the end they require the same thinking.

I'm in the focus business. As a consultant and coach, I ask simple questions that often elicit very creative and intelligent responses from others (and even myself!), which can in turn add value to the situation and work at hand. People aren't any smarter after they work with me than they were before—they just direct and utilize their intelligence more productively.

What's unique about the practical focus of *Getting Things Done* is the combination of effectiveness and efficiency that these methods can bring to every level of your reality. There are lots of inspirational sources for the high-level "purpose, values, vision" kind of thinking, and many more mundane tools for getting hold of smaller details such as phone numbers and appointments and grocery lists. The world has been rather barren, however, of practices that relate equally to both levels, and tie them together.

"What does this mean to me?" "What do I want to have be true about it?" "What's the next step required to make that happen?" These are the cornerstone questions we must answer, at some point, about everything. This thinking, and the tools that support it, will serve you in ways you may not yet imagine.

An idealist believes that the short run doesn't count. A cynic believes the long run doesn't matter. A realist believes that what is done or left undone in the short run determines the long run.
—Sidney J. Harris

The Power of Natural Planning

The value of all this natural project planning is that it provides an integrated, flexible, aligned way to think through any situation.

Being comfortable with challenging the purpose of anything you may be doing is healthy and mature. Being able to "make up" visions and images of success, before the methods are clear, is a phenomenal trait to strengthen. Being willing to have ideas, good or bad, and to express and capture all of them without judgments is critical for fully accessing creative intelligence. Honing multiple ideas and types of information into components, sequences, and priorities aimed toward a specific outcome is a necessary mental discipline. And deciding on and taking real next actions—actually moving on something in the physical world—are the essence of productivity.

Being able to bring all these ingredients together, with appropriate timing and balance, is perhaps the major component of professional competence for this new millennium. But it's not yet the norm in professional behavior; far from it. It's still a daunting task to apply this awareness to all the aspects of personal and professional life. But even when only portions of the model are inserted, tremendous benefit ensues.

The feedback I have gotten over the years in my consulting, teaching, and coaching with this model has continued to validate that even the slightest increase in the use of natural planning can bring significant improvement. To see brainstorming about almost every aspect of their lives becoming a standard tool for many people is terrific. To hear from executives who have used the model as a way to frame key meetings and discussions, and have gotten great value from doing that, is gratifying. It all just affirms that the way our minds naturally work is the way that we should focus to make anything happen in the physical world.

The model is simply the basic principle of determining outcomes and actions for everything we consider to be our work. When those two key focus points become the norm in our day-to-day lives, the baseline for productivity moves to another level. The addition of brainstorming—the most creative means of expressing and capturing ideas, perspectives, and details about projects—makes for an elegant set of behaviors for staying relaxed and getting things done.

Shifting to a Positive Organizational Culture

It doesn't take a big change to increase the productivity standards of a group. I continually get feedback indicating that with a little implementation, this method immediately makes things happen more quickly and more easily.

The constructive evaluation of activities, asset allocations, communications, policies, and procedures against purposes and intended outcomes has become increasingly critical for every organization I know of. The challenges to our companies continue to mount, with pressures coming these days from globalization, competition, technology, shifting markets, and raised standards of performance and production.

"What do we want to have happen in this meeting?" "What is the purpose of this form?" "What would the ideal person for this job be able to do?" "What do we want to accomplish with this software?" These and a multitude of other, similar questions are still sorely lacking in many quarters. There's plenty of talk in the Big Meetings that sounds good, but learning to ask "Why are we doing this?" and "What will it look like when it's done successfully?" and to apply the answers at the day-to-day operational level—*that* is what will create profound results.

Empowerment naturally ensues for individuals as they move from complaining and victim modalities into outcomes and actions defined for direction. When that becomes the standard in a group, it creates significant improvement in the atmosphere as well as the output. There are enough other problems to be concerned with; negativity and passive resistance need to continually give way to a focus on the desired results at the appropriate horizons.

The microcosm of how people deal with their in-baskets, e-mail, and conversations with others will be reflected in the macro-reality of their culture and organization. If balls are dropped, if decisions about what to do are resisted on the front end, if not all the open loops are managed responsibly, that will be

A vision without a task is but a dream, a task without a vision is drudgery, a vision and a task is the hope of the world.
—From a church in Sussex, England, ca. 1730

magnified in the group, and the culture will sustain a stressful fire-and-crisis siege mentality. If, in contrast, individuals are implementing the principles of *Getting Things Done*, the culture will expect and experience a new standard of high performance. Problems and conflicts will not go away—they remain inherent as you attempt to change (or maintain) anything in this world. The operational behaviors of this book, however, will provide the focus and framework for addressing them in the most productive way.

Conclusion

I HOPE THIS book has been useful—that you have started to reap the rewards of getting more done with less effort and stress. And I *really* hope you have tasted the freedom of a "mind like water" and the release of your creative energies that can come with the application of these techniques. Those who begin to implement these methods always discover there's more here than meets the eye, and you may have begun to experience your own version of that.

I'll bet *Getting Things Done* has validated much of what you already know and have been doing to some degree all along. Perhaps, though, it will make it much easier for you to apply that common sense more systematically in a world that seems to increasingly confound us with its intensity and complexity.

My intent is not to add more to the plethora of modern theories and models about how to be successful. I have tried, on the contrary, to define the core methods that don't change with the times, and which, when applied, always work. Like gravity, when you understand the principle, you can operate a lot more effectively, no matter what you're doing. Perhaps this is the Leading Edge of Back to Basics!

Getting Things Done is a road map to achieve the positive, relaxed focus that characterizes your most productive state. I invite you to use it, like a road map, as a reference tool to get back there whenever you need to.

To consistently stay on course, you'll have to do some things that may not be habits yet: keep everything out of your head; decide actions and outcomes when things first emerge on your radar, instead of later; and regularly review and update the complete inventory of open loops of your life and work. I hope by now you at least have established a reference point for the value these behaviors create. Don't be surprised, though, if it takes a little while to make them automatic. Be patient, and enjoy the process.

Here are some final tips for moving forward:

- Get your personal physical organization hardware set up. Get your workstation organized. Get in-baskets. Create a personal filing system—for work and home. Get a good list-management organizer that you are inspired to play with. I also suggest that you give yourself permission to make any changes that you have been contemplating for enhancing your work environments. Hang pictures, buy pens, toss stuff, rearrange your work space. Support your fresh start.

- Set aside some time when you can tackle one whole area of your office, and then each part of your house. Gather everything into your system, and work through the *Getting Things Done* process.

- Share anything of value you've gleaned from this with someone else. (It's the fastest way to learn.)

- Review *Getting Things Done* again in three to six months. You'll notice things you might have missed the first time through, and I guarantee it will seem like a whole new book.

- Stay in touch with people who are broadcasting and reflecting these behaviors and standards. (We're available. Visit http://www.davidco.com anytime for tons of free support material, conversations about these best practices, current information about supportive products and services, and access to our global network of people sharing the best practices in productivity. For anything, contact us at David Allen & Co. at info@davidco.com.

Have a great rest of your life!

Index

PIATKUS BOOKS

If you have enjoyed reading this book, you may be interested in other titles published by Piatkus. These include:

0 7499 1401 7	10-Day MBA, The	Steven Silbiger	£12.99
0 7499 2258 3	Body Talk at Work	Judi James	£9.99
0 7499 2330 X	Business Etiquette for the 21st Century	Lynne Brennan	£10.99
0 7499 2494 2	Career Comeback	Bradley G. Richardson	£9.99
0 7499 1686 9	Complete Time Management System, The	C. Godfrey and J. Clark	£9.99
0 7499 1675 3	Continuos Quality Improvement	Alasdair White	£9.99
0 7499 1893 4	Corporate Charisma	H. Adler and P. Temporal	£9.99
0 7499 2348 2	Digital Aboriginal	Mikela Tarlow	£10.99
0 7499 1814 4	Enterprise One to One	D. Peppers and M. Rogers	£14.99
0 7499 2237 0	Engaged Customer, The	Hans Peter Brondmo	£12.99
0 7499 2397 0	Fierce Conversations	Susan Scott	£12.99
0 7499 2264 8	Getting Things Done	David Allen	£10.99
0 7499 1233 2	How to Make Money from Freelance Writing	Andrew Crofts	£8.99
0 7499 1882 9	Interviewing Skills for Managers	Tony and Gillian Pont	£8.99
0 7499 2026 2	Journalism for Beginners	Joan Clayton	£10.99
0 7499 2388 1	Make it Happen!	Kathryn M. Redway	£9.99
0 7499 2489 6	Masters of Doom	David Kushner	£8.99
0 7499 2360 1	More Time Less Stress	Judi James	£9.99
0 7499 2416 0	Mrs Moneypenny: Survival in the City	Mrs Moneypenny	£12.99
0 7499 2528 0	Napoleon Hill's Keys to Success	Napoleon Hill	£7.99
0 7499 1587 0	Napoleon Hill's Positive Action Plan	Napoleon Hill	£8.99
0 7499 2529 9	Napoleon Hill's Unlimited Success	Naploleon Hill	£7.99

0 7499 2283 4	Network Your Way To Success	John Timperley	£10.99
0 7499 1643 5	NLP for Managers	Harry Alder	£10.99
0 7499 1492 0	One to One Future, The	D. Peppers and M. Rogers	£14.99
0 7499 1693 1	Perfect CV, The	Tom Jackson	£9.99
0 7499 2403 9	Perfect Store, The	Adam Cohen	£7.99
0 7499 2479 9	Ready for Anything	David Allen	£9.99
0 7499 2351 2	Same Words, Different Language	Barbara Annis	£12.99
0 7499 2378 4	So You Want To Write	Marge Piercy	£9.99
0 7499 2218 4	Total Memory Workout	Cynthia R. Green	£9.99
0 7499 1809 8	Train Your Brain	Dr Harry Alder	£9.99

All Piatkus titles are available from:

Piatkus Books Ltd, c/o Bookpost, PO Box 29, Douglas, Isle of Man, IM99 1BQ

Telephone (+44) 01624 677 237
Fax (+44) 01624 670 923
Email: bookshop@enterprise.net
Free Postage and Packing in the United Kingdom
Credit Cards accepted. All Cheques payable to Bookpost

Prices and availability are subject to change without prior notice. Allow 14 days for delivery. When placing orders, please state if you do not wish to receive any additional information.

In ***Ready for Anything,*** David Allen, personal productivity guru and bestselling author of *Getting Things Done*, inspires you to work better, not harder in order to enhance your productivity.

This new book will enable you to identify what drives you, what holds you back and how to be ready for anything. With over 50 productivity principles to help you clear your head and focus, Allen shows you how to create structures that work and how to put them in motion. His principles include:

- Too controlled is out of control
- You can't win if you don't know what the game is
- Creating the space for success facilitates success
- A change in focus equals a change in result

With motivational insights and inspirational quotes, ***Ready for Anything*** shows you how to make things happen with less effort, stress and inefficiency, and lots more energy, creativity and clarity. If you want to work and live at your very best, this is the perfect inspirational and motivational book for you.

'David Allen's strategies for getting on top of your workload are invaluable. Read this book!' Praise for *Getting Things Done* by Ken Blanchard, co-author *The One Minute Manager* and *Whale Done!*